Off the
Beaten Path®

michigan

Help Us Keep This Guide Up to Date

Every effort has been made by the author and editors to make this guide as accurate and useful as possible. However, many changes can occur after a guide is published—establishments close, phone numbers change, hiking trails are rerouted, facilities come under new management, etc.

We would love to hear from you concerning your experiences with this guide and how you feel it could be improved and be kept up to date. While we may not be able to respond to all comments and suggestions, we'll take them to heart, and we'll make certain to share them with the author. Please send your comments and suggestions to the following address:

The Globe Pequot Press
Reader Response/Editorial Department
P.O. Box 480
Guilford, CT 06437

Or you may e-mail us at: editorial@GlobePequot.com

Thanks for your input, and happy travels!

INSIDERS' GUIDE®

OFF THE BEATEN PATH® SERIES

Off the Beaten Path®

EIGHTH EDITION

michigan

A GUIDE TO UNIQUE PLACES

JIM DuFRESNE

INSIDERS' GUIDE®

GUILFORD, CONNECTICUT
AN IMPRINT OF THE GLOBE PEQUOT PRESS

The prices, rates, and hours listed in this guidebook were confirmed at press time. We recommend, however, that you call establishments to obtain current information before traveling.

To buy books in quantity for corporate use or incentives, call **(800) 962–0973, ext. 4551,** or e-mail **premiums@GlobePequot.com.**

INSIDERS' GUIDE ®

Copyright © 1988, 1990, 1993, 1996, 1999, 2001, 2003, 2005 by Jim DuFresne

Illustrations on pages 7, 29, 46, 84, 87, 108, 117, 136, 147, 167, 178, and 198 by Steve Baldwin
Illustrations on pages 59 and 210 by Carole Drong
Text design by Linda Loiewski
Maps created by Equator Graphics © The Globe Pequot Press
Spot photography throughout © Claudia Adams/Alamy Images

ISSN 1542-4804
ISBN 0-7627-3527-9

Manufactured in the United States of America
Eighth Edition/Third Printing

To that wonderfully warm
and huggable person
I call Mom

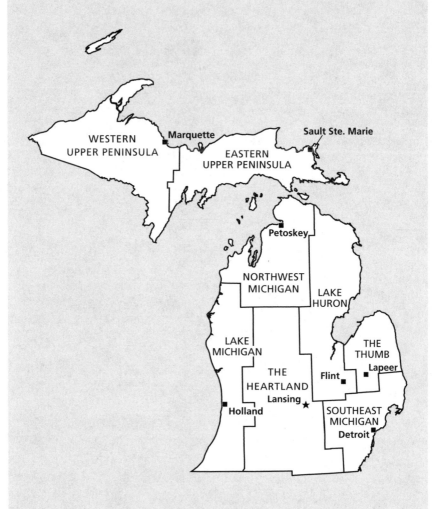

Contents

Introduction

If you look at a map of the United States or spin a globe, you'll discover that the most prominent state is Michigan. It always stands out, regardless of the size of the map or how obscured the detail.

Michigan is set off from much of the country by water. Four of the five Great Lakes surround it and have turned its borders into 3,200 miles of lakeshore where you can sit in the sand and look out on the watery horizon of the world's largest freshwater seas.

Michigan is inundated with water. It's not only outlined by blue, but its history was shaped by the Great Lakes. Today travelers search the state over for a bit of their own sand and surf, and there is no short supply. Stand anywhere in the state and you are no more than 85 miles from the Great Lakes and only 6 miles from one of the 11,000 sparkling inland lakes or 36,000 miles of streams and rivers. Come winter, Michigan's water turns fluffy and white and gently lands all around, much to the delight of skiers.

Michigan is water, yet beaches and boating, swimming and sunbathing are only part of the state's attractions. To the adventurous traveler, to those who love to swing off the interstate highways onto the country roads that wander between the woods and the lakes, there are quaint villages to discover and shipwrecks to explore, art fairs and mushroom festivals to enjoy, wine-tasting tours to savor, a stretch of quiet trail to soothe the urban soul.

All you need is time, a good map of Michigan, and this book. The map can be obtained by writing the Michigan Travel Bureau at P.O. Box 30226, Lansing 48909; by calling, toll-free, (800) 543–2937; or by checking the Web site www.michigan.org. The map will lead you away from the six-lane highways to the scenic country roads and then back again when you are ready to return home.

Michigan Off the Beaten Path points out those half-hidden gems that travelers rejoice in discovering, from a lighthouse that has become a country inn to party-fishing boats that let novice anglers stalk and catch the Great Lakes' tastiest offering, the yellow perch. Because addresses, phone numbers, and hours of operation can change from summer to summer, the regional chapters and the appendix contain a list of tourist associations that can provide the most up-to-date information.

The same holds true for prices. Inflation, with its annual increases in everything from room rates and restaurant prices to entry fees at parks and museums, will quickly outdate anything listed. Therefore, only the prices for substantial items (rooms, meals, and major attractions) have been provided in this book to help readers judge whether a restaurant or hotel is affordable.

Most of all, more than this book and a map, you need time. Don't short-change Michigan. Don't try to cover half the state in a weekend holiday. You will only be disappointed at the end of your trip. You could spend a summer exploring Michigan and never leave the shoreline. I have spent a lifetime here, yet my never-ending list of places to go and adventures to undertake only grows longer with each journey in the Great Lakes State.

Michigan Facts

- **Nickname:** Great Lakes State
- **Capital:** Lansing
- **Population:** 9,938,444, eighth in the country
- **Area:** 58,513 square miles, twenty-third in the country
- **Admitted to Union:** Michigan became the twenty-sixth state when it was admitted on January 26, 1837.
- **Major Cities:** Detroit, population 1,027,974; Grand Rapids, 195,000; Warren, 144,868; Flint, 140,761; Lansing, 127,321; Ann Arbor, 110,900; Kalamazoo, 77,460
- **Famous Residents:** Henry Ford, Thomas Edison, Gen. George Custer, President Gerald Ford, Charles Lindbergh, Diana Ross, Stevie Wonder, and Brace Beemer, the actor who played the Lone Ranger on the radio
- **National Park Units:** Isle Royale National Park, Pictured Rocks National Lakeshore, Sleeping Bear Dunes National Lakeshore
- **Travel Information:** The Michigan Travel Bureau, P.O. Box 30226, Lansing 48909; (800) 543–2937; www.michigan.org, will send you a free travel guide to Michigan along with a road map. The West Michigan Tourist Association, 950 28th Street SE, Suite E-200, Grand Rapids 49508; (800) 442–2084 or (616) 456–8557; www.wmta.org, covers accommodations, attractions, and visitor facilities in the western half of the Lower Peninsula. The Upper Peninsula Travel and Recreation Association, P.O. Box 400, Iron Mountain 49801; (800) 562–7134 or (906) 774–5480; www.uptravel.com, covers the Upper Peninsula.
- **State Parks:** For a guide to the Michigan State Parks system, contact the Michigan Department of Natural Resources, Parks & Recreation Division, Box 30257, Lansing 48909; (517) 373–9900.
- **Major Newspapers:** *Detroit Free Press, Detroit News, Grand Rapids Press, Flint Journal, Lansing State Journal*
- **Public Transportation:** Michigan's major regional air center is Metro Airport, located in Romulus 15 miles southwest of Detroit. The main carrier

is Northwest Airlines (800–225–2525), which uses Detroit as a major hub. Both Greyhound Bus Service (800–229–9424; www.greyhound.com) and Amtrak (800–872–7245; www.amtrak.com) maintain service throughout the state.

- **Climate:** Michigan is split in the middle by the 45th Parallel; this northern position means that it has a very temperate, four-season climate. Summers reach the high 90s but rarely break triple digits. Winters can dip to minus 10 or 20 degrees at times in the northern half of the state but usually hover between 10 and 20 degrees in southern Michigan. Thanks to the Great Lakes, Michigan receives an abundance of snow, with some towns like Munising and Calumet totaling more than 250 inches by the end of March. Autumn colors are spectacular in the state, with trees beginning to change in late September in the Upper Peninsula and late October in Southern Michigan.

Southeast Michigan

Southeast Michigan, a region of seven counties, revolves around metropolitan Detroit, which sprawls into three of them. And Detroit revolves around automobiles. It's as simple as that.

Known best throughout the country as Motor City, Detroit carries several other titles, including Motown, after the recording company that produced such famous singers as Diana Ross and Stevie Wonder before it fled to Los Angeles from its studio on Woodward Avenue. The city is also home to the nation's oldest state fair (the Michigan State Fair dates to 1849) and the largest farmers' market.

Detroit and its neighboring suburbs wear many faces; some are good, some others are unjustly earned, but the least recognized one is that of a destination for travelers. Detroit is the sixth largest city in the country, yet despite its size many tourists consider it very much "off the beaten path." Depart from the city and the rest of Southeast Michigan changes quickly, from the urban sprawl to the rolling hills and lakes of northern Oakland County, the blue water of St. Clair and Port Huron, and the culture and carefree college ways of Ann Arbor, the home of the University of Michigan.

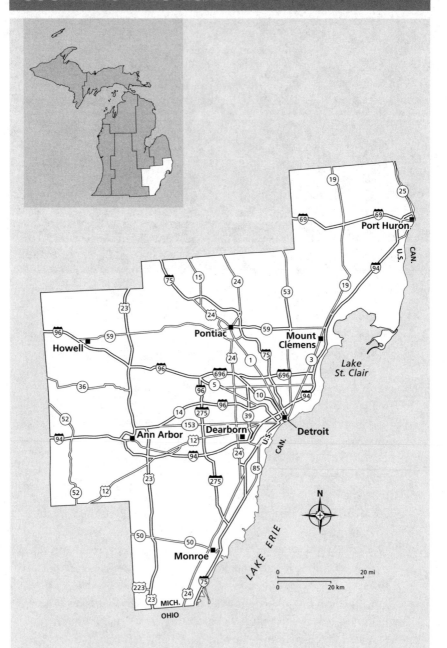

Wayne County

Until the 1870s, Detroit was a commercial center for farmers, but at the end of that century the first automobiles appeared, as Ransom E. Olds and Henry Ford began tinkering with "horseless carriages." By 1903, Ford had organized the Ford Motor Company, and when he pioneered the assembly-line method of building cars and introduced the Model T, the vehicle for the common man, Detroit's place as the automobile capital of the world was established.

Cars are a way of life in Detroit. Michigan boasts of having the first mile of concrete rural highway (1909), the first traffic light (1915), and the first urban freeway free of those annoying stoplights (1942). The best-known place to view this history of cars and their immense effect on the American way of life is **The Henry Ford**, home of Greenfield Village and Henry Ford Museum, (313–271–1620), a 260-acre complex with one hundred historic buildings in Dearborn that has become the nation's largest indoor and outdoor museum.

Keep in mind that there is a museum and a village, each a separate attraction with a separate admission price and requiring at least a good part of a day to view. The Henry Ford Museum's main attraction is "The Automobile in American Life," an ode to the motor car culture that is a social history of twentieth-century America. Adjacent Greenfield Village features old buildings

AUTHOR'S TOP TEN PICKS

African American History,
Detroit;
(313) 494–5800

Ann Arbor Hands-On Museum,
Ann Arbor;
(734) 995–5437

Belle Isle Aquarium,
Detroit;
(313) 852–4141

Eastern Market,
Detroit;
(586) 393–8800

Ford Wyoming Drive-in,
Dearborn;
(313) 846–6910

Greenfield Village,
Dearborn;
(313) 271–1620

People Mover,
Detroit;
(313) 962–7245

River Raisin Battlefield Visitor Center,
Monroe;
(734) 243–7137

Walter P. Chrysler Museum,
Auburn Hills;
(888) 456–1924

Wright Museum of Motown Museum,
Detroit;
(313) 875–2264

shipped in from all over the country, including Thomas Edison's laboratory from Menlo Park, New Jersey, Henry Ford's birthplace, and the Wright Brothers' cycle workshop.

The complex is located at 20900 Oakwood Boulevard and reached by following signs from Southfield Freeway. Admission is $14 for the museum, $20 for the village, or $48 for a combination ticket good for two days. Serious history buffs purchase a two-day ticket.

For a more intimate view of the auto barons themselves, visit one of the many mansions that auto money built and historical societies have since preserved. **Fairlane,** the Henry Ford estate, is a fifty-six-room mansion located nearby on the University of Michigan–Dearborn campus. Built in 1915 at what was then an astronomical $1.8 million, the home is an extension of Ford's ingenuity wrapped up in his love for functionalism. It often hosted such dignitaries as Edison, President Herbert Hoover, and Charles Lindbergh. Tours begin underground among the massive turbines and generators that were designed by Ford and his friend Edison in the six-level powerhouse that made the estate self-sufficient in power, heat, light, even ice.

funfacts

Michigan's largest city has the distinction of lying north of the Canadian border. Visitors are often surprised when they learn that to reach Windsor, Ontario, they have to drive south on the Ambassador Bridge or through the Detroit-Windsor Tunnel.

From the outside the house looks modest compared with other historic mansions. But inside you'll find such luxuries as a central vacuum cleaner, a sixty-five-extension phone system, a one-lane bowling alley, and a pool that has been covered and turned into a delightful restaurant that serves lunch. Guided tours lead you through the house and underground tunnels, show you where Edison used to sleep, and tell of April 7, 1947, when the Rogue River flooded and knocked out the powerhouse. That night, without heat, light, or phone service, Ford suffered a cerebral hemorrhage and died by candlelight.

To reach U of M–Dearborn, head west of Southfield Expressway on Michigan Avenue and then north on Greenfield Road, where signs point the way to the small campus. Guided tours of the National Historic Landmark are offered year-round. From April through December, Fairlane (313–593–5590) is also open daily with tours offered on the hour from 10:00 A.M. to 3:00 P.M. Monday through Saturday and every half hour 1:00 to 4:30 P.M. Sunday. There are shorter hours in the winter. Admission is $10.00 for adults, $6.00 for children.

Movie stars and fresh air . . . you do remember drive-in theaters, don't you? At the **Ford Wyoming Drive-in** in Dearborn, it's hard to forget them.

Contrary to the popular belief that drive-ins are cinematic dinosaurs of the be-bop era, this motorized movieland in the hometown of Henry Ford is still packing them in.

Ford Wyoming is the largest drive-in complex in Michigan, with eight theaters—that's right, eight separate screens, each showing a different movie. On a good weekend there will be more than 2,000 cars and between 5,000 and 8,000 people watching a film.

Ford Wyoming Drive-in (313–846–6910 or 582–2200) is reached from I–94 by taking exit 210 and heading north on Wyoming Avenue. Some of the screens are entered from Wyoming Avenue and some from Ford Road.

To most people Detroit is Motor City, but to music lovers it will always be Motown, the birthplace of the famous record company that Berry Gordy Jr. founded in 1958. Gordy started out with $800 and a small recording studio that was built in the back of his Grand Boulevard home. From Studio A emerged the distinct "Motown Sound" and such performers as Marvin Gaye, the Miracles, Gladys Knight and the Pips, the Supremes, the Jackson 5, and a very talented blind singer named Steveland Morris Hardaway, known now as Stevie Wonder. Eventually the famous HITSVILLE U.S.A. sign was hung on the front of the home, and Motown expanded into seven additional houses along the street before setting up its Woodward office.

The company continued recording in Studio A until 1972, when it moved its operation to Los Angeles. What remains today at Hitsville U.S.A. is **Motown Museum,** a state historic site. The museum is two adjoining houses filled with gold record awards, old album covers, publicity photos, and even some old Temptations costumes that are viewed to the beat of Motown hits played

TOP ANNUAL EVENTS

International Freedom Festival,
Windsor and Detroit, end of June;
(313) 923–8259

Ann Arbor Street Art Fairs,
Ann Arbor, July;
(800) 888–9487

Port Huron to Mackinac Island Yacht Race (Boat Night),
Port Huron, July;
(800) 852–4242

Michigan State Fair,
Detroit, August;
(313) 369–8310

Woodward Dream Cruise,
Birmingham, August;
(248) 433–3550

Ford International Jazz Festival,
Downtown Detroit,
Labor Day weekend;
(313) 963–7622

continuously in every room. For most visitors the intriguing part is Studio A and its control booth, looking as it did many years ago when Motown was a struggling recording company.

Motown Museum (313–875–2264) is located at 2648 West Grand Boulevard, 2 blocks west of the exit off the Lodge Freeway. The museum is open Tuesday through Saturday 10:00 A.M. to 6:00 P.M. Admission is $8.00 for adults, $5.00 for children.

Although Detroit has its mansions and its auto barons, it is known primarily as a blue-collar town, an assembly-line haven that has made it as ethnically diverse as any city in the country. Detroiters love their heritage, ethnic foods, music, and the traditions of an old way of life. The ethnic pride and the love of traditional foods can best be seen at the *Eastern Market,* a farmers' market that is said to be the largest of its kind (open to retailers rather than wholesalers) in the country. Two areas, one open-air, the other enclosed, and both decorated with huge murals on the outside, are the heart of the market. On Tuesday and Saturday they overflow with shoppers, farmers, and vendors bartering for the freshest fruit, vegetables, flowers, meats, and cheeses to be found in the city. Everything from the farm is on sale here, from homemade bratwurst to live rabbits, and the market makes for an enjoyable stroll, even if you don't intend to buy anything.

Ringing the market are butcher shops, fish markets, and stores specializing in spices, nuts, and foods imported from around the world. The oldest shop is *R. Hirt Jr. Company* in a three-story redbrick building that overlooks the market stalls. Rudolph Hirt Jr. began his business in 1887 with a stall in the old Detroit Central Market, selling eggs, butter, and cheese from local farms. When land in Cadillac Square became too valuable to be used as a farmers' market, Hirt was one of the first to build a store in the new Eastern Market on land the city set aside in 1892.

Big Explosion

In the spirit of international cooperation, Windsor and Detroit team up in late June for the Freedom Festival, which is highlighted with a fireworks display over the Detroit River. The fireworks are lit from a barge in the middle of the river and usually are watched by more than a million people oohing and aahing with every explosion. It is the largest fireworks show in North America.

If you're planning to attend, get there early, bring a lawn chair, and find a spot downtown within a few blocks of the river. Hart Plaza, naturally, is the prime spot to watch this brilliant performance.

The building still stands, and the old wooden cheese locker behind the counter is still used, although a much larger one has been built on the second floor. The second one was needed because 40 percent of Hirt's business is selling cheese: more than 250 kinds, from well-known Swiss cheese and French brie to the little-known Michigan Raw Milk Pinconning that is made in the Upper Peninsula. The shop also sells imported crackers and cookies, teas, jams, at least thirty kinds of mustard, olive oil, and other gastronomic items, all left stacked in their opened cases to make for leisurely and informal browsing. On the third floor, Hirt sells wicker baskets of all descriptions and sizes. You could purchase a basket on the third floor and then easily fill it with enough mouthwatering items on the first floor for a memorable gourmet dinner in the park.

R. Hirt Jr. Company

To reach the Eastern Market, head downtown on I–75 and exit east on Mack Avenue. The market is 2 blocks east of the expressway, near Russell Avenue. R. Hirt Jr. is open Monday through Friday 7:00 A.M. to 3:00 P.M., and Saturday 7:00 A.M. to 2:00 P.M.

Restaurants also reflect the ethnically diverse, hardworking Detroiters who at nightfall put aside their jobs and enjoy themselves immensely with good food served in large portions at very reasonable prices. Coney Island hot dogs and baseball are a summer tradition in the Motor City. Begin with the Detroit Tigers, an American League club that moved into its new stadium, Comerica Park, in 2000; after the ninth inning, head over to **Lafayette Coney Island,** Detroit's premier hot-dog place. Located where Lafayette and Michigan Avenues merge near Kennedy Square downtown, the porcelain white eatery with its male waiters is an institution in Detroit. The fare is Coney dogs (with loads of chopped onions, chili, and mustard), loose burgers (loose hamburger in a hot-dog bun), and bean soup served on Formica counters and tables with paper napkins and truck-stop china. Yet arrive at midnight and you'll see patrons dressed in tuxedos enjoying a late-night hot dog after the symphony, seated next to a couple of rabid baseball fans with a team pennant. Lafayette Coney Island (313–964–8198) is open twenty-four hours daily with hot dogs and loose burgers priced at around $2.00.

A few blocks over at Monroe Street is lively **Greektown,** where a dozen restaurants, nightclubs, and Greek bakeries make it the liveliest spot in downtown Detroit. My favorite restaurant is the **New Hellas Cafe,** where flaming cheese and the cry of "Opa!" is a Detroit tradition. The best African-American cuisine in Detroit is **Southern Fire** (313–393–4930) at 575 Bellevue Street. It's the place for ribs, fried catfish, collard greens, and sweet potato pie. Detroit's Polish community is centered around the city of Hamtramck, where Pope John Paul II once performed mass. At the **Polish Village Cafe** (313–874–5726) at Yehmans Street and Joseph Campau Avenue, you can dig into stuffed cabbage, pork goulash, and pierogi for less than $8.00.

It may not be "off the beaten path," but Detroit's Central Automated Transit System is definitely above the city streets. Better known as the **People Mover,** the mass transit project was opened in 1987 after several years of controversial delays and cost overruns. The 2.9-mile elevated track circles the downtown heart of Detroit. Its automated cars stop every three minutes at thirteen stations, each decorated with beautiful mosaics and other artwork. The ride costs only 50 cents and lasts fourteen minutes, but it gives an excellent overall view of the city from a superb vantage point. The best stretch comes when the cars wind around Cobo Hall and passengers see a panorama of the Detroit River and the skyline of Windsor, the Canadian city to the south. The People Mover (313–962–7245) operates from 7:00 A.M. to 11:00 P.M. Monday to Thursday, until midnight Friday and Saturday, and until 8:00 P.M. Sunday.

funfacts

Lafayette Coney Island dates back to 1924 when Greek entrepreneur Bill Keros opened the restaurant, using the New York–style Coney Island stand concept. When his brother opened up American Coney Island right next door, they began slathering the hot dogs with chili to attract customers, inventing the Detroit version of a Coney Island. Today both restaurants are still battling it out side-by-side on Lafayette Avenue.

The Detroit River, which connects Lake St. Clair with Lake Erie, was the avenue that the city's first residents—the French in 1701—used to arrive in Southeast Michigan. The river remains a focal point of activities for Detroiters, with several parks lining its banks and one—Belle Isle—located in the middle of it. Reached by a bridge at East Jefferson and Grand Boulevard, the island park features the **Belle Isle Aquarium** (313–852–4141), which opened to the public in 1904, making it one of the oldest freshwater aquariums in the country.

The center features thousands of fish in dozens of large tanks, everything from a school of piranhas and a 4-foot-long alligator gar to common bluegill, bass, and rainbow trout. One of the most popular tanks contains an electric eel, and when this fish is fed, at 10:30 A.M., 12:30 P.M., and 2:30 P.M. daily, it is an electrifying affair. The handlers drop a microphone into the tank so onlookers can hear the fish-made electric charges. The aquarium is open daily 10:00 A.M. to 5:00 P.M. There is a small admission fee.

Almost next door to the aquarium on the island is **Dossin Great Lakes Museum** (313–852–4051), which traces the sailing history of the Great Lakes in several rooms of displays and hands-on exhibits and a video room. A highlight of the museum is the preserved pilothouse from a Great Lakes freighter, which actually looks out on the Detroit River. The museum is open from 11:00 A.M. to 5:00 P.M. Saturday and Sunday. A small donation is requested at the door.

If the day is nice, you can spend an afternoon at Hart Plaza at the foot of Woodward Avenue overlooking the Detroit River and Windsor. For an even better view of the waterfront, **Diamond Jack River Tours** (313–843–7676) offers two-hour cruises on the Detroit River that depart from Hart Plaza. The cruises are $14 per person.

Detroit's Cultural Center, clustered around Woodward Avenue and Kirby Street, is dominated by the **Detroit Institute of Arts** (313–833–7900). Thanks to auto baron wealth accumulated in the early 1900s, the DIA is considered one of the top art collections in the country. It is known for its Italian Renaissance, Dutch-Flemish, and German expressionist art, but the most viewed work is probably Diego Rivera's mural, *Detroit Industry*, which fills a room and reflects the city's blue-collar work ethic. Hours are 11:00 A.M. to 4:00 P.M. Wednesday through Thursday, 10:00 A.M. to 9:00 P.M. Friday, and 10:00 A.M. to 5:00 P.M. Saturday and Sunday. Adult admission is $4.00.

Within easy walking distance of the DIA at East Warren Avenue and Brush Street, is the **Wright Museum of African American History** (313–494–5800), the largest such museum in the country; its collection ranges from art to clubs and golf shoes used by Tiger Woods to capture the World Match Play. In November 2004, the museum unveiled its new per-

funfacts

Michigan's first public whipping post stood at Woodward and Jefferson Avenues in Detroit from 1818 to 1831. At the intersection now is the giant sculptural fist. The controversial statue honors Joe Louis, Detroit's famous son who became world heavyweight boxing champion in 1937.

manent exhibit entitled "And Still We Rise." The impressive, $8-million exhibit uses multimedia displays to trace the 400-year history and culture of African Americans. Hours are 9:30 A.M. to 8:00 P.M. Tuesday, 9:30 A.M. to 5:00 P.M. Wednesday through Saturday, and 1:00 to 5:00 P.M. Sunday. Admission is $8.00 for adults and $5.00 for children.

Detroit's Cool Jazz

There's nothing like spending an evening in Detroit area nightclubs listening to jazz and blues. A list of clubs with the type of music they feature is found in **Metro Times**, a free entertainment newspaper. Some of the better-known clubs for local blues and jazz include Rhinoceros at 265 Riopelle Street and Baker's Keyboard Lounge at 20510 Livernois Avenue. In Hamtramck there is the Attic Bar at 11667 Joseph Campau Avenue, a true blues bar where customers take over the piano when a band isn't around.

Also located in the Cultural Center is the *New Detroit Science Center* (313–577–8400) at 5020 John R Road. The center was founded in the early 1970s and was among the first in the country to feature an IMAX Dome Theater. In 1999 the Science Center broke ground on a $30-million expansion, and two years later it reopened to rave reviews from children and their amazed parents.

The New Detroit Science Center features 110,000 square feet of scientific exploration, with five hands-on exhibit laboratories for future scientists and two demonstration stages where real scientists, at times, defy gravity. You can still see a more-real-than-life movie in the IMAX Dome Theater or gaze at the universe in Dassault Systemes Planetarium. Hours are 9:00 A.M. to 5:00 P.M. Monday through Friday, 10:30 A.M. to 6:00 P.M. Saturday, and noon to 6:00 P.M. on Sunday. The center is closed on Monday in the winter. Admission is $7.00 for adults and $6.00 for children.

In 1882 the Plymouth Iron Windmill Company began to manufacture and give away small BB guns to farmers to encourage them to purchase one of its windmills. Within four years, the northwest corner of Wayne County was well "windmilled," but the company kept producing the air rifles. Eventually Plymouth Iron Windmill Company became Daisy Manufacturing Company, and this small town was known as the "air rifle capital of the world" until the operations were moved to Arkansas in 1958.

You can learn about the start of Daisy air rifles and see a collection of the earliest models at the *Plymouth Historical Museum.* The museum also has many other exhibits, period rooms, and even a depiction of "downtown Plymouth" in the early 1900s, but it is the display of Daisy air rifles that brings back fond memories of tin cans in the backyard to so many of us.

To reach the Plymouth Historical Museum (734–455–8940) from I–275, get off at exit 28, head west on Ann Arbor Road, and then turn north on Main Street. Hours are 1:00 to 4:00 P.M. Wednesday, Thursday, Saturday, and Sunday. There is a small admission fee.

Monroe County

General George Armstrong Custer may have staged his ill-fated "last stand" at the Little Bighorn River in Montana, but he grew up in Monroe, Michigan. Custer was actually born in Rumley, Ohio, but spent most of his youth, until he entered a military academy at the age of sixteen, living with his half sister in this city along Lake Erie. Even after he became a noted brigadier general during the Civil War, Custer continued to return to Monroe, and in 1864 he married Elizabeth Bacon, his boyhood sweetheart, here.

Custer's intriguing life can be traced at the *Monroe County Historical Museum,* which features the largest collection of the general's personal artifacts in the country. The Custer exhibit room occupies a fourth of the museum floor, and focuses on his youth in Monroe and his distinguished Civil War career, rather than his well-known days on the western plains. There is an overcoat of buffalo hide that he wore during a winter campaign in 1868 and a buckskin suit that is impressive with its beadwork and porcupine quills. Custer was an avid outdoorsman and also a fine taxidermist. It comes as a surprise to many that Custer enjoyed mounting the game animals he hunted, and housed in the museum along with his favorite Remington buffalo rifle are many mounted game animals.

The museum also has displays on Monroe's early history, which dates back to French missionaries in 1634. But it is the life and tragic death of General Custer that most people find fascinating. The Monroe County Historical Museum (734–240–7780) is at 126 South Monroe Street in the heart of the city and is open Wednesday through Sunday from 10:00 A.M. to 5:00 P.M. During the summer through September, it is open daily. There is a small admission fee.

Unless you are a military buff, you might not realize that the Massacre of the River Raisin was among the largest battles in the War of 1812 and produced more American casualties than any other conflict. Now the city's newest museum, the *River Raisin Battlefield Visitor Center,* is dedicated to what many historians believe became the turning point in the conflict with Great Britain.

After the disastrous opening months of the War of 1812 in which Mackinac Island, Chicago, and Detroit had fallen, two of them without even a shot fired, an elderly Revolutionary War veteran, General James Winchester, was sent to Michigan with almost 1,000 men. The large American force set up camp on an open field on the north side of the river. But in the pre-dawn darkness of January 22, almost 600 British regulars with 6 cannons and 800 Indians attacked. The fighting raged for twenty minutes and then turned into a panicked flight for Ohio for Winchester's army. Of the 400 Americans who ran, 220 were killed, another 147, including Winchester himself, were captured, and only 33 managed to escape to safety. The next day Indians returned to plunder the homes, scalp the wounded, and toss the bodies into burning homes. More than sixty unarmed Americans were killed, and a nation was horrified. Soon, "Remember the Raisin!" became a battle cry that led U.S. troops to victory in the old Northwest.

All this history has been carefully preserved and clearly presented at the battlefield visitor center. Its most impressive display is a fourteen-minute fiber-optic map presentation. On two wall-size maps, the story of the River Raisin is retold with the Americans, British, and Indians, as colorful lights, maneuvering and taking up positions in front of you. The visitor center (734–243–7136) is reached from I–75 by taking exit 14 and heading west on Elm Street. The center is open 10:00 A.M. to 5:00 P.M. Friday through Tuesday from Memorial Day through Labor Day, and on Saturday and Sunday the rest of the year. There is no admission charge.

Washtenaw County

Trendy Ann Arbor, the cultural capital of Southeast Michigan (and some say the entire state), is the site of the University of Michigan, the "Harvard of the West." The university dominates the city, its buildings and campus entwined in the town's landscape. It provides many of Ann Arbor's top attractions, such as the **Kelsey Museum of Archaeology** (734–764–9304), a renowned collection of art and artifacts, including mummies, from Egyptian, Greek, Roman, and classical Mediterranean cultures. On Saturdays in the fall, Ann Arbor is U of M football; the largest stadium crowds in the country (112,000) gather to cheer on the Wolverines.

funfacts

The University of Michigan was founded in 1837 when the state legislature set aside U of M's original forty-acre campus. Classes were held in the old Mason Hall in the fall of 1841 with a student body of seven and faculty of two.

But there is another side to this college town, one that children will appreciate, and it begins at the **Ann Arbor Hands-On Museum.** This is no stuffy hall with an endless row of glass-enclosed displays. The entire museum is devoted to participatory exhibits—more than eighty on four floors—and the concept that kids learn by doing. Housed in the classic Central Fire House, the museum was dedicated on September 28, 1982, the one hundredth anniversary of the building. Inside, visitors try exhibits such as the sand pendular, a suspended funnel that you fill with sand and swing to make various patterns. There is also the bubble capsule, where participants step into a ring of soap film and slowly raise a cylinder bubble around them until it pops. Some exhibits use computers and deal with complex theories; others are as simple as the mystery boxes: A child sticks in a hand and attempts to guess what is touched. All the exhibits come with a printed explanation that is appreciated mostly by the parents.

The Ann Arbor Hands-On Museum (734–995–5437) is recommended for children eight years of age and older. It is at Huron Street and Fifth Avenue, which can be reached by following Business US 23 (Main Street) from M 14 north of the city or from I–94 by exiting to US 23 and then to Washtenaw Avenue. Hours are Monday through Saturday from 10:00 A.M. to 5:00 P.M. and Sunday from noon to 5:00 P.M. Admission is $7.50 for adults and $6.00 for children.

There are no mountains in Southeast Michigan, but that doesn't stop the region from being a mecca for mountain biking. In large part because of cycle-crazy Ann Arbor, the trails at **Pinckney Recreation Area** have been transformed into a playground for off-road cycling. It's estimated that more than 120,000 mountain bikers from Ohio, Indiana, and Illinois as well as Michigan visit the park annually to ride the challenging 17.5-mile Potawatomi Trail, the 5-mile Crooked Lake Trail, or the 2-mile Silver Lake Trail.

The trailhead for all trails is in the park's Silver Lake Day-Use Area reached from US 23 by taking exit 49 and heading west on North Territorial Road to Dexter-Townhall Road, then heading north on Dexter-Townhall Road past the park headquarters (734–426–4913) to the day-use area. In Ann Arbor bicycles can be rented at the Student Bike Shop (734–662–6986) at 607 South Forest Street.

strange as it sounds

The center of the University of Michigan campus is the Diag, a parklike opening that extends from State Street to South University Avenue. The bronze seal in the center was donated by the Class of 1953, and legend has it that any freshman who steps on it before taking his or her first exam at U of M will fail the test.

Nearby on the west side of State Street is the Michigan Union. It was on the steps of this imposing building that John F. Kennedy first announced his vision of the Peace Corps in 1960 while campaigning for the White House.

Oakland County

It's 4:00 P.M. in **Birmingham** and you're sipping tea from fine china in a setting that includes fresh-cut flowers, silver platters of cakes and other tempting edibles, a fire in a fireplace of imported Italian marble, and a tuxedo-clad piano player, er, excuse me, pianist.

Big Leaguers in Motown

There is plenty of big-league sports action in Southeast Michigan. The Detroit Pistons and the Detroit Shock play men's and women's basketball, respectively, at the Palace of Auburn Hills (tickets: 248–377–0100). The Detroit Red Wings, the 2002 Stanley Cup winners, play at Joe Louis Arena (313–396–7544), though it's almost impossible to get Red Wing tickets. The Detroit Tigers (313–471–2555) play baseball at impressive Comerica Park, while next door the Detroit Lions (800–616–7627) play football at brand-new Ford Field. These side-by-side stadiums opened in Detroit in 2000 and 2002.

If you just want to see where the big leaguers play, the Palace (248–377–0100) offers tours Monday through Friday from 9:00 A.M. to 4:00 P.M. Tours include going behind the scenes to see the Palace broadcast center, visitors' locker rooms, the press lounge, and the owner's suite. Admission is $5.00 for adults and $3.00 for children.

Must be tea at the Townsend. The afternoon ritual, in all its elegance, takes place throughout the week in the *Townsend Hotel,* the most affluent hotel in this ritzy suburb of Detroit. Built in 1988, the hotel has eighty-seven rooms and fifty-two suites on three floors, and among its guests have been entertainers such as Madonna, Michael Jackson, Paul McCartney, and New Kids on the Block. (Remember them?) Just about anybody who plays in Detroit stays at the Townsend.

Have afternoon tea here, and who knows? Maybe you'll see Billy Idol stroll in. It has happened before. From Woodward Avenue in downtown Birmingham, turn west onto Townsend Street, and the hotel is reached in 3 blocks. There is one seating for afternoon tea at 3:00 P.M. Call the Townsend Hotel at (248) 642–7900 for reservations.

The newest museum in Southeast Michigan focuses on one of the state's most popular attractions: classic cars. In 1999 the *Walter P. Chrysler Museum,* with its collection of seventy-five cars, opened on the grounds of Daimler-Chrysler's huge Auburn Hills complex. The sleek $10 billion center is the first on-site museum built by a North American auto company.

Inside are interactive displays, a video wall, life-size dioramas, and time-lines that detail the history of the car company that Walter Chrysler founded in 1924. But the main attraction here is the cars themselves. Just inside the front door is a massive 75-foot stainless steel pylon that holds aloft a 1941 Thunder-bolt and a red 1989 Viper concept car. Called "The Tower," the display slowly rotates to give visitors a full view of the impressive cars. Other vehicles on exhibit include rare DeSoto, Hudson, Nash, and Rambler models, as well as trucks and concept cars.

To reach the museum (888–456–1924), depart I–75 at exit 78 and head east on Chrysler Drive into the DaimlerChrysler complex. Signs will direct you to the museum. Hours are 10:00 A.M. to 6:00 P.M. Tuesday through Saturday and noon to 6:00 P.M. Sunday. Admission is $6.00 for adults and $3.00 for children.

The urban sprawl of Southeast Michigan runs its course to Pontiac, but from there the terrain changes quickly to the rolling hills, lakes, and woods of northern Oakland. A drive of less than an hour from the heart of Detroit can remove you from the city and bring you to the porch steps of a rustic cabin on a small pond in a wooded area where white-tailed deer often pass by. **Roston Cabin** in Holly Recreation Area makes a weekend spent in the woods as comfortable and warm as sitting around the fireplace at night. The cabin is snug and tight, but still rustic and secluded enough to make it seem like an adventure in the woods—even though the car is parked right outside.

Built by the Roston family as a weekend cottage in the early 1940s, the cabin was obtained by the park, which began renting it out in 1984. It's a classic cabin built with walls of logs, polished planked floors, and red-checkered curtains on the windows. There is electricity, and the kitchen features an electric stove and refrigerator as well as a table, benches, and a wood stove. The sleeping room is larger, with a set of bunks and an easy chair facing a fieldstone fireplace. Overlooking the cozy room is a loft, the warmest part of the cabin at night, with four more mattresses. Outside you'll find a vault toilet, woodshed, a hand pump for water, and a barbecue grill.

It's necessary to reserve the cabin in advance by calling the park headquarters, and, surprisingly, the most popular time to rent it is during the winter when families arrive to cross-country ski on the unplowed park roads around the lakes. The overnight rate for the cabin is $50, and reservations can be made by contacting Holly Recreation Area (248–634–8811). The recreation area is reached by taking Grange Hall Road (exit 101) east off I–75.

Many people exit I–75 at Grange Hall Road and head west to explore the historical town of Holly. Established in the early 1800s, Holly was a sleepy little hamlet until 1855, when the Detroit-Milwaukee Railroad reached the town, bringing immediate growth and prosperity with the twenty-five trains that passed through daily. Martha Street, near the tracks, was the site of the Holly Hotel, many saloons, and frequent brawls. In 1880 an uproar between local rowdies and a traveling circus left so many beaten and bruised that the street became known as **Battle Alley.** The most famous moment in Battle Alley's history was

funfacts

The country's first shopping mall, Northland, was built in Southfield in Oakland County in 1954.

on August 28, 1908, when Carry Nation, the notorious "Kansas Saloon Smasher," arrived in Holly at the request of the local Prohibition committee. The next day Nation, with umbrella in hand and her pro-temperance supporters a step behind her, invaded the saloons, smashing whiskey bottles, clubbing patrons, and preaching about the sins of "demon rum." Nation created the biggest flurry at the hotel, where she entered the "Dispensing Room" and attacked the painting of a nude over the bar.

strangeasitsounds

The 1950s are alive and well at Eddie's Drive-in (586–469–2345), a landmark burger place at 36111 Jefferson Avenue in Harrison Township. It's a nightly show in the summer when hep cats and cool chicks show off their hot rods while waitresses on roller skates serve you shakes and fries to the be-bop music of that golden era. Eddie's is open from April to mid-October.

Today the residents of Holly celebrate the occasion with a *Carry Nation Festival* the second weekend of September, highlighted by a reenactment of that special day in 1908 along with a parade, arts and crafts booths, and much food, entertainment, and, yes, a few swigs of the very stuff Nation campaigned against. Battle Alley and its hundred-year-old Victorian buildings have been restored as a string of twelve specialty shops that include antiques markets both along the alley and on nearby streets.

The *Holly Hotel,* which was built in 1891 and suffered through two devastating fires, the second in 1978, has since been completely restored, including the painting of the nude. It is now listed on the National Register of Historic Places but no longer provides lodging. Instead, the hotel is a fine restaurant, known for both its classic and its creative cuisine, all set in a Victorian tradition that reflects its birth during the railroad era. The main dining room, with its pedestal tables, soft glow of gas lamps, and red velvet wing-back chairs, is the stage for such entrees as medallions of beef with morel mushroom sauce, fillet of beef Wellington, and sautéed Michigan rainbow trout. The hotel also provides gourmet picnic baskets that include not only appetizers, dinner, desserts, and wine but also linen, flatware, candles, and a map of good picnic spots in the area.

The Holly Hotel (248–634–5208) is open for lunch Monday through Saturday from 11:00 A.M. to 3:00 P.M. and for dinner Monday through Thursday from 4:00 to 10:00 P.M., Friday and Saturday from 5:00 to 11:00 P.M., and Sunday from 10:30 A.M. to 8:00 P.M. Dinner prices range from $23 to $33, and reservations are recommended.

Michigan has more than its share of unusual bed-and-breakfasts. You can book a room in a lighthouse, on a two-masted schooner, at a farm, in a home

Visiting the North Pole in Michigan

Our timing was perfect; on the March day we visited the Arctic Ring of Life exhibit at the **Detroit Zoo**, the temperature was in the midteens.

At Glacier Overlook we had our hands buried in our pockets and our backs against the wind when suddenly a polar bear appeared, strolled across the pack ice, and then belly flopped into water that was littered with small icebergs.

It looked—and felt—as if we were at the North Pole.

Which is exactly what the officials at the Detroit Zoo were hoping to achieve when they unveiled "the world's largest polar bear exhibit" in 2001.

The $14.9-million Arctic Ring of Life covers 4.2 acres and is designed to simulate a trek through the three environments found north of the Arctic Circle: tundra, open sea, and pack ice.

A one-way path first winds through the tundra, where you can see arctic foxes prance around or a pair of snowy owls blink back at you. From there you descend into the open sea via the Polar Passage.

This passage is a showstopper, a 70-foot-long, acrylic tunnel that takes you through the exhibit's 300,000-gallon sea environment. On one side are a half dozen seals lazily swimming and eyeing you through the transparent walls. On the other side it's possible to watch the powerful elegance of an 800-pound polar bear underwater. It's a fascinating experience watching seals swim over your head.

From the tunnel you venture into the pack ice environment by first entering an ice cave with a howling winter gale and icy walls that are covered with polar bear prints.

From the cave you reemerge outside and follow the path as it leads you past a handful of viewing points of the pack ice where polar bears can be seen swimming among the icebergs in the open water.

The Detroit Zoo (248–398–0900) is open from 10:00 A.M. to 5:00 P.M. from April 1 to October 31 and from 10:00 A.M. to 4:00 P.M. the rest of the year. Admission is $10.50 for adults and $6.50 for children.

To reach the zoo from I–696, exit north on Woodward Avenue just west of I–75. There are entrances to the zoo on both Woodward Avenue and Ten Mile Road.

that doubles as a microbrewery. Now you can also make reservations to spend a night at the country's first B&B train.

Coe Rail has renovated a pair of classic Pullman sleeper cars to offer people the opportunity to wake up on the rails. Owners claim their **Star Clipper Train** is the "first railroad to offer bed-and-breakfast service on rail."

If you don't have a night to spare, just drop by for dinner. Coe Rail has also re-created the romance of dining on the rail with prime rib, seafood, or such entrees as Duet au Poivre Pork in the train tradition of elegance with sparkling crystal, fine china, fresh-starched linens, and ever-changing scenery through the windows. Each evening features a three-hour rail excursion, with guests indulging in a five-course dinner while the train passes the new Depot Park in Wixom, the wooded West Bloomfield Bird Sanctuary, and Woodpecker Lake.

Star Clipper Bed and Breakfast (248–960–9440) is reached from I–96 by taking exit 159 and heading north on Wixom Road to Pontiac Trail. Continue north on Pontiac Trail into Walled Lake. Coe Rail Depot is on Pontiac Trail just past Maple Road. The Star Clipper departs Tuesday, Wednesday, Thursday, and Saturday at 7:00 P.M., Friday at 7:30 P.M., and Sunday at 5:00 P.M., year-round. A night on the train, which is offered only on Saturday, includes dinner and is $289 per couple. The dinner excursion only is $77.

Macomb County

In the fall one of the favorite activities in Southeast Michigan is a trip to a cider mill. Parents pack the kids in the car and head out to the edge of the county where a river turns an old wooden waterwheel. The wheel is the source of power for the mill, which crushes apples to extract the dark brown juice and refine it into cider, truly one of Michigan's culinary delights. After viewing the operation, visitors can purchase jugs of cider, cinnamon doughnuts, and sticky caramel apples and then retreat to a place along the river. Here they enjoy a feast in the midst of brilliant fall colors, in the warmth of an Indian summer, and with the fragrance of crushed apples floating by.

Cider mills ring the metropolitan Detroit area, but one of the oldest and most colorful lies right on the border of Oakland and Macomb Counties west of Rochester on Avon Road (Twenty-Three Mile Road). **Yates Cider Mill** was built in 1863 along the banks of the Clinton River and began its long history as a grist-mill. It has been a water-powered operation ever since, but in 1876 it began making cider, and today the waterwheel still powers the apple elevator, grinders, and press as well as generating electricity for the lights inside. The mill can pro-duce 300 gallons of cider per hour, all of which is needed in the fall to meet the demand of visitors who enjoy their treat around the huge red barn or across the street on the banks of the Clinton River. Yates Cider Mill (248–651–8300) is open daily from 9:00 A.M. to 7:00 P.M. September through November, and from noon to 5:00 P.M. Saturday and Sunday December until May.

You won't find much apple cider to sip, but an equally interesting mill in Macomb County is the focal point at **Wolcott Mill Metropark.** Built in 1847 on the North Branch of the Clinton River, Wolcott Mill was a grist and feed operation for more than a century, commercially milling as late as 1967. Today the mill's grain-grinding machinery is still turning for visitors while exhibits and interpreters provide a glimpse of a bygone era.

The 2,380-acre park also includes several other historical buildings, a short nature trail, and a farm learning center where children can have contact with barnyard animals. Wolcott Mill Metropark (586–749–5997) is southeast of Romeo, with the mill entrance off Kunstman Road just north of Twenty-Nine Mile Road. Building hours for the park are 9:00 A.M. to 5:00 P.M. daily, with longer weekend hours during the summer and fall. There is a vehicle fee to enter the park.

If there was ever a factory tour made for Christmas, it's the one offered at the *Lionel Train Company* near Mt. Clemens. The famous toy train company was founded in 1900 in New York City after Joshua Lionel Cowen combined his newly invented dry cell battery with a small electric motor and a model train. His original intention was to create a window display that would attract shoppers into the large department stores. But what the holiday shoppers wanted to buy was the train itself, and railroading with toy trains was born.

The most important dates to Michigan toy train lovers, however, are 1970, when Lionel moved its operations to the Mt. Clemens area, and February 1992, when it opened its Lionel Trains Visitor Center. The tours include cardboard engineer hats for children, a short film on the history of the company, and a visit to the center's layout room, which features a 560-square-foot stage complete with mountains, towns, tunnels, and 1,000 feet of track for eight Lionel trains and more than a hundred cars.

funfacts

The first underground railroad tunnel in the world was opened between Port Huron and Sarnia, Ontario, in 1891. It is 11,725 feet long with 2,290 feet underground.

To reach the visitor center (586–949–4100), head east on M 59 through Utica and then turn north on Romeo Plank Road and east on Twenty-Three Mile Road. The posted entrance to the Lionel Train Company is reached in 7 miles. Tours are offered at 10:00 A.M., 3:00 P.M., and 4:00 P.M. on Wednesday and Thursday, 10:00 A.M., 1:30 P.M., and 2:30 P.M. on Friday, and at 10:00 A.M., 11:00 A.M., and noon on Saturday. There is no admission fee, but tours are by reservation only.

St. Clair County

This county is often referred to as the Bluewater region of Michigan because it is bounded by Lake St. Clair to the south, Lake Huron to the north, and the St. Clair River to the east. M 29 circles the north side of Lake St. Clair and then follows the river to Port Huron, passing small towns and many bait shops, marinas, and shoreline taverns advertising walleye and perch fish fries. The most charming town on the water is St. Clair, 15 miles south of Port Huron and a major shipbuilding center in the early 1900s. The city recently renovated its downtown section, centering it on **Palmer Park,** which residents claim has one of the longest boardwalks in the world facing freshwater. The favorite activity on the 1,500-foot riverwalk is watching the Great Lakes freighters that glide by exceptionally close, giving land-bound viewers a good look at the massive boats and their crews. The second favorite activity is walleye fishing. The St. Clair River is renowned for this fish, and anglers can be seen throughout the summer tossing a line from the riverwalk, trying to entice the walleye with minnows or night crawlers.

Above the walkway is a wide, grassy bank filled with sunbathers, kids playing, and, in mid-June, the arts and crafts booths of the **St. Clair Art Fair,** a popular festival along the river. Call the St. Clair Art Association (810–329–9576) for the exact dates and times. The riverwalk ends to the north at the **St. Clair Inn** (810–329–2222), a historic hotel that was built in 1926 and today features outdoor dining in a courtyard overlooking the river.

Port Huron, a city of 30,000, is the site of the Bluewater Bridge, the international crossing between Michigan and Sarnia, Ontario. It is also recognized

Edison in Port Huron

Port Huron's most famous resident was not its happiest one. Thomas Edison moved to the city with his family when he was seven years old but quit school after only three days when a teacher wrote that the future inventor was "addled." His mother taught him at home, and Edison, already fascinated with science and chemistry, turned the family basement into his personal laboratory.

To pay for the chemicals and equipment, he took a job selling candy and newspapers on the Grand Trunk Railroad's commute to Detroit and back. The Port Huron Depot that he worked out of is now the **Thomas Edison Depot Museum**.

But Edison left the town as a teen to seek telegraph work and eventually his fortune out east at Menlo Park, New Jersey. "I do not think that any living human being will ever see me there again," he wrote to his father when he was thirty years old and already a well-known inventor. "I don't want you to stay in that hole of a Port Huron, which contains the most despicable remnants of the human race that can be found on earth."

Historians said that over time, Edison softened his views on Port Huron and later in life did return several times, mostly to attend family funerals.

throughout the state as the start of the Port Huron–Mackinac Sailboat Race in late July. On the eve of the event, known as **Boat Night,** the downtown area of Water, Lapeer, and Quay Streets, which borders the docks on the Black River, becomes congested with block parties. Sailors, local people, and tourists mingle in a festival that spreads throughout the streets, the yacht clubs, and even onto the sailboats themselves.

Port Huron has several museums, and one of the most interesting honors its favorite son; the **Thomas Edison Depot Museum** (810–982–0891) is located under the Bluewater Bridge at 510 Thomas Edison Parkway. The museum is housed in the historic Fort Gratiot Depot, built in 1858, this is where Edison picked up the Grand Trunk Railroad train, on which he sold candy and newspapers as a youth. Exhibits portray Edison's younger days and what led him to become the greatest inventor of our times. Outside the depot, a restored baggage car contains Edison's mobile print shop, which he used to publish the *Weekly Herald,* the world's first newspaper to be printed on a moving train. Edison sold the newspaper on the train for two cents a copy and eventually had a circulation of more than 400.

The museum is open 11:00 A.M. to 5:00 P.M. daily from Memorial Day to Labor Day, and Thursday through Monday the rest of the year. Admission is $5.00 for adults and $3.00 for children.

A short walk from the depot museum is the **Port Huron Museum of Arts and History** (810–982–0891) at 1115 Sixth Street. The museum combines an art gallery with collections of natural history and artifacts from Port Huron's past. Included are bones and displays of the prehistoric mammoths that roamed Michigan's Thumb 10,000 years ago and memorabilia of Thomas Edison's boyhood home, which was located in the city. A popular attraction is the reconstructed pilothouse of a Great Lakes freighter. All the furnishings were taken from various ships, and visitors can work the wheel, signal the alarm horn, and ring the engine bell. All around the pilothouse is a huge mural that gives the impression you are guiding the vessel into Lake Huron. The museum, housed in a 1904 Carnegie library, is open 11:00 A.M. to 5:00 P.M. daily. Admission is $5.00 for adults and $3.00 for children.

Places to Stay in Southeast Michigan

ANN ARBOR

Comfort Inn,
2455 Carpenter Road,
(734) 973–6100

Weber's Inn,
3050 Jackson Road,
(734) 769–2500

AUBURN HILLS

Courtyard by Marriott,
1296 Opdyke Road,
(248) 373–4100

DEARBORN

Dearborn Inn,
20301 Oakwood Boulevard,
(313) 271–2700

Econo Lodge,
23730 Michigan Avenue,
(313) 565–7250

Super 8 Motel,
2101 South Telegraph Road,
(313) 274–0001

DETROIT

Atheneum Hotel,
1000 Brush Street,
(313) 962–2323

Omni Hotel,
1000 River Place,
(313) 259–9500

Shorecrest Motor Inn,
1361 East Jefferson Avenue,
(313) 568–3000

MOUNT CLEMENS

Comfort Inn,
1 North River Road,
(586) 465–2185

PORT HURON

Thomas Edison Inn,
500 Thomas Edison Parkway,
(810) 984–8000

TROY

Drury Inn,
575 West Big Beaver Road,
(248) 528–3330

WARREN

Baymont Inn,
30900 Van Dyke Road,
(586) 574–0550

SELECTED SOUTHEAST MICHIGAN TOURISM BUREAUS

**Ann Arbor Area
Convention and Visitors Bureau,**
120 West Huron Street,
Ann Arbor 48104;
(800) 888–9487;
www.annarbor.com

Bluewater Area Tourist Bureau
(Port Huron and St. Clair),
520 Thomas Edison Parkway,
Port Huron 48060;
(800) 852–4242;
www.bluewater.org

**Metropolitan Detroit
Convention and Visitors Bureau,**
211 West Fort Street,
Detroit 48226;
(800) 338–7648;
www.visitdetroit.com

Monroe County Tourism Bureau,
106 West Front Street,
Monroe 48161;
(800) 252–3011;
www.monroeinfo.com

**Ypsilanti Area Visitors and
Convention Bureau,**
106 West Michigan Avenue,
Ypsilanti 48197;
(800) 265–9045;
www.ypsilanti.org

OTHER ATTRACTIONS

Cranbrook Institute of Science,
Bloomfield Hills

Detroit Science Center,
Detroit

Eddy Discovery Center,
Chelsea

Fox Theatre,
Detroit

Holocaust Memorial Center,
West Bloomfield

Meadowbrook Hall,
Rochester

U of M Exhibit Museum of Natural History,
Ann Arbor

U of M Museum of Art,
Ann Arbor

Yankee Air Museum,
Belleville

Motel 6,
Thirteen Mile and Van Dyke Roads,
(586) 826–9300

Places to Eat in Southeast Michigan

ANN ARBOR

Arbor Brewing Co.
(brew pub),
114 East Washington Avenue,
(734) 213–1393

Blue Nile (Ethiopian),
221 East Washington Avenue,
(734) 998–4746

Gandy Dancer (seafood),
401 Depot Street,
(734) 769–0592

Zingerman's Delicatessen,
422 Detroit Street,
(734) 663–0974

CLARKSTON

Union (American),
54 South Main Street,
(248) 620–6100

DEARBORN

Big Fish (seafood),
700 Town Center Drive,
(313) 336–6350

DETROIT

Dakota Inn Rathskeller
(German),
17324 John R Road,
(313) 867–9722

Fishbone's Rhythm
Kitchen Cafe (Cajun),
400 Monroe Street,
(313) 965–4600

Jacoby's (German),
624 Brush Street,
(313) 962–7067

New Hellas Cafe,
583 Monroe Street,
(313) 961–5544

Roma Cafe (Italian),
3401 Riopelle Street,
(313) 831–5940

Traffic Jam (brew pub),
511 West Canfield Street,
(313) 831–9470

Tres Vite (American),
2203 Woodward Avenue,
(313) 964–4144

The Whitney (fine dining)
4421 Woodward Avenue,
(313) 832–5700

Xochimilco (Mexican),
3409 Bagley Street,
(313) 843–0179

FARMINGTON

Bone Yard Bar-B-Que (ribs),
31006 Orchard Lake Road,
(248) 851–7000

FERNDALE

Howe's Bayou (Cajun),
22848 Woodward Avenue,
(248) 691–7145

NORTHVILLE

Geniti's Hole-in-the-Wall
(Italian),
108 East Main Street,
(248) 349–0522

OAK PARK

Bread Basket Deli,
26052 Greenfield Road,
(248) 968–0022

ROYAL OAK

BD's Mongolian Barbecue
(stir-fry),
310 South Main Street,
(248) 398–7755

Inn Season Cafe
(vegetarian),
500 East Fourth Street,
(248) 547–7916

SOUTHFIELD

Sweet Lorraine's Cafe
(American),
29101 Greenfield Road,
(248) 559–5985

TROY

Charley's Crab (seafood),
5498 Crooks Road,
(248) 879–2060

WATERFORD

Lion's Den (American),
4444 M 59,
(248) 674–2251

WEST BLOOMFIELD

The Lark (country inn),
6430 Farmington Road,
(248) 661–4466

The Thumb

Within the mitten that is the Lower Peninsula of Michigan, there is a special area known as "the Thumb." The state's most recognized appendage is shaped by Saginaw Bay to the west and Lake Huron to the east. The bodies of water not only outline the peninsula but also have wrapped it in rural isolation, the Thumb's trademark and the reason it is called "the getaway close to home."

Home is likely to be one of three of the state's largest urban areas: Detroit, Flint, or Saginaw, all less than a two-hour drive from the four counties that compose the region. Yet the Thumb is a world away. In this place where interstate highways give way to country roads and indistinguishable suburbs turn into distinct villages, the bustle and heartbeat of the city is replaced by the rural charm of the country.

You don't have nightclubs in the Thumb or dominating skylines or symphony orchestras. But you have more than 90 miles of lakeshore to view, small museums to discover, and an easy way of life whose rural pace will soothe the soul and rest a weary urban mind.

Lumber companies opened up the Thumb in the early 1800s, but after the trees were gone and the loggers went north, the region slipped into the small-town realm of agriculture.

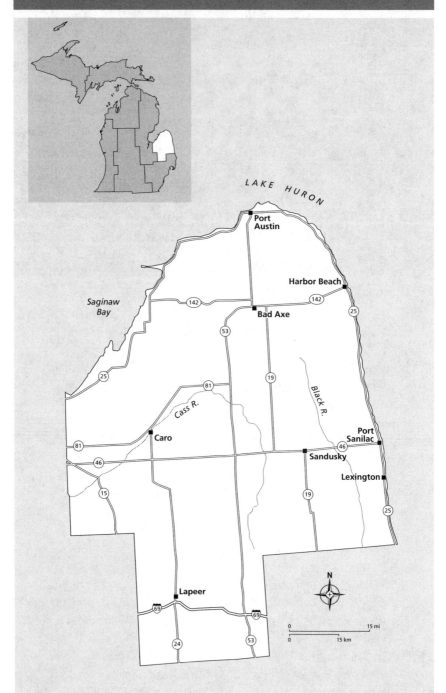

LAKE HURON

Port
Austin

Harbor Beach

Saginaw
Bay

142

142

25

Bad Axe

53

19

Black R.

25

81

Cass R.

Port
Sanilac

81

Caro

46

Sandusky

46

Lexington

15

19

25

N

Lapeer

69

69

0   15 mi

24

53

0   15 km

Today the area is still predominantly a farm belt, and from its rich soil come corn, sugar beets, grains, beans, and the lush grass that supports vast dairy herds and livestock. Huron County produces more navy beans per acre than anyplace else in the world.

In recent years tourist dollars have become a significant part of the economy, but the region will never turn into one of the strips of motels and ice-cream stands that characterize much of the Lake Michigan shoreline, the heart of Michigan tourism. The Thumb lies on the other side of the state, away from the mainstream of summer traffic. And many travelers, who come for the fine beaches, country markets, and picturesque lighthouses, leave it cherishing that out-of-the-way character the most.

Lapeer County

A misconception of the Thumb held by many Michigan natives is that the region is flat, without so much as a ripple between the shoreline of Saginaw Bay and the lapping waters of Lake Huron. A drive through Lapeer County dispels that notion immediately. The rolling hills that are the trademark of northern Oakland County continue north through the heart of the peninsula. In southern Lapeer County these hills have an enhancement that makes them

AUTHOR'S TOP TEN PICKS

The Bank 1884 Restaurant,
Port Austin;
(989) 738–5353

**Be Good to Your
Mother-in-Law Bridge,**
Croswell;
(810) 679–3346

Bird Creek County Park,
Port Austin;
(989) 738–7600

Huron City Museum,
Huron City;
(989) 428–4123

Murphy Museum,
Harbor Beach;
(989) 479–9554

Pioneer Log Cabin Village,
Bad Axe;
(989) 269–2630

Pointe Aux Barques Lighthouse,
Huron City;
(989) 428–4749

Port Crescent State Park,
Port Austin;
(989) 738–8663

Sanilac County Historical Museum,
Port Sanilac;
(810) 622–9946

Sanilac Historic Site,
New Greenleaf;
(517) 373–3559

unique in Michigan: the distinct white rail fences of horse country. Follow County Road 62 between M 24 and M 53 and dip south along the gravel crossroads of Blood, Garder, or Barber, and you'll pass through one of the greatest concentrations of horse farms in the state. Come in late spring when the grass is green, a new coat of whitewash covers the fences, and the mares and foals are trotting through the fields—and this area could easily be mistaken for the bluegrass region of Kentucky.

The heart of Michigan's horse country is **Metamora,** a village of 500 that lies just east of M 24 and is crowned by the towering steeple of the Pilgrim Church (built in 1878). Settlers first began arriving in the area in 1838, but Metamora earned a spot on the map when it became a stop for a stagecoach route that turned into the Detroit–Bay City Railroad in 1872. Whether travelers were carried by horse or by rail, the resting place was the same: a large rambling carriage house built in 1850 on one corner of County Road 62 and Metamora Road.

Back then it was known as the Hoard House, after its proprietor, Lorenzo Hoard, who charged travelers, weary from a long day on the road, only 50 cents a room. Today it's called the **White Horse Inn,** and while it no longer has rooms for rent, it is still serving meals today, making it the oldest operating restaurant in the county. Half of the inn is the dining room, completely sealed off from the barnlike barroom and decorated in dark oak, leaded-glass windows, and red plaid carpeting. On Tuesdays both halves are filled with customers, as the inn offers its weekly all-you-can-eat fish fry for $8.00 per person. The rest of its menu is equally tempting, especially its White Horse Wellington, a flaky pastry filled with tenderloin, mushrooms, and cheese. The inn also has a list of daily seafood specials such as Rainbow Trout a la Praline, boneless trout dusted with a seasoned flour and sautéed in butter with pecans.

The White Horse Inn (810–678–2150) is open for dinner Monday through Thursday from 11:30 A.M. to 9:00 P.M., Friday and Saturday from 11:30 A.M. to 10:00 P.M., and Sunday from 9:00 A.M. to 8:00 P.M. Menu prices range from $10 to $22 for dinners; reservations are recommended on the weekends.

North of Metamora along M 24 is **Lapeer,** a town of 6,270. Settlers began arriving in the area in 1828 and borrowed their village name from *la pierre*, the French translation of the Indian name for the Flint River, which lies nearby. Lapeer became the county seat in 1831, and eight years later the county courthouse was built on the town common.

Lapeer is still the center of government, and the **Lapeer County Court- house** still stands at the corner of Court and Nepessing Streets. It is an impressive building featuring a Greek Revival style with four fluted Doric columns. It's topped by a three-tiered tower and a Roman dome and is noted as the "oldest

Lapeer County Courthouse

courthouse still being used in Michigan today," even though the county has long since built a newer, all-brick building across the street. The old court- house keeps its title because every summer, the judge, the jury, and a handful of history buffs move to the other side of the street to hear a few cases in the second-floor courtroom of this landmark structure.

The first floor is now the **Lapeer Historical Society Museum,** and for a small admission fee, visitors can wander through the turn-of-the-twentieth- century judge's chambers or the first sheriff's office in the county. The Court- house Museum is open from early June through November 15. Hours are 1:00 to 5:00 P.M. Tuesday through Friday.

More history and a lot of country charm can be found just up the road from Lapeer at the **Past Tense Country Store** (810–664–5559). The store is only minutes from downtown Lapeer and can be reached by driving north on M 24 and then turning east on County Road 7 (Daley Road). The first intersec- tion on Daley is Farnsworth Road, and visible to the south from this intersection is one of the most impressive houses in the region. The huge, twenty-three- room home was built by the Farnsworth family, who were part of the first wave of settlers to farm the county. There are several buildings on the old farm, including the original barn that Lucie Hiner renovated into the Past Tense Country Store in 1971.

The store is an intriguing place, worth browsing through even if you are not in a buying mood. It is part country store, part antiques shop, and part museum. Walk in on a chilly day and the rush of warm air from the wood- burning stove greets you. Then you'll notice the hundred-year-old German barrel piano and the classic red Texaco gasoline pump next to it. The store itself is four rooms, each stocked to the rafters with such items as handmade

TOP ANNUAL EVENTS

Swinging Bridge Festival,
Croswell, June;
(810) 679–2299

Caseville Walleye Tournament,
Caseville, July;
(800) 606–1347

Michigan Sugar Festival,
Sebewaing, June;
(989) 883–2150

Fish Sandwich Festival,
Bay Port, August;
(989) 453–0109

Log Cabin Day,
Bad Axe, June;
(989) 269–6936

baskets, dried flowers, candles, knickknacks, and children's toys, including one of the most amazing teddy bear collections you'll ever see outside a museum. Upstairs are numerous pieces of antique furniture, while one room is devoted to Christmas, with an old sled in the middle and walls covered with ornaments.

Above every shelf of merchandise, Hiner draws you back into the rural history of Lapeer with small artifacts she has saved. Above the wall of hard candy, a requirement in every country store, are rows of cleaning products and cans of food, all from an era long gone. Some you'll recognize, like Oxydol, Quaker Oats, or Calumet Baking Powder, though the packaging hardly resembles the modern-day counterparts. Many you will not (Quick Arrow Soup Chips or Red Moon Early Peas), for they have long since vanished from supermarkets.

Hiner and her family live in the Farnsworth house and operate the store, which is open Monday through Saturday from 10:00 A.M. to 6:00 P.M. and Sunday from noon to 6:00 P.M.

Sanilac County

M 25, the state road that leads out of Port Huron, follows the shoreline of Sanilac County and continues along the entire coast of the Thumb, ending in Bay City. While the road does not offer a watery view at every bend, there are more than enough panoramas of Lake Huron and shoreline parks to make it one of the more scenic drives in the Lower Peninsula.

Heading north on M 25, the first town you reach in Sanilac County is Lexington, which was incorporated in 1855 and boomed at the turn of the twentieth century. Back then the bustling town of 2,400 was a common stop for Great Lakes shipping and boasted an organ factory, a brewery, a flour mill, and six saloons. In 1913 the great storm that swept across Lake Huron destroyed the town's docks and virtually isolated it. Lexington slipped into a standstill until the automobile and roads revived it in the 1940s, and today the town of almost 800 has worked harder than any other community in the Thumb to promote its future by preserving its past.

Lexington's streets are lined with turn-of-the-twentieth-century homes and buildings, including four listed on the National Register of Historic Places. One of them is the **Charles H. Moore Public Library,** at Main and Huron Streets next to the village hall. The brick building was built in 1859 as the Devine Law Office but somehow passed into the hands of Moore, a local seaman who died in 1901, leaving the building to his three daughters. When a dispute erupted in 1903 as to where to put the town library, the daughters offered the former law office as a permanent site.

It has been the library ever since and today holds nearly 12,000 books, including a rare-book collection. Librarians will tell you that as many people wander through just to view the renovated interior as to check out a book. The wood trim and stained-glass windows have been fully restored inside, as has the graceful wooden banister that leads you past a picture of the "old seaman" to the upstairs. It's hard to imagine a more pleasant place to read than the sunlit room of the second floor, which features desks, tables, and office chairs that were originally used by the law firm.

The Moore Library (810–359–8267) is open Monday from 3:00 to 7:00 P.M., Wednesday and Friday from 10:00 A.M. to 5:00 P.M., and Saturday from 10:00 A.M. to 1:00 P.M.

Moore was also responsible for another building in Lexington that is now a National Historic Site. When the seaman built his home in the 1880s, he located it just a block from the lake where he plied his trade. The huge Queen Anne–style home at Simons and Washington Streets was constructed from white

Port Sanilac Lighthouse

Port Sanilac's most distinctive landmark is its lighthouse, a redbrick house and whitewashed tower overlooking the town harbor and the watery horizon of Lake Huron. Built in 1886, the 80-foot tower was originally a kerosene-fueled continuous white light. In 1889 it was changed to red, and in 1926 the lighthouse was wired for electricity and changed to a flashing light with a range of 12 to 15 miles. Although the lighthouse is not open to visitors, it's a photographer's delight thanks to its contrasting colors.

The Port Sanilac Lighthouse is on Lake Street, 1 block east of M 25.

pine that loggers were shipping out of the port of Lexington. In 1901, Mary, the youngest daughter, used the house as a backdrop for her marriage to Albert E. Sleeper, a newly elected state senator. When Sleeper's political career led to his election as governor in 1917, the house became an important summer retreat for the couple, who were eager to escape the busy public life in Lansing.

Today the home is still used as a summer retreat as the ***Captain's Quarters Inn,*** Lexington's first bed-and-breakfast. Guests spend summer evenings much the way the governor and his wife did—on the wraparound porch in wicker rockers (there are seven now instead of two), enjoying the cool breezes off Lake Huron. Reservations are recommended and can be made by writing the Captain's Quarters Inn, P.O. Box 39, Lexington 48450, or phoning (810) 359–2196.

From Lexington M 25 continues north along Lake Huron and in 11 miles reaches the next lakeside town, ***Port Sanilac.*** Like Lexington, Port Sanilac's early history and wealth can be seen in the old homes that border its streets. One is the Loop-Harrison House, a huge Victorian mansion just south of town on M 25 that now serves as the ***Sanilac County Historical Museum.*** The home was built in 1872 by Dr. Joseph Loop, who arrived in Sanilac in 1854 and began a practice that covered a 40-mile radius. The home and its extensive furnishings passed down through three generations of the family until Captain Stanley Harrison, grandson of the good doctor, donated it to the Sanilac Historical Society in 1964.

trivia

Michigan's oldest continuously operating hardware store is Raymond Hardware on M 25 in downtown Port Sanilac. Founded in 1850 by Uri Raymond, the high-roofed building is a classic hardware store that sells "anything and everything."

The Historical Society has kept the home intact, and visitors can wander through two floors of rooms that have remained virtually the same since the 1870s, right down to the original carpet, the cooking utensils in the kitchen, and the doctor's instruments in his office. There are also a dairy museum out back and a furnished 1882 pioneer log cabin. The museum (810–622–9946) is open Memorial Day through Labor Day from 11:00 A.M. to 4:30 P.M. Wednesday through Friday, and from noon to 4:30 P.M. on Saturday and Sunday. There is a small admission fee.

Closer to town on M 25 is another impressive home that has become the ***Raymond House Inn,*** Port Sanilac's bed-and-breakfast. The home was built in 1871 by Uri Raymond, one of the founding fathers of the town, who established what is now Michigan's oldest continuously operating hardware store just up the street. The exterior of this Victorian-style home makes it hard to miss with its redbrick facade, high peaked roofs, and white gingerbread trim.

Bark Shanty Point

Port Sanilac dates back to the summer of 1830 when a group of lumbermen arrived to peel the bark from the hemlocks in the area for tanning leather. Their accommodations were in a hastily built shanty that was covered in bark. The crude shelter was left standing on the shore after the men departed in the fall, and it quickly became a landmark to sailors who referred to the spot as Bark Shanty Point. Eventually a settlement emerged, and in 1857 the residents decided that the name of a famous Wyandot Indian chief was a little more dignified for their community than Bark Shanty Point.

Inside, high ceilings, classic moldings, winding staircases, and large rooms add to the inn's turn-of-the-twentieth-century charm.

Shirley Denison bought the house after three generations of Raymonds had lived in it. Denison is a restorative artist from Washington, D.C., but she spent her childhood summers in Port Sanilac, where her grandfather was a local boat and lumber baron. She was enchanted by the antique furniture that filled the rooms, including the old-fashioned parlor and the six bedrooms she rents out on the second floor. The inn is open from April through December, with a rate of $95 for double occupancy (private bath). Write to Denison at P.O. Box 438, Port Sanilac 48469, or call (810) 622–8800 for a reservation.

For dinner or what many say is the best fish fry in the Thumb, head almost directly across the street to yet another century-old Victorian home known as the **Bellaire Hotel.** Inside you'll find more arches, ceiling-high windows, and parquet floors. More important to the patrons, however, are the dining rooms and what emerges from the kitchen. Local people call them "porch dinners," for you sit in a glass-enclosed room overlooking the gardens that surround the hotel. Diane Douros, who has operated the Bellaire since she and her husband bought it in 1945, is best known for her perch and pickerel dinners. The meal is complete only if it is topped off with a piece of her tart lemon meringue pie. The Bellaire (810–622–9981) is at 120 South Ridge Road, and its entrees are priced from $10 to $15.

The stretch of M 25 from Port Sanilac to Forestville is especially scenic and passes three roadside parks on high bluffs from which you can scramble to the Lake Huron shoreline below. For those who want to explore the center of the Thumb, the Bay City–Forestville Road, the only intersection in tiny Forestville, provides a good excuse to turn off M 25. Head west, through the hamlets of Charleston and Minden, and look for the PETROGLYPHS sign at the corner of Bay City–Forestville and Germania Roads. **Sanilac Historical Site** is located just south on Germania and is marked by a large Department of Natural Resources sign. Situated in the wooded heart of the Thumb, the park features a large slab of stone with petroglyphs, Indian carvings that archaeologists believe to be between 300 and 1,000 years old and the only ones in the Lower Peninsula. The department has erected a large pavilion over the rock, which contains dozens of carvings. The most prominent one features a bowman with a single long line depicting his arm and arrow. A short trail leads from the parking lot a few hundred yards inland to the pavilion and then continues beyond as a 1.5-mile interpretive trail.

There is no entrance fee. From Memorial Day to Labor Day, the Michigan Bureau of History staffs the park from 11:30 A.M. to 4:30 P.M. Wednesday through Sunday with guides who help visitors recognize the carvings and lead guided walks.

ajohndeere museum

The Deckerville Historical Museum is located on a farm and includes a log cabin, railroad depot, windmill, and sawmill, but its most noted collection is its exhibit of John Deere tractors. The museum has more than twenty on display with all of them in working order and some dating to the 1930s.

The museum is a mile north of Deckerville at 4208 Ruth Road and is open Saturdays from May through September from 9:00 A.M. to 5:00 P.M. There is a small admission fee.

Another reason to head inland in summer and fall is to pick berries—sweet, juicy, and back-breakingly close to the ground. Next to the town of Croswell is the **Croswell Berry Farm** (810–679–3273) at 33 Black River Road. This farm features strawberries in June and early July, then extends the picking season with blueberries, and finishes up the year with raspberries that are harvested as late as November. Hours are 8:00 A.M. to 4:00 P.M. daily.

One final reason to head inland to Croswell is to get some advice for keeping your marriage intact from a bridge that Dear Abby would appreciate. In the middle of this Sanilac County village is the **Be Good to Your Mother-in-Law Bridge**, which was first constructed in 1905 and has been rebuilt three times since then with David Weis, a local businessman, assisting in the effort.

Best known in town for offering sage advice to newlyweds, it was Weis who hung a sign at one end of the bridge that advises them to be good to their mothers-in-law and at the other end one that admonishes them to love one another. It's such good advice that the bridge has become something of a ritual with both newlyweds and longtime married couples, who are photographed under the black-and-white sign and then walk hand in hand across the structure.

They hold hands partly out of devotion to each other and partly to keep their balance. The 139-foot suspension footbridge is held up by four thick cables that make you bounce with each step across. The wooden slats sway, jiggle, and dip toward the Black River, coming within 8 feet of its murky surface. Some people are even more nervous about crossing the 4-foot-wide swinging bridge than strolling up to the altar.

Small tree-lined parks are at each end of the bridge, while a short walk away on Wells Street is the *Croswell Museum,* a former railroad depot that features a horse-drawn hearse, local artifacts, and plenty of fading photographs of the town's beloved swinging bridge. The parks and bridge are open daily from dawn to dusk. The Croswell Museum is open Saturday and Sunday from 1:00 to 5:00 P.M.

Huron County

The country charm of M 25 continues into Huron County as it winds north toward Port Austin on the Tip of the Thumb. Along the way it passes several museums, including two in Harbor Beach, a quiet rural town of 2,000 residents.

Murphy Museum preserves the birthplace of Governor Frank Murphy, best known for refusing to use the National Guard to end the 1937 Flint Sit-Down Strike at General Motors. By pushing for collective bargaining, Murphy, in effect, paved the way for the United Auto Workers and unionization of the auto industry. Murphy also served as mayor of Detroit, U.S. attorney general, and a U.S. Supreme Court justice from 1940 to his death in 1949. The house is packed with historical artifacts relating to one of Michigan's most influential residents.

The Fires of 1881

What began as small fires in the middle of a hot, dry summer turned into the Thumb's worst disaster when on September 5, 1881, a gale swept in from the southwest. The high winds turned the fires into an inferno that raged for three days and burned more than a million acres in Sanilac and Huron Counties alone.

The fire put a sudden end to the logging era in the region while killing 125 people and leaving thousands more destitute. Aid to victims was the first disaster relief effort by the new American Red Cross. Its prompt response quickly won the support of the country.

Murphy Museum (989–479–9554) is at 142 South Huron Street in downtown Harbor Beach and is open from Memorial Day to Labor Day from 9:00 A.M. to 4:00 P.M. daily. There is a small admission charge. Just north of town on M 25 at the Harbor Beach harbor is the *Grice Museum,* which features a farmhouse from the late 1800s, a barn, and a rural school.

Another small museum along M 25 is at *Lighthouse County Park,* 15 miles north of Harbor Beach. The museum is on the first floor of the classic Pointe Aux Barques Lighthouse, which was built in 1857 and is still used by the U.S. Coast Guard. The lighthouse actually overlooks two parks; the county park around it features seventy-four campsites with electricity for recreational vehicles, a swimming beach, a boat launch, and a picnic area. Out in Lake Huron is an underwater park, the Thumb Area Bottomland Preserve, which the state set up in 1985 to protect the nine known shipwrecks that lie offshore. Many of the relics that are gathered from the wrecks are stored in the Lighthouse Museum, which is open weekends during the summer. There is no admission charge for the park (989–428–4749) or the museum.

trivia

A historical marker at a rest area along M 25 is dedicated to the Storm of November 1913, another deadly disaster in the history of the Thumb. The devastating storm blew in with little warning, sinking more than 40 ships, killing 235 sailors, and destroying almost every dock along Michigan's Lake Huron shoreline.

Where Lighthouse Road loops back to M 25 is the Thumb's most impressive attraction, *Huron City.* The town was founded in the mid-1850s by lumberman Langdon Hubbard, who needed a port for his 29,000-acre tract of timberland, which included most of northern Huron County. It quickly became the largest town in the county, with several hundred residents and two sawmills that produced 80,000 feet of lumber a day. After the Great Fire of 1881 that swept across the Thumb devastated Hubbard's logging efforts, he sold his land to immigrant farmers (after opening a bank to lend them the money), and for a while Huron City hung on as a farming community.

By the early 1900s, Huron City had withered away to a ghost town when it experienced a revival—a religious awakening, you might say. One of Hubbard's daughters had married William Lyon Phelps, a Yale professor and an ordained minister, and each summer the couple returned to Huron City and stayed at Seven Gables, the rambling Hubbard home. Eventually Dr. Phelps began preaching in the nearby church on Sunday. Local people soon discovered the magic of his oratory: simple solutions and relief from the problems of everyday life. The church, which originally held 250, was quickly enlarged to

1,000 in the 1920s as people throughout Michigan heard of the preacher and began finding their way to Huron City for his Sunday afternoon service.

Dr. Phelps died in 1937, but Huron City survived when the granddaughter of the founder preserved the community as a museum town. Twelve buildings are on the site, nine of them furnished and open to the public. They include a country store, a church, a lifesaving station, a settler's cabin, the old inn, a barn with antique farm equipment, and the Phelps Museum, which was built in honor of the minister in the early 1950s. Huron City (989–428–4123) is open July 1 through Labor Day from 10:00 A.M. to 6:00 P.M. Thursday through Saturday and Monday, and 11:00 A.M. to 6:00 P.M. Sunday. The admission fee is $10 for adults but includes an hour-long guided tour that tells the stories behind the buildings.

Where Lake Huron and Saginaw Bay meet is Port Austin, the town at the Tip of the Thumb. M 25 winds through the center of Port Austin and near its two busiest spots in the summer, the city marina and, just east of the marina's breakwall, delightful **Bird Creek County Park.** This seven-acre park includes a beautiful sandy beach and a half-mile boardwalk where people fish during the day and gather nightly to watch the sunset over Saginaw Bay.

Travelers will find some antique accommodations in this New England–style town that boomed with lumber barons in the mid-1800s. One of them is the **Garfield Inn,** a huge red mansion on Lake Street that is named after a U.S. congressman who stayed in the home in the 1860s and once delivered a stirring speech from its balcony endorsing Civil War hero Ulysses Grant for president. That man was James Garfield, who later became the twentieth president of the United States. The inn, which became a restaurant, bar, and bed-and-breakfast in 1985, has been named a National Historic Site, and among its more striking features are the mahogany bar and the winding cherrywood staircase that leads to the ten bedrooms upstairs, seven of which are rented out.

Grindstone Capital of the World

Where M 25 begins to curve around the top of the Thumb, you can take Pointe Aux Barques Road to Grindstone City. Amazingly, this tiny village was once the world's leading producer of natural-sandstone grinding wheels. Sandstone was first quarried in 1834 by Captain Aaron G. Peer, who shipped it to Detroit, where it was used to pave the intersection of Woodward and Jefferson Avenues. Two years later the first grindstone wheel was turned out, and for nearly a century Grindstone City grindstones were shipped all over the world. Today you can still see many of the huge grindstones, some 6 feet in diameter, on the beach and around the village's boat harbor.

The Garfield Inn (989–738–5254 or 800–373–5254) is open from April 1 to January 1. Rooms based on double occupancy run from $95 to $125. The restaurant is open at 5:00 P.M. for dinner daily during the summer, on Friday and Saturday only during the winter.

In keeping with the restored atmosphere of the Port Austin inns, there is the *Bank 1884 Restaurant* for, unquestionably, the finest dining in town. Built in 1884 as the Winsorsnover Bank on the corner of Lake and State Streets, the red-washed, brick building ceased being a place of financial business in 1957. In 1982 Anthony and Marilynne Berry began renovating the building, and two years later they opened its doors as a restaurant. The interior features stained glass over the classic stand-up bar, a teller's cage on the first floor, and walls of oversize photographs depicting early Huron County. The changing menu usually has shrimp scampi, prime rib, and En Papilote—walleye prepared with a crabmeat dressing and baked in parchment paper. During the summer the Bank 1884 is open daily from 5:00 to 10:30 P.M. During May and after Labor Day until mid-December, the restaurant is open only on weekends. Prices for entrees range from $17 to $23, and reservations (989–738–5353) are strongly recommended for the weekends.

funfacts

Huron County accounts for more than 90 percent of the country's production of navy beans.

West of Port Austin, M 25 begins to follow the shoreline of Saginaw Bay and is especially scenic in its 19-mile stretch to Caseville. It passes many views of the bay and its islands, numerous roadside parks, and the finest beaches in the Thumb. One of the parks is *Port Crescent State Park,* popular with sunbathers and swimmers for the long stretches of sandy shoreline. The park also offers opportunities and facilities for camping, hiking, and fishing, and it contains the Thumb's only set of dunes, a unique place for beachcombers to explore. There is an entrance fee to Port Crescent State Park (989–738–8663) and a $23 charge to camp overnight.

Even more than for sand and sun, Saginaw Bay has always been known as an angler's destination for yellow perch. Visitors, especially families, can still enjoy good fishing even without a boat or knowledge of where to go by joining a perch party boat. The large charter boats hold between twenty and forty anglers and usually depart twice a day for half-day fishing trips. In Port Austin, **Miss Port Austin** (989–738–5271) offers party-boat charters that depart at 7:30 A.M. and 2:30 P.M. daily. The fee is $35 per angler. You need to bring your own pole; the boat provides the bait and takes you where the perch are biting. Perch fishing is easy, and on a good day you may need a bucket to bring home your catch.

To enjoy your perch without having to put a minnow on your hook, stay on M 25 as it curves southwest toward Bay Port. From the 1880s until the late 1940s, this sleepy village was known as the "largest freshwater fishing port in the world," as tons of perch, whitefish, walleye, and herring were shipped as far away as New York City in refrigerated railroad cars. Today it honors its fishing past on the first Sunday in August with its annual *Bay Port Fish Sandwich Day.* The small festival includes arts and crafts, softball games, and lots of sandwiches—close to 8,000 are served during the event.

A small commercial fishery is still operating in Bay Port, a place to go for fresh walleye, perch, whitefish, and herring. From the center of town, head for the waterfront docks of the *Bay Port Fish Company* (989–656–2121) for the catch of the day or to watch fishermen work on the boats or nets in the evening. The company, which is open from 9:00 A.M. to 3:00 P.M. daily, also sells smoked fish.

In the heart of Huron County is *Bad Axe,* the county seat and a city of 4,000 residents. The town's most interesting attraction is *Pioneer Log Cabin Village* (989) 269–2630. This unique outdoor museum features a home, blacksmith shop, chapel, general store, barn, and one-room schoolhouse. All the buildings are log cabins that were built in Huron Cabin and moved to Bad Axe. The cabins are fully furnished to reflect the pioneer lifestyle of the nineteenth century and often are staffed during the summer by guides in period costumes.

The village is located in Bad Axe City Park on South Hanselman Street and is open Sunday from 2:00 to 5:00 P.M. from May through September. There is no admission fee.

West of Bad Axe is Pigeon in the heart of Huron County's flat-as-a-pancake farm country. This is Michigan's largest agricultural area, and it's best viewed on a *Farm Tour.* The self-guided tours begin with a stop at the Village Qwick

One Bad Axe

Rudolph Papst is credited by many with giving Bad Axe its name. While surveying for a new road across the heart of Huron County in 1861, he discovered a "bad axe" near his campsite one night and labeled the spot Bad Axe Corners on his map.

In 1872 county supervisors wanted the government moved from Port Austin to a more central location in the county and chose Bad Axe Corners, which in reality was little more than a junction in a dense forest. But five acres were quickly cleared, and in 1873 a courthouse was built. Since then Bad Axe has grown to be Huron County's largest city while its residents have resisted several attempts to give it a more dignified name.

Stop on M 142 in Pigeon where you can pick up a map and self-guided tour tape. From there the tape directs you to fifteen stops that include an egg farm, hog farm, bean plant and cooperative elevator, and dairy farms. For more information about the tour or special events that many of the farms stage, call the Pigeon Chamber of Commerce at (989) 453–7400.

Places to Stay in Michigan's Thumb

BAD AXE
Franklin Inn,
1060 East Huron Street,
(989) 269–9951

CASEVILLE
Farmstead Inn,
5048 Conkey Road,
(989) 856–3110

Sunset Bay Resort,
6010 Port Austin Road,
(989) 856–4400

HARBOR BEACH
Train Station Motel,
2044 North M 25,
(989) 479–3215

Wellock Inn,
404 South Huron Avenue,
(989) 479–3645

LEXINGTON
Captain's Quarters Inn,
7277 Simons Street,
(810) 359–5770

Lex-on-the-Lake Lodges,
5795 Main Street,
(810) 359–7910

Lusky Lakefront Cottages,
8949 Lakeshore Drive,
(810) 327–6889

PORT AUSTIN
Breakers-on-the-Bay,
1404 Port Austin Road,
(989) 738–5101

Garfield Inn,
8544 Lake Street,
(989) 738–5254

Krebs Cottages,
3478 Port Austin Road,
(989) 856–2876

Lakeside Motor Lodge,
8654 Lake Street,
(989) 738–5201

PORT HOPE
Stafford House,
4489 Main Street,
(989) 428–4554

PORT SANILAC
Raymond House Inn,
111 South Ridge Street,
(810) 622–8800

Places to Eat in Michigan's Thumb

BAD AXE
Franklin Inn (American),
1060 East Huron Street,
(989) 269–9951

CASEVILLE
Bay Cafe (American),
6750 Main Street,
(989) 856–3705

OTHER ATTRACTIONS

Sleeper State Park,
Caseville

Luckhard Museum,
Sebewaing

Pigeon Historical Museum,
Pigeon

Boathouse,
6567 Main Street,
(989) 856–4506

Shaker's Diner,
6685 Main Street,
(989) 856–2663

HARBOR BEACH

Harbor Light Inn
(American),
1090 North Lakeshore Road,
(989) 479–6005

Randolph's (Italian),
722 State Street,
(989) 479–3595

Williams Inn (American),
1724 South Lakeshore
Road,
(989) 479–3361

METAMORA

White Horse Inn,
1 East High Street,
(810) 678–2150

PORT AUSTIN

Bank 1884
(fine dining),
Lake and State Streets,
(989) 738–5353

Farm Restaurant
(American),
699 Port Crescent,
(989) 874–5700

Garfield Inn (fine dining),
8544 Lake Street,
(989) 738–5254

Lighthouse Cafe
(American),
42 West Spring Street,
(989) 738–5239

PORT HOPE

Four Seasons Cafe,
4411 Main Street,
(989) 428–3200

PORT SANILAC

Bellaire Lodge (American),
120 South Ridge Street,
(810) 622–9981

Mary's Diner (American),
14 North Ridge Street,
(810) 622–9377

SELECTED CHAMBERS OF COMMERCE AND TOURISM BUREAUS

Bad Axe Chamber of Commerce,
P.O. Box 87,
Bad Axe 48413;
(969) 269–6936;
www.badaxemich.com

Caseville Chamber of Commerce,
P.O. Box 122,
Caseville 48725;
(800) 606–1347

Huron County Visitors Bureau,
350 East Huron Street,
Bad Axe 48413;
(800) 358–4862;
www.huroncounty.com

Port Austin Chamber of Commerce,
P.O. Box 274,
Port Austin 48467;
(989) 738–7600;
www.portaustinarea.com

The Heartland

By the 1830s "Michigan Fever" had become an epidemic. Scores of pioneer families from the East Coast floated through the Erie Canal, made their way to Detroit, and then took to the newly completed Detroit-Chicago Road, which cut across the southern half of the Lower Peninsula. They soon discovered the rolling prairies of Michigan, where the soil was very rich and the land very cheap—the federal government was selling it for only $1.25 an acre.

From this onrush of settlers between 1825 and 1855, some of the state's largest cities emerged: Kalamazoo, Lansing, Battle Creek, Jackson, and Grand Rapids, all in this central region. But the Heartland of Michigan, the only area without direct links to the Great Lakes, is still an agricultural breadbasket. It is faded red barns and rolling fields of oats, the birthplace of Kellogg's Corn Flakes, and the home of a village antiques dealer who scours area farms for the furniture and knickknacks that fill her store.

The vibrant cities, each with a distinct downtown that never sleeps, are popular destinations for travelers who can zip from one to the next on interstate highways six lanes wide. But the unique nature of this region is found by rambling along its two-lane county roads, which take you past the horse-drawn

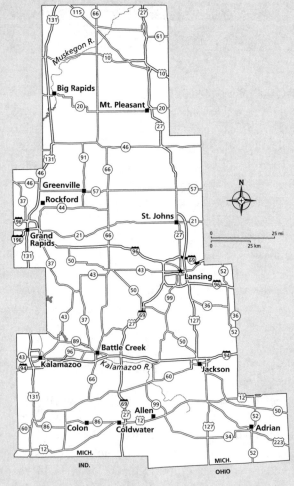

carriages of Amish country, down main streets of small villages, and along roadside stands loaded with the summer's harvest. In these out-of-the-way places, you can sample the fruits of Michigan's Heartland.

Lenawee County

At the northern edge of Lenawee County are the famed Irish Hills, an area of green rolling hills with intermittent lakes and ponds. US 12 cuts through the middle of this popular area and has become an avenue of manufactured tourist attractions: miniature golf courses and Go Kart tracks, a dinosaur amusement park, another park called Stagecoach Stop U.S.A., motels, gift shops, and even an international speedway that holds Indy car races. So overwhelming are these modern-day sights that it's easy to pass by one of the most interesting attractions and probably the only one that is free, *Walker Tavern.*

Located in *Cambridge State Historic Park,* the white clapboard tavern overlooks US 12, and rightfully so. The highway was originally an Indian trail and then became a stagecoach route known as the Detroit-Chicago Road. The stagecoach era lasted from 1835 to 1855, and on these rickety wagons, passengers traveled 50 miles a day with the hope of reaching Chicago in five days. The string of frontier taverns along the way was a crucial part of the system.

AUTHOR'S TOP TEN PICKS

Antiquing in Allen,
Allen;
(517) 869–2788

Capital Tours,
Lansing;
(517) 373–2353

Gerald R. Ford Museum,
Grand Rapids;
(616) 254–0400

Gilmore Classic Car Club of America Museums,
Hickory Corners;
(269) 671–5089

Hidden Lake Gardens,
Tipton;
(517) 431–2060

Jerry's Diner Village,
Rockford;
(616) 866–3663

Kalamazoo Aviation History Museum,
Kalamazoo;
(269) 382–6555

Kellogg's Cereal City USA,
Battle Creek;
(800) 970–7020

Michigan Library and Historical Center,
Lansing;
(517) 373–3559

Van Andel Museum Center,
Grand Rapids;
(616) 456–3977

Walker Tavern

They provided not only overnight accommodations (two or three travelers would share a bed for 25 cents a night) but also meals for the weary passengers who had just spent the day bouncing along the rough dirt road.

By the 1830s Walker Tavern had a reputation as a fine place to dine. Proprietor Sylvester Walker ran not only the inn but a small farm as well, while his wife, Lucy, performed miracles baking in the stone fireplace. A typical supper at Walker Tavern might include stewed chicken, biscuits, corn bread, and applesauce cake or pumpkin pie. The tavern still stands on its original site, and the pub, sitting room, and kitchen have been renovated. Next to the tavern is a reconstructed wheelwright shop, featuring the tools used to build and repair the fragile wooden wheels as well as the covered wagons and carriages of the era. Visitors begin the self-guided walking tour at the Interpretive Center with a film in its theater and an exhibit on the settling of Michigan.

Cambridge State Historical Park (517–467–4414) is at US 12 and M 50, 25 miles south of Jackson. The tavern complex is open from 10:00 A.M. to 5:00 P.M. daily from Memorial Day through Labor Day.

Also located in the Irish Hills is Lenawee County's other outstanding attraction, ***Hidden Lake Gardens.*** Glaciers were responsible for the rolling terrain of the gardens, and when the ice sheet finally melted away, it left a topography of prominent knolls, ridges, valleys, and funnel–like depressions. Harry A. Fee was responsible for preserving it. The Adrian businessman fell in love with the scenic land formations and in 1926 purchased 226 acres, including its namesake lake. He began developing the landscape and supervising its early plantings before giving the gardens to Michigan State University in 1945. The visitor center was added in 1966, the plant conservatory four years later, and today Hidden Lake Gardens covers 670 acres with 6 miles of picturesque, winding, one-way roads, 5 miles of hiking trails to its remote corners, and more than 2,500 introduced species of plants.

Upon entering the gardens most people head for the visitor center, which includes an orientation and information area, a gift shop, and a walk-through exhibit concourse. Next door is the plant conservatory, where 8,000 square feet of glass houses plants from around the world. Along with the kumquats and vanilla plants in the tropical house and the old-man cacti in the arid dome, there is the 80-by-36-foot temperate house used to display unusual houseplants and seasonal flowers. From the conservatory visitors can follow a winding drive around Hidden Lake and then ascend through a unique forest carpeted in ivy before topping out at Gobblers Knob with a view of the surrounding ridges and hardwood trees below. The network of one-way roads also leads visitors past a glacial pothole, through an oak upland forest, and around an open meadow, and ends, of course, at a picnic area.

The entrance to the gardens (517–431–2060) is located on M 50, 2 miles west of Tipton or 7 miles west of Tecumseh. The gardens, visitor center, and plant conservatory are open daily from 9:00 A.M. to 8:30 P.M. April through October and 8:00 A.M. to 4:00 P.M. November through March. There is a small per-person admission fee.

There are many mansions-turned-restaurants in Michigan, but few evoke an aura of gracious living and fine dining the way the *Hathaway House* does. A National Historic Site, the home was built by David Carpenter, who arrived in Blissfield in 1836 as a twenty-one-year-old with $25. Seventeen years later, Carpenter was a wealthy merchant, and he decided to build a home that would reflect his position as one of the county's most prominent residents. The eighteen-room Hathaway House resembles a southern mansion. Inside guests are seated

TOP ANNUAL EVENTS

Clare Irish Festival,
Clare, March;
(800) 715–3550

Alma Highland Festival and Games,
Alma, May;
(989) 463–8979

East Lansing Art Festival,
May;
(517) 337–1731

World's Longest Breakfast Table,
Battle Creek, June;
(800) 397–2240

Abbott's Magical Get-Together,
Colon, August;
(269) 432–3235

Civil War Muster,
Jackson, August;
(517) 788–4320

Riverfest,
Lansing, September;
(517) 483–4499

Michigan Wine and Harvest Festival,
Kalamazoo and Paw Paw,
September;
(269) 657–5568

Historic Homes Tour,
Marshall, September;
(269) 781–5163

Celebration on the Grand,
Grand Rapids, September;
(800) 678–9859

in six distinctively decorated rooms that were previously the east and west parlors, the card room, and the library, among others. In this restaurant you can still run your hand along the original cherry banister of the sweeping staircase, be warmed during the winter by one of five fireplaces, and admire the classic woodwork.

funfacts

Adrian's Croswell Opera House is the third oldest continuously operated theater in the country. The Opera House (517–263–6868) dates back to 1866 and today still features live theater productions.

Afterward you can drop in at the Main Street Stable. What used to be the carriage house in the back of Carpenter's mansion is now a lively little pub that still features a rustic interior of hand-hewn beams, wooden benches, and lanterns hanging from the ceiling.

The Hathaway House (517–486–2141) is reached from US 23 by taking exit 5 and heading 10 miles west on US 223. Hours are 5:00 to 9:00 P.M. Tuesday through Thursday, 11:30 A.M. to 9:00 P.M. Friday and Saturday, and 1:00 to 8:00 P.M. Sunday. Dinner entrees range from $11 to $30.

Hillsdale County

In 1827 a surveying crew from the Detroit-Chicago Road was working in the fertile prairie of the St. Joseph Valley when one crew member, Captain Moses Allen, fell in love with the area. His homestead led to a small hamlet of homes and shops known as Allen's Prairie, the first white settlement west of Tecumseh. This is the birthplace of Hillsdale County, but today **Allen** is better known as the Antiques Capital of Michigan.

It began as a weekend flea market in the late 1960s and soon drew crowds of antiques hunters from several states to the junction of US 12 and M 49. Eventually some of the antiques dealers who rented the summer stalls began to set up permanent businesses in Allen. Today this quaint village of fewer than 300 residents supports more than a dozen antiques malls, each housing several dealers and other shops along a mile-long stretch of US 12, the town's main street. Some of the shops are located in redbrick buildings near the intersection, others in old homes or weathered barns that are packed with furniture and other large antiques.

The largest shop is **Allen Antique Mall** (517–869–2788), which is west of town on US 12 and has four buildings jammed with collectibles. The best times to visit Allen are on the weekends of Memorial Day, Fourth of July, or Labor Day when the community holds open-air antiques festivals and even more dealers converge on the town and set up booths along the streets.

If you are heading south to Allen, swing through the picturesque village of Litchfield 14 miles to the north at the other end of M 49. Near the center of town is the Litchfield Town Hall, and featured in the huge storefront display windows is the *Litchfield Community Hand Tool Collection.* In one window are seventy-five tools from the turn of the twentieth century, in the other another sixty-three, all numbered to correspond to a list taped on the window and in surprisingly good condition. In the three smaller windows on the second floor, more tools are hung in display as the town's collection continues to grow and grow. Someday it might have to use all these tools to build a museum for them.

The *Tristate Corner* in Hillsdale County is hardly a major tourist attraction. But there is enough interest in this geographical oddity that the Hillsdale County Historical Association maintains a stone monument dedicated to where three states—Michigan, Indiana, and Ohio—come together, the only such spot in the Midwest that doesn't involve a river.

> ## funfacts
>
> Somerset Center's McCourtie Park, located in the northeast corner of Hillsdale County, was once the Prohibition-era playground of cement mogul William McCourtie and features seventeen sculpted cement bridges across a winding stream.

The monument is actually in Michigan, but it explains exactly where the corner is (130 feet to the south) because when you actually reach this obscure spot, a farm field on a county dirt road, you want to make sure you're standing in all three states at the same time.

It's not as famous as Four Corners, the spot where Arizona, New Mexico, Colorado, and Utah come together, but on the other hand, as the locals say, it won't burn two weeks of your vacation to visit.

From Camden, in the southwest corner of Hillsdale County, head south on M 49 and then west on Territorial Road. In less than 3 miles, turn south on Cope Road and look for the stone monument on the left-hand side of the road.

St. Joseph County

Michigan is known for many things, but to the average tourist, magicians and magic are not generally among them. Yet Harry Houdini died in Michigan, and the state has deep roots in the art of illusion and the related conjuring culture. One of the most famous American magicians in the 1920s, Harry Blackstone, toured the country with his act. At one time he passed through the village of **Colon** and then returned in 1926 and purchased property. Blackstone toured in the winter but spent his summers in Colon creating new illusions and rehearsing his show. One summer Australian magician Percy Abbott came to Colon to visit Blackstone and fell in love with a local girl and the quiet area. Abbott, eager to end his days of traveling, moved to Michigan and formed a partnership with Blackstone to begin a magic-apparatus manufacturing company.

The partnership went sour after only eight months, but the Australian magician went ahead with his plans and in 1933 set up *Abbott's Magic Manufacturing Company.* Today this sleepy farming village is the home of the world's largest magic company, an interesting stop even if you've never done a card trick. The walls inside are plastered with posters and photographs of magicians, for all the famous performers, from Doug Henning to David Copperfield, have done business with this company. A display room in the factory, an all-black brick building, has cases and shelves filled with a portion of the 2,000 tricks and gadgets Abbott's Magic builds. And there is always a resident magician on hand to show you how they work.

langley
coveredbridge

The longest of Michigan's handful of remaining covered bridges is just north of Centreville along Covered Bridge Road. Built in 1887, the Langley Covered Bridge is 282 feet long and uses three spans to cross the St. Joseph River.

A year after beginning his company, Abbott also instituted an open house for magicians as a sales incentive, and that quickly evolved into Colon's annual festival, Magical Get-Together. Every August more than a thousand amateur and professional magicians flood the village for a series of shows at the high school auditorium. Abbott's Magic Manufacturing Company (269–432–3235) is at 124 St. Joseph Street, 1 block off M 86, and is open from 9:00 A.M. to 5:00 P.M. Monday through Friday and 9:00 A.M. to 4:00 P.M. on Saturday.

More magic memorabilia can be viewed at the *Colon Community Museum,* which is housed in an 1893 church at 219 North Blackstone Road. Although many artifacts deal with the town's first pioneer families, one area is devoted to the personal items and photographs of Blackstone and Abbott. The museum is open Tuesday, Thursday, and Sunday from 2:00 to 4:30 P.M. There is no admission charge.

Jackson County

The Lower Peninsula lacks the waterfalls that grace the countryside in the Upper Peninsula, but in Jackson there are the *Cascades.* Billed as the largest constructed waterfalls in North America, the Cascades were a creation of "Captain" William Sparks, a well-known Jackson industrialist and philanthropist.

They date to the early 1930s, when Sparks was developing a 450-acre park as a gift to the city and wanted it to showcase something different, something no other Michigan city had.

What he developed were the Cascades, a series of eighteen waterfalls with water dancing down the side of a hill from one to the next. Six fountains, varying in height and patterns, supply more than 3,000 gallons per minute, while 1,200 colored lights turn the attraction into a nightly event of constantly changing light, color, and music. The total length of the falls is 500 feet, and energetic viewers climb the 129 steps that run along each side of the Cascades, dodging the spray along the way. Others prefer to sit in the amphitheater seats to watch the water and light show that takes place nightly from Memorial Day to Labor Day.

The Cascades (517–788–4320) can be reached from I–94 by taking exit 138 and heading south for 3 miles. Signs point the way to the falls. There is an admission fee.

Ten miles southwest of Jackson is the Victorian town of Concord, the proper setting for the *Mann House,* a Michigan historical museum. The three-story house was built in 1883 by Daniel and Ellen Mann, two of the earliest settlers in the area. They raised two daughters, Jessie and Mary Ida, who continued to live in the house and maintained the original furnishings, most dating to the 1870s. The younger daughter died in 1969 but bequeathed the historic house and all its contents to the people of Michigan through the Michigan Historical Commission.

The house can be toured today, and its eight rooms are a well-preserved trip back to life in the 1880s. The table is set in the dining room; a chess game waits to be played in the parlor; toys, books, and knickknacks fill the children's rooms. As soon as you walk through the wrought-iron gate at the street, you

More Magic in Marshall

If you need more conjuring, head to Marshall for the *American Museum of Magic.* Founded in 1978, the museum is located in a restored 1868 building, and its collection of almost a half million pieces of memorabilia takes up three floors. There are props from all the great magicians of the nineteenth and twentieth centuries, including the milk can escape apparatus that saved Houdini's career.

The American Museum of Magic (616–781–7674) is at 107 East Michigan Avenue in downtown Marshall. You must call the museum in advance to set up a tour. There is a small admission fee.

The Parlour

Late one night, when the *Parlour* is humming with people, ice-cream dishes clanging, and waitresses hustling orders from the kitchen, a woman screams and no one takes notice. It's her first trip to the landmark ice-cream parlor, and a waitress has just placed in front of her the largest Black Cow she has ever seen. The fountain glass itself is 12 inches high, and still the rich mixture of root beer and ice cream is cascading over the top, because at the Parlour, they put five scoops of vanilla—count 'em, five—in their Black Cow.

"Oh my goodness," said the woman, in a near state of calorie shock. "All I asked for was a root beer float, and look what they brought me."

If you're a die-hard ice-cream lover, then the Parlour is heaven on earth, or at the very least a parfait paradise. Operated by the Jackson Dairy, this hot fudge haven is basically four U-shaped lunch counters plus a handful of booths for those of us who like to pig out anonymously. Everybody else has to sit across from total strangers and indulge in five scoops of cherry ripple drowning in a sea of marshmallow syrup. Then again, maybe it's better they are strangers.

Or else, who cares? When you enter the Parlour, you have momentarily forgotten about your waistband if you ever thought about it to begin with. The most popular item is the Deluxe Pecan Combo: three scoops of ice cream smothered in hot fudge and hot caramel, sprinkled with pecans, and buried in real whipped cream. You don't eat this sundae, you attack it, using your spoon like a shovel to remove large portions from the sides before it avalanches onto your place mat.

There's also the Hot Fudge Ice Cream Cake, nicknamed "Awful, Awful." It's two thick slices of chocolate cake covered with four scoops of ice cream and drenched in hot fudge and whipped cream. But the greatest creation at the Parlour, the reason it was once voted the best ice-cream shop in the state, is the Dare to Be Great Sundae—twenty-one scoops of ice cream, or roughly a half gallon of assorted flavors, with four soup ladles of toppings and a mountain of nuts, and, of course, totally smothered in real whipped cream. It's served in a punch bowl for obvious reasons.

The Parlour (517–783–1581) is at Wildwood Avenue and Daniel Road in Jackson and reached from I–94 by taking exit 137. Head south on Lawrence and then east on Wildwood Avenue.

enter an era gone by. The Mann House (517–524–8943) is at 205 Hanover Street in Concord and is open from 9:30 A.M. to 4:30 P.M. Wednesday through Sunday from Memorial Day to Labor Day. There is no admission fee.

Deer hunting is not just an outdoor sport in Michigan, it's a passion. Every November more than 750,000 hunters participate in the 16-day firearm deer season. Add in the people who participate in the archery and muzzleloading deer seasons, and the number tops a million.

These hunters's shrine is the *Michigan Whitetail Hall of Fame Museum,* just off I–94 near Jackson. At this unusual "hall of fame" you can feed live deer, or, if you are around on June 1, see newborn fawns. Inside the hall is a gallery of more than one hundred trophy racks, the stuff that deer hunters dream about while sitting in their blinds every November.

The Michigan Whitetail Hall of Fame, (517) 522–3354, is at 4220 Willis Road and reached by taking exit 150 at Grass Lake and following the signs. Hours are 10:00 A.M. to 5:00 P.M. Monday through Friday and 10:00 A.M. to 6:00 P.M. Saturday and Sunday. Admission is $4.00 for adults and $1.00 for children.

funfacts

The Republican Party was born on the corner of Second and Franklin Streets in Jackson. The hall where the founders had originally planned to meet on July 6, 1854, was too small for the 1,500 people who arrived to form a new political party. So the crowd walked 8 blocks to an oak grove and met there "under the oaks."

Calhoun County

Homer is a small town in the southeast corner of the county, and its most impressive structure is a century-old gristmill on the banks of the Kalamazoo River. The U.S. government once wanted to turn the mill's black walnut beams into propellers for World War I airplanes. Another historic building in town, though considerably smaller, is a fun place to have breakfast on the Fourth of July: the *Homer Fire Museum.* The redbrick structure with its arched windows and decorative cornice was built in 1876, five years after Homer was incorporated as a village. It has always been the classic fire hall on the main street, but in its early days it also served as a jail, town hall, and place for public meetings and local theater performances. It's the oldest building in town, and when Homer residents decided to replace it, they preserved the old fire hall by attaching the new fire station to it.

In 1983 it was set up as a museum, with suits and equipment donated by former firefighters. By far the most impressive item on display had always been there, a horse-pulled steam pumper built in 1887. Homer bought it from Union City in 1904 for $1,200 and placed it in the fire hall, where it has been ever since. The best time to see the displays is on the Fourth of July, when the town holds its annual Fire Hall Pancake Breakfast from 7:00 to 11:00 A.M. Almost 500 people enjoy the all-American morning meal in the new fire station on tables set up among the modern equipment. Then they wander into the old hall to see how fires were put out in days past. The museum does not have regular hours, but those who are passing through can go to the Homer City Offices

Sojourner Truth Museum Exhibit

The **Kimball House Museum** is a restored 1886 Victorian home furnished with antiques and devoted to the history of Battle Creek. But by far the most interesting exhibit is dedicated to Sojourner Truth. This famous anti-slavery reformer was born into slavery in Hurley, New York, in 1797 but was freed when the state emancipated slaves in 1829. A mystic who believed she heard God's voice, Truth began to preach in the streets of New York City in 1829 and then along the Eastern Seaboard after embracing the abolitionist movement in 1843. She added women's rights to her causes a few years later, and in 1864 she was received by President Abraham Lincoln at the White House.

Eventually Truth relocated to Battle Creek but continued to stump the country on speaking tours, advocating women's rights. Illiterate all her life, Truth was nevertheless a charismatic speaker who drew large crowds to her lectures and quickly became Battle Creek's first nationally known figure.

The second-floor exhibit at the Kimball House Museum features a handful of Truth's mementoes, including her crude attempt to write her name. The museum is at 196 Capital Avenue, 3 blocks north of Michigan Avenue. Hours are 1:00 to 4:00 P.M. Friday and the second and fourth Sunday of the month.

(517–568–4321) next to the fire station, and an employee will open up the museum for you. There is no admission fee.

Battle Creek is best known as the Cereal Bowl of America, dating back to 1876 when Dr. John Harvey Kellogg joined the staff of the Battle Creek Sanitarium. Kellogg spent the next twenty-five years developing the sanitarium into an institution recognized around the world for its "health building and training" regimen of hydrotherapy, exercise, and vegetarian diet. Along the way he found a way to process grains into appetizing breakfast food for his sanitarium guests. Cornflakes and other cereals quickly revolutionized the eating habits of people everywhere, and by the early 1900s more than forty cereal manufacturers were based in Battle Creek, including Kellogg's.

The fascinating story behind the breakfast cereal industry is best told at **Kellogg's Cereal City USA.** Opened in the summer of 1998, the two-and-a-half-story, 45,000-square-foot center contains 15,000 square feet of interactive displays along with theaters and galleries. A detailed replica of Kellogg's cereal production line demonstrates the process of manufacturing cereal. At the Marketplace gift shop, you can purchase Kellogg's apparel, and the Collectibles Cafe features novelty food made with cereal.

Tony the Tiger? Yeah, he's there too, and the kids think It's Grrrreat!

Kellogg's Cereal City USA (800–970–7020) is at 171 West Michigan Avenue. From I–94 take exit 103 and follow Michigan Avenue west into the downtown area. Cereal City is open from 9:30 A.M. to 5:00 P.M. daily from Memorial Day through Labor Day. During the rest of the year, it is open from 10:00 A.M. to 4:00 P.M. Tuesday through Friday, 10:00 A.M. to 5:00 P.M. Saturday, and noon to 5:00 P.M. Sunday. Admission is $7.95 for adults and $4.95 for children.

Not every attraction in Battle Creek is wrapped around sugar-frosted flakes. Just south of the city in a wooded area along Harper Creek is ***Binder Park Zoo,*** one of Michigan's most unusual displays of fauna and flora. Instead of a series of cages and animal houses in the middle of a city, Binder Park is a walk through

Strange As It Sounds

It looked so plain when the woman behind the counter handed it to me, wrapped in waxed paper and placed in a brown paper bag. But there it is: a buttered turkey sandwich, slices of moist meat on a bun, topped with mayonnaise. It's the kind of sandwich you'd make after Thanksgiving dinner with the leftover rolls and that platter of turkey still sitting in the kitchen.

But here at a place they call Turkeyville, U.S.A., you don't have to wait until Uncle Harry and the kids go home. You can order one year-round because this simple sandwich—turkey, butter, mayonnaise on soft white bread—is the foundation of a multimillion-dollar company. Cornwell's Turkeyville, U.S.A. has been called "the oldest, best-known, and possibly largest all-turkey specialty restaurant in North America."

The Cornwells have done to the turkey what the Zehner family has done to the chicken in Frankenmuth: turned a meal into a tourist attraction. Today the restaurant is an entertainment complex serving an average of 1,000 people a day, grossing more than $2 million annually, and feeding more than 400 busloads a summer—and pretty much does it all on the backs of 15,000, 30-pound toms a year. In 1985, when a photo of founders Wayne and Marjorie Cornwell was featured in People magazine with an item proclaiming their buttered bun "the world's best turkey sandwich," people around here knew the Cornwells had hit the big time.

After you've had your fill of turkey, you can wander into Cornwell's Ice Cream Parlour or browse Country Junction, a huge gift shop. Also on the grounds are the Antique Barn, St. Julian Wine Tasting shop, Turkey Barn, a play fort for the kids, and a gazebo with a band playing throughout the summer.

From I–94, take I–69 north to exit 42 and then head west on North Drive North, also known as Turkeyville Road. The restaurant is reached in a half mile. Cornwell's Turkeyville, U.S.A. (800–228–4315) is open from 11:00 A.M. to 8:00 P.M. daily from April through October with reduced hours in the winter.

woods along boardwalks, brick walkways, and wood-chip trails, passing animal exhibits that have been designed around the existing flora and terrain.

There is the Northern Forest Boardwalk, where you can view timber wolves, great horned owls, and a Sitka deer; a Great Plains area, with bison, a prairie dog colony, and snowy owls; hungry trout that you can feed in Harper Creek; and a turtle log and viewing area in the pond. In other areas you will see giant tortoises, zebras, cheetahs, and even a bald eagle, but the most impressive section is Binder's zoo within a zoo. The newest addition to the park is Miller Children's Zoo, the largest animal-contact area in the state. Kids have a chance to feed and touch dozens of animals, including donkeys, rabbits, pygmy goats, draft horses, and pigs. Constructed around these contact stations are intriguing play areas. There's the Pig Pen, with models of pigs that children can play on; the dinosaur area, with a 100-foot-long brontosaurus and a fossil-find pit; a giant spiderweb to climb; and a farm area with a silo slide and cow climber.

Binder Park Zoo (269–979–1351) is reached from I–94 by taking exit 100 south along Beadle Lake Road and following the signs to the entrance. The zoo is open from mid-April to mid-October from 9:00 A.M. to 5:00 P.M. Monday through Friday, 9:00 A.M. to 6:00 P.M. Saturday, and 11:00 A.M. to 6:00 P.M. Sunday. Admission is $8.95 for adults and $6.95 for children.

Kalamazoo County

The **Air Zoo of Kalamazoo** is dedicated to the aircraft of World War II and the role they played in the Allies' success. It's a "living museum" that not only displays many planes in its hangar at the southeast corner of the city's municipal airport but also restores them to working condition. Visitors are treated to exhibits and historic films in the video room and to a close-up view of more than a dozen historic planes inside and more planes outside. They can even watch mechanics work on restoring the latest acquisitions.

The museum has more than sixty planes and historic crafts on display in two buildings. Planes include a Curtiss P-40 "Flying Tiger" and three Grumman cats—"Wildcat," "Hellcat," and "Bearcat," which led to the museum's name.

The Air Zoo (269–382–6555) is at 2101 East Milham Road and is open Monday through Saturday from 10:00 A.M. to 8:00 P.M. in the summer and 10:00 A.M. to 6:00 P.M. the rest of the year. You can drive to the hangar or, if you have your own plane, fly in. Admission is $19.50 for adults and $15.50 for children ages six through fifteen; five and under are free.

Also on the edge of Kalamazoo is the **Celery Flats Interpretive Center.** This is a truly unique facility that teaches the history of the efforts of Dutch immigrants to convert wetlands into one of the most productive celery-growing areas in the world. From the 1890s through the 1930s, fields of green-tipped celery covered Portage, Comstock, and Kalamazoo; the celery was touted as "fresh as dew from Kalamazoo."

The historic area offers an 1856 one-room schoolhouse, a 1931 grain elevator, and historical displays on celery, as well as an opportunity to rent canoes to explore the surrounding wetlands. Celery Flats (269–329–4522) is open from May through August from noon to 5:00 P.M. Friday and Sunday and 10:00 A.M. to 7:00 P.M. Saturday. In September the hours are noon to 5:00 P.M. Saturday and Sunday. From I–94 take exit 76A and head south 2.5 miles on South Westedge Avenue and then east a half mile on Garden Lane. There is a small admission fee.

Barry County

In 1962 Donald Gilmore, the son-in-law of Dr. W. E. Upjohn, founder of one of the nation's leading pharmaceutical firms, was restoring a 1920 Pierce-Arrow touring car in the driveway of his Gull Lake summer home. The project dragged on into the fall, and by the time it was finished, Gilmore had to erect a tent around the car and light a kerosene heater. This was no way to work on a classic car. So Gilmore purchased three farms north of his home and then scouted the countryside for old wooden barns, which he had dismantled and moved.

The wooden structures held his growing collection, and in 1966 Gilmore opened his barn doors to the public on ninety acres of rolling farmland. The Classic Car Club of America added its collection to what had become the Hickory Corners Museum in 1984, and today the *Gilmore-Classic Car Club of America Museums* form a complex of twenty-two barns displaying 120 vintage automobiles in mint condition. The car that attracts the most attention is a 1929 Duesenberg. Some visitors, however, are fascinated with Rolls-Royces, and the museums contain fifteen of them, including eight in one barn, ranging from a 1910 Silver Ghost to a 1938 Phantom III.

There is also a 1927 Bugatti Grand Sport Roadster, the "Gnome-Mobile" from the Disney movie of the same name, as well as other transportation displays, including a replica of the Wright Brothers' Kitty Hawk flier. Those intrigued by hood ornaments can view a collection of more than 800 that captures everything from a windblown angel to an archer taking aim at the road ahead. They come from as far away as the former Soviet Union and include leaded-glass ornaments from France.

The complex (269–671–5089) is located at M 43 and Hickory Road, 7 miles north of Richland. From I–94, take exit 80 and head north to M 43. The museums are open from 9:00 A.M. to 5:00 P.M. Monday through Friday and 9:00 A.M. to 6:00 P.M. Saturday and Sunday May through October. Admission is $7.00 for adults and $5.00 for children ages seven to fifteen.

Nearby is the **Kellogg Dairy Center.** Founded in 1984 by Michigan State University, this experimental dairy is a working farm that combines research and teaching. It's also a popular spot for urban folks to visit and learn what it's like down on the farm. There is a visitor center with educational exhibits and a viewing area of the computerized milking parlor. There also is a self-guided tour through the farm that takes about an hour, or longer if you stop to pet and feed every calf.

The Kellogg Dairy Center (269–671–2507) is reached from I–94 by taking exit 85 and heading north 7 miles on Thirty-fifth Street. Turn east on M 89 and in 3 miles north on Fortieth Street to reach the posted entrance. Hours are 8:00 A.M. to sunset daily. There is no admission charge.

Ingham County

What was once a hardware store and then an ice-cream parlor in the heart of old Okemos was turned into a restaurant in 1982 by Jennifer Brooke and William White, whose extensive travels around the world gave them a love for Mexican, Thai, Southwestern, and many other types of food. Food, however, was only White's second love. His first was playing the tuba, something he had been doing since he was eleven years old.

Adorning the walls of the **Travelers Club International Restaurant and Tuba Museum** are more than two dozen tubas—over-the-shoulder baritones and alto horns—and memorabilia that White has collected over the years, including a photo of the Great Band Race staged in London in 1918, basically five guys running and playing instruments at the same time. White's most valuable piece is the only known double E-flat helicon tuba, which was made in 1915 and nicknamed "The Majestic Monster." His most unusual: the double bell euphonium; it has two horns. The Travelers Club International Restaurant (517–349–1701) is reached from I–96 by taking exit 110 and heading north on Okemos Road. Hours are 9:00 A.M. to 10:00 P.M. Sunday through Thursday and 8:00 A.M. to 10:30 P.M. Friday and Saturday.

One of the best urban park developments in Michigan is Lansing's **River Trail.** The 6-mile-long park is a greenbelt that stretches on both sides of the

Grand River from Kalamazoo Avenue just north of I–496 to North Street, 3 mi
downstream. A riverwalk, made of long sections of boardwalk near or on
river, runs along the entire east side of the park, with bridges that lead to m
walkways on the west side. Interesting attractions are found throughout the
park, and you could easily spend an entire day walking from one to the next.

At the south end is the **R. E. Olds Transportation Museum** (517–372–
0422), dedicated to the history of transportation in Lansing, where at one time
or another fifteen makes of automobile were manufactured. Almost twenty
cars, from the first Oldsmobile, built in 1897, to an Indy 500 pace car, fill the
old City Bus Garage along with old motoring apparel and other memorabilia.
The museum is open Tuesday through Saturday from 10:00 A.M. to 5:00 P.M. and
Sunday from noon to 5:00 P.M. There is an admission fee.

Right next door you'll find the **Impression 5 Museum** (517–485–8116),
which is described as an "exploratorium" for children and their parents, stress-
ing hands-on exhibits. The 240 exhibits on several floors range from a music
room, filled with unusual instruments to be played, to a touch tunnel, where
everything is explored using only your tactile sense. Impression 5 is open the
same hours as the R. E. Olds Museum, and there is an admission fee.

Continuing north along the east side, you'll walk under Michigan Avenue
and past views of the state capitol, around Sun Bowl Amphitheater and the
city's Farmers' Market (open Tuesday, Thursday, and Saturday), and eventually
reach the **Brenke River Sculpture and Fish Ladder.** The structure is a swirl
of steps and stone benches leading down to the fish ladder that curves its way
around scenic North Lansing Dam. Come mid-September you can watch
salmon and steelhead trout leap from one water ledge of the ladder to the next
on the way to their spawning grounds.

The park really comes alive during RiverFest, held Labor Day weekend,
which includes, among other activities, a lighted boat parade and a fireworks

Riverwalk in Lansing

display. On any clear evening there is a magnificent view of the capitol's lighted dome, shimmering over the Grand River.

For a closer look at Michigan's most famous government building, join a **State Capitol Tour** and be prepared for the building's stunning interior. In 1992 a major renovation of the century-old capitol was completed at a cost of more than $45 million. When the building was originally dedicated on January 1, 1879, it was one of the first state capitols to emulate the dome and wings of the U.S. Capitol in Washington, D.C., and today it is considered by most as an outstanding example of Victorian craftsmanship. All tours begin in the rotunda, where visitors stand on the floor of glass tiles imported from England and stare at the stars in the top of the dome 172 feet above. In between are portraits of governors on the second level and, on the main floor, flags carried by Michigan regiments during battles from as long ago as the Civil War. Tours also include a look into the restored state Senate and House of Representative chambers as well as other offices and rooms, each accompanied by bits and pieces of Michigan's history.

To reach the state capitol from I–96, follow I–496 through Lansing and take the Walnut exit. State capitol signs point the way to the building and parking nearby. Capitol Tour Guide Service (517–373–2353) offers the tours every

Planet Walk

For most children one of the most enjoyable aspects of the River Trail is the Planet Walk, a cleverly simple but thoroughly enjoyable trek through our solar system. It is also very enlightening. Most maps of our solar system have condensed the distances to fit the sun and nine orbiting planets on the same page. You learn the names of the planets, but distances in the universe, the 93 million miles from the sun to Earth or the 3.7 billion miles to Pluto, are simply too large for children to comprehend from textbooks.

That's the idea behind the Planet Walk. The one-way walk of 2 miles is strung out along River Front Park, beginning and ending at two of Lansing's most enjoyable attractions: the Impression 5 Museum and Potter Park Zoo. In between it's a 45- to 60-minute walk from the sun to Pluto, a hike in which every step represents a million miles.

Not only are the distances properly scaled but so are the size and mass of the sun and each planet. The sun, located near the entrance to the Impression 5 Museum, is a 20-inch golden sphere looking like an over-inflated basketball.

From there it's a few quick steps to reach Mercury, the size of a pencil eraser. The first four planets are reached within a few hundred feet. But the rest are spread out, and it's probably three-quarters of a mile between Saturn and Uranus alone.

> ## Wilderness Capital
>
> When Michigan was organized as a state in 1837, Detroit was its capital, as it had been in the territorial days. After much debate, the capital was moved to a more central location in 1847. Lansing did not exist then, and its first capitol, completed in 1848, was built in a wilderness. Among the towns that wanted to be Michigan's seat of government is Marshall, which went as far as to set aside land for the capitol and even build a "Governor's Mansion" in 1839.

half hour Monday through Friday from 9:00 A.M. to 4:00 P.M. Visits by groups of more than ten must be scheduled in advance. There is no charge for tours.

Almost as impressive as the state capitol is the **Michigan Library and Historical Center,** which opened in 1988. Nationally recognized for its architectural design, the 312,000-square-foot center houses the Michigan Historical Museum, the State Archives, and the Library of Michigan, the second largest state library in the country.

Most people, however, visit the center to see the museum. The Michigan Historical Museum features twelve permanent galleries displaying facades of a lumber baron's mansion and the state's first territorial capitol, a walk-through copper mine tunnel, and an impressive woodland diorama. Other rooms feature a working sawmill, historic cars, a stake fort, and many other exhibits relating to the history of the Great Lakes State. To view the museum and the capitol is a full day for most families.

The Michigan Library and Historical Center (517–373–3559) is at 717 West Allegan Street, within easy walking distance of the capitol. Hours are 9:00 A.M. to 4:30 P.M. Monday through Friday, 10:00 A.M. to 4:00 P.M. Saturday, and 1:00 to 5:00 P.M. Sunday. There is no admission charge.

Ionia County

When autumn arrives in Michigan and the leaves begin turning shades of red, yellow, and orange, many people instinctively head north to view the fall colors. But the southern portions of the state also enjoy their share of autumn brilliance, and one of the best drives is a 15-mile route that is lined by hardwood forests and rolling farm fields and crosses three covered bridges, including the oldest one in Michigan, **White's Covered Bridge.**

Nestled in a wooded area and spanning the Flat River, White's Covered Bridge was built in 1867 by J. N. Brazee for $1,700 and has faithfully served the public ever since. It is a classic covered bridge, its trusses hand-hewn and

The Roadside Table

For those who like obscure historical sites, Ionia County has one of the best in the state. Located at Morrison Lake Road and Grand River Avenue, south of the town of Saranac, is the place known simply as the Roadside Table. It was at this very spot that in 1929 county engineer Allen Williams used a stack of leftover guardrail planks to build a table, the first public picnic table ever placed on a highway right-of-way. Today, of course, there are roadside tables and rest areas in all fifty states, and the only sights more common on our nation's highways are billboards and McDonald's restaurants. Along the road, the site is marked only by a small white historical site sign, but a green state historic site plaque detailing the story has been erected next to the tables. The state still maintains the tables and garbage barrels, even though most of the traffic now flows along I–94 to the south.

secured with wooden pegs and hand-cut square nails. The bridge is 14 feet wide and 116 feet long, and you can still drive a car across it; most travelers park on the other side and return on foot for a closer inspection. The bridge is reached by driving to the hamlet of Smyrna in Ionia County (5 miles southwest of Belding) and then heading south on White's Bridge Road.

Continue south on White's Bridge Road for 4 miles, and turn west (left) onto Potters Road for a short distance to Fallasburg Bridge Road, which will lead you over another covered bridge in Fallasburg County Park just inside Kent County. Brazee and his construction company also built the **Fallasburg Covered Bridge.** Its design is similar to White's bridge, and it was built with the same high standards that have allowed both these structures to exist for more than a century. Above both entrances to the Fallasburg Bridge is a stern warning: $5 FINE FOR RIDING OR DRIVING ON THIS BRIDGE FASTER THAN A WALK. The county park is a pleasant stretch of picnic tables and grills on the grassy slopes of the Flat River.

From the park, take Lincoln Lake Avenue south into the town of Lowell and head west on M 21 along the Grand River until you finally cross it into the town of Ada, where signs will point the way to the **Ada Covered Bridge.** The original bridge that crossed the Thornapple River was built in 1867 by Will Holmes but was destroyed by fire in 1980. The residents of Ada immediately opened their hearts (and their wallets), and the bridge was quickly rebuilt and restored. The Ada Bridge is open to pedestrian traffic only.

Kent County

The favorite son of Grand Rapids is Gerald R. Ford, a local congressman who eventually became the thirty-eighth president of the United States. In 1981 the **Gerald R. Ford Museum** opened, and today the center, dedicated to Ford's life and his days in office, is one of the city's top attractions. More than two million visitors have passed through the center, which features two floors of exhibits and displays that underwent a $5.3-million makeover in 1997.

The museum still features a full-scale reproduction of the Oval Office as it appeared in Ford's administration but now has several new galleries that feature hands-on and computerized exhibits. Among them is a TelePrompTer that allows you to give a Ford speech, videos of President Richard Nixon resigning, and a holographic device that puts you into ten rooms of the White House, including the famous Lincoln Bedroom.

The Gerald R. Ford Museum (616–451–9263) is at 303 Pearl Street NW on the west bank of the Grand River, and is reached by exiting US 131 at Pearl Street. Hours are 9:00 A.M. to 5:00 P.M. daily. Admission is $5.00 for adults and free for children.

Long before the presidential seal was stamped on this portion of Kent County, Grand Rapids was known as the City of Furniture. In 1853 it was a small frontier town surrounded by forests with a seemingly endless supply of lumber and situated on the banks of the Grand River, which provided power for the mills. In this setting William "Deacon" Haldane opened a cabinet shop and soon was building not only cupboards but also cradles, coffins, and tables and chairs. By the end of the decade, there were several shops, and soon "Grand Rapids–Made Furniture" became the standard of excellence.

funfacts

Grand Rapids entered the national furniture market with exhibits at the Philadelphia Centennial Exposition in 1876. Today the city still accounts for 40 percent of the business and office furniture market.

As impressive as the Ford Museum is, it now has a rival practically next door. In 1995 the **Van Andel Museum Center** opened to the public, replacing the old Grand Rapids Public Museum. The $40-million structure is on the Grand River, and overlooking the water is its centerpiece, a glass pavilion housing a working 1928 carousel with hand-carved horses and a Wurlitzer organ. Rides are 50 cents, and it's debatable who has more fun—children or their parents.

Other exhibits in the three-story building include a replica of a Union Depot waiting room, a 76-foot finback whale suspended from the ceiling, an entire street from Grand Rapids in the 1890s, a high-tech planetarium, and many interactive and hands-on exhibits that focus on natural science and the unique western Michigan environment.

The Van Andel Museum Center (616–456–3977) is at 272 Pearl, just east of the Pearl exit off US 131. Hours are 9:00 A.M. to 9:00 P.M. Monday through Thursday and 9:00 A.M. to 5:00 P.M. Friday through Sunday. There is an admission fee of $7.00 for adults and $2.50 for children ages three to seventeen.

Jerry's Diner Village

I'm drawn into the large parking lot off US 131 by the warm glow of a huge neon sign that says ROSIE'S. But when I step out, it's Elvis that greets me. "All Shook Up" is crackling over the speakers attached to the streamlined diner of shiny stainless steel and glass brick.

I step through the door and am hit by an aroma of french fries, mom's homemade apple pie, and meat loaf, and then slip into a half-moon booth and order a hot roast beef sandwich that comes with an ice-cream scoop of potatoes smothered in a sea of gravy.

To those of us who love road food, this is our temple—a cathedral with spin-around stools and a lunch counter wiped every five minutes by a waitress in bobby socks and tennis shoes. What isn't pink tile or stainless steel here is red vinyl.

You've heard of Disneyland in California? Now there's Dinerland in Rockford, a wild combination of fine art, tacky souvenirs and miniature golf, road food and gourmet dining, and not one but three authentic diners salvaged and saved by artist Jerry Berta.

The main diner is Rosie's, which Berta saved and moved 700 miles from New Jersey to Rockford in 1989. Built in 1946 by the Paramount Dining Car Company, the classic diner was used in several movies and more than one hundred commercials but was made famous by actress Nancy Walker when she cleaned up spills in it with "the quicker picker-upper," Bounty paper towels. In 1991, Berta opened it up as a restaurant because so many people were stopping in at his Diner Store wanting to buy hamburgers or milk shakes instead of his art.

The diners are 15 miles north of Grand Rapids. From US 131 take exit 101 and head east a quarter mile. Rosie's (616–866–3663) is open from 6:00 A.M. to 9:00 P.M. Monday through Thursday, 6:00 A.M. to 10:00 P.M. Friday and Saturday, and 6:00 A.M. to 8:00 P.M. Sunday.

When the state began stocking salmon in the Great Lakes in the 1960s, the fish would spawn up the Grand River but had problems getting beyond the Sixth Street Dam in Grand Rapids. The solution was the *Fish Ladder Sculpture,* a unique sculptured viewing area designed by local artist Joseph Kinnebrew. Located at 606 Front Street NW, just on the north side of I–196, the ladder is a series of seven small ledges on the west bank of the river that let the salmon easily leap around the dam. The rest of the sculpture is a platform above the ladder that provides a close view of the large fish as they jump completely out of the water from one ledge to the next.

The first salmon begin arriving in early September, and the run is over in October. Local people say the third week of September is when you'll see the major portion of the spawning run. Spectators won't be the only ones there, however, as the river will be filled with anglers trying to interest the fish in a lure, a spectacle in itself.

Fred Meijer, founder of the chain of Meijer's stores, is also responsible for **Frederik Meijer Gardens,** the largest tropical conservatory in the state. Meijer funded the project after members of West Michigan Horticultural Society pointed out to him that their side of the state had no large public gardens.

Opened in 1995, the one-hundred-acre complex features plants from around the world, waterfalls, streams, and more than sixty bronze sculptures by Marshall Fredericks and other renowned artists. Along with the main conservatory are smaller garden areas including Arid Gardens, Victorian Garden, and Gardener's Corner where specialty plants are sold. Winding through the complex is the "magnificent mile," a system of barrier-free nature trails and boardwalks that overlook wetlands, ponds, and meadows.

The gardens (888–957–1580) are northeast of Grand Rapids. From I–96 take exit 38 and head north on East Beltline Road and then east on Bradford Street to reach the gardens. Hours are 9:00 A.M. to 5:00 P.M. Monday through Saturday and noon to 5:00 P.M. Sunday. Admission is $10.00 for adults, $6.00 for children five to thirteen, and $3.00 for children three and four.

Just 15 miles north of Grand Rapids is the small town of Rockford, which dates back to the 1840s when a dam and sawmill were built along the Rogue River. Soon a railroad line passed through Rockford, and the town became a trading center with warehouses, a train depot, mills, and a bean-processing plant built along the river. What connected them on land was an unnamed alley that eventually became known as Squires Street. In 1970, the bean plant was renovated into the Old Mill, a cider mill and restaurant. This led to more historical buildings being bought and turned into a strip of specialized shops and stores.

Today **Squires Street Square** is the heart of Rockford, a charming 3-block section of more than forty shops and restaurants. You'll find stores in old warehouses, barns, a former shoe factory, a carriage house, even in railroad cars. The Rockford Historical Museum occupies the Power House, which sits on the banks of the Rogue River and at one time was a generator plant for a local factory. All the businesses are within walking distance of each other, and most are open Monday through Saturday. Rockford can be reached from US 131 by taking exit 97 and following Ten Mile Road east a short way.

Mecosta County

Big Rapids may be the county seat of Mecosta County, but in recent years the city has also become known as the Tubing Capital of Michigan. Owners of **Sawmill Canoe Livery,** which began renting out large truck inner tubes in

Hot Dog Hall of Fame (No Kidding!)

To travelers passing through Rockford, the Corner Bar appears from the outside to be just that, a small-town tavern on the corner of Main Street and Northland. Once you step inside, though, you soon realize that this pub, decorated in brass nameplates, sports memorabilia, and newspaper clippings, is packed with history and hot-dog legends. For starters, the Corner Bar is the oldest brick building in Rockford. Built in 1873, it survived several fires, including the Great Main Street Fire of 1896, and today is exceeded in age only by a wood-frame house behind the railroad depot.

At one time the building was a dry-goods store, then a hardware store, and finally, at the turn of the twentieth century, its most enduring business moved in. It became a saloon noted for its hot dogs. People came from all around to enjoy hot dogs served in steamed buns and topped with special sauce, a good heaping of relish, and chopped onions. Among the patrons one night in 1967 were several members of the Detroit Lions football team who amazed their waitress when they challenged each other to eat twelve hot dogs apiece. By the following year owner Donald R. Berg had turned that twelve-dog challenge into the Hot Dog Hall of Fame, Michigan's most unusual hall of fame, where twelve hot dogs at $1.40 apiece can immortalize your appetite with a brass nameplate on the wall. The present record of forty-two-and-a-half hot dogs was set in 1982. The bar (616–866–9866) is open from 11:00 A.M. to 10:00 P.M. Monday, Tuesday, and Thursday, 11:00 A.M. to 11:00 P.M. Wednesday, Friday, and Saturday, and 11:00 A.M. to 9:00 P.M. Sunday.

1979, say the portion of the Muskegon River that runs through Big Rapids from their livery to Highbanks Park is the most tubed waterway in the state, with more than 30,000 people floating down every summer. It's easy to see why on a hot day. Tubing is a lazy and carefree way to beat the heat; you simply place the tube in the water, sit in it, and float. No skills or paddling are needed.

The run takes about two hours, and tubers often take small coolers (larger ones require their own tube) and plenty of suntan lotion with them. For a small fee the livery provides the tube and transportation back from Highbanks Park, and on a hot August day, there will be hundreds floating along the Muskegon at every bend. Sawmill Canoe Livery (231–796–6408) is at 230 Baldwin Street and rents tubes from May to September. A two-hour float in a tube is $6.00 per person.

Places to Stay in Michigan's Heartland

BATTLE CREEK

Battle Creek Inn,
5050 Beckley Road,
(800) 232–3405

Hampton Inn,
1150 Riverside Drive,
(269) 979–5577

COLDWATER

Chicago Pike Inn,
215 East Chicago Street,
(800) 471–0501

EAST LANSING

Kellogg Hotel,
on the Michigan State
campus,
(800) 875–5090

Marriott East Lansing,
300 M.A.C. Avenue,
(517) 337–4440

GRAND RAPIDS

Amway Grand Plaza Hotel,
187 Monroe Street,
(800) 253–3590

Courtyard by Marriott,
11 Monroe Avenue,
(616) 242–6000

Days Inn Airport,
5500 Twenty-eighth Street,
(616) 949–8400

Fountain Hill Bed & Breakfast,
222 Fountain Street NE,
(800) 261–6621

JONESVILLE

Munro House Bed & Breakfast,
202 Maumee Street,
(517) 849–9292

KALAMAZOO

Country Inn,
1912 East Kilgore Road,
(269) 382–2303

Hall House Bed & Breakfast,
106 Thompson Street,
(269) 343–2500

Radisson Plaza Hotel,
100 West Michigan Avenue,
(269) 343–3333

SELECTED CHAMBERS OF COMMERCE AND TOURISM BUREAUS

Grand Rapids/Kent County Convention & Visitors Bureau,
171 Monroe Avenue NW, Suite 700,
Grand Rapids 49503;
(800) 678–9859;
www.visitgrandrapids.org

Greater Battle Creek Visitor and Convention Bureau,
77 East Michigan Avenue, Suite 100,
Battle Creek 49017;
(800) 397–2240;
www.battlecreekvisitors.org

Greater Lansing Convention and Visitors Bureau,
1223 Turner Street, Suite 200,
Lansing 48906;
(888) 252–6746;
www.lansing.org

Jackson Convention and Tourist Bureau,
6007 Ann Arbor Road,
Jackson 49201;
(800) 245–5282;
www.jackson-mich.org

Kalamazoo County Convention and Visitors Bureau,
346 West Michigan Avenue,
Kalamazoo 49007;
(800) 530–9192;
www.discoverkalamazoo.com

Stuart Avenue Inn,
229 Stuart Avenue,
(269) 342–0230

LANSING

Radisson Hotel,
111 North Grand River
Avenue,
(517) 482–0188

Red Roof Inn,
3615 Dunckel Road,
(517) 332–2575

Sheraton Lansing Hotel,
925 South Creyts Road,
(517) 323–7100

MARSHALL

Arbor Inn,
15435 West Michigan
Avenue,
(269) 781–7772

National House Inn,
102 South Parkview Avenue,
(269) 781–7374

MENDON

Mendon Country Inn,
440 West Main Street,
(800) 304–3366

STANTON

Clifford Lake Hotel,
561 West Clifford Lake Drive,
(989) 831–5151

Places to Eat in Michigan's Heartland

ADA

The Thornapple Daily Grill,
445 Thornapple Village Drive,
(616) 676–1233

BATTLE CREEK

Arcadia Brewing Company
(brew pub),
103 West Michigan Avenue,
(269) 963–9690

Mexicali Restaurant
(Mexican),
595 Columbia Avenue,
(269) 963–8188

Pancake House (breakfast),
185 Capital Avenue,
(269) 964–6790

EAST LANSING

Beggar's Banquet
(American),
218 Abbott Road,
(517) 351–4573

El Azteco (Mexican),
225 Ann Street,
(517) 351–9111

Harpers (brew pub),
131 Albert Street,
(517) 333–4040

OTHER ATTRACTIONS

Grand Rapids Art Museum

Grand Rapids Children's Museum

Honolulu House,
Marshall

John Ball Zoological Gardens,
Grand Rapids

Kalamazoo Valley Museum,
Kalamazoo

Kellogg Bird Sanctuary,
Augusta

Kingman Museum of Natural History,
Battle Creek

Kresge Art Museum,
East Lansing

Leila Arboretum,
Battle Creek

Michigan State University Museum,
East Lansing

**Michigan's Women's
Historical Center & Hall of Fame,**
Lansing

Potter Park Zoo,
Lansing

GRAND RAPIDS

Cygnus (Mediterranean),
Amway Grand Plaza,
(616) 774–2000

Gibson's Restaurant
(American),
1033 Lake Drive SE,
(616) 774–8535

**Grand Rapids Brewing
Company** (brew pub),
3689 Twenty-eighth
Street SE,
(616) 285–5970

Schnitzelbank (German),
342 Jefferson Avenue,
(616) 459–9527

JACKSON

Bella Notte Ristorante
(Italian),
137 West Michigan Avenue,
(517) 782–5727

The Parlour (ice cream),
1401 Daniel Road,
(517) 783–1581

KALAMAZOO

Club Car Restaurant
(American),
6225 West D Avenue,
(269) 342–8087

François Macaroni Factory
(fine dining),
116 Portage Street,
(269) 381–4958

Theo & Stacy's (Greek),
5225 Portage Road,
(269) 345–3000

LANSING

Clara's Lansing station
(fine dining),
637 East Michigan Avenue,
(517) 372–7120

Mad Cap Cafe,
207 West Madison Street,
(517) 267–1460

Nuthouse Sports Grill
(American),
420 East Michigan Avenue,
(517) 484–6887

MARSHALL

Schuler's (American),
115 South Eagle Street,
(616) 781–0600

ROCKFORD

Rosie's Diner (American),
4500 Fourteen-Mile
Road NE,
(616) 866–3663

Lake Huron

The Lake Huron shoreline, the eastern side of Michigan, is a region that has come full circle in its history and its appearance. The first inhabitants of the area were Indians who traveled lightly through the woods and lived off the land but rarely disfigured it. When Europeans arrived, they were awed by what was perceived as an endless forest, woods so thick with towering white pines that the sun rarely reached the forest floor.

All that changed in the mid-1800s. Lumbering companies that had exhausted the forests in Maine were looking for pine to cut for new settlements on the Great Plains, which were desperate for wood in their treeless region. Michigan met those needs as the greatest lumber-producing state in the nation between 1850 and 1910, with an estimated 700 logging camps and more than 2,000 mills. Massive log drives filled the Saginaw and Au Sable Rivers, which were avenues to the sawmill towns on Lake Huron. In mill towns like Saginaw and Bay City, sawmills lined the riverbanks, and huge mansions lined the streets as more wealth was made off Michigan's white pine than by miners in the Klondike Gold Rush.

By the turn of the twentieth century, all that was left were the stumps. The lumbering era had devastated the region, turning it into treeless areas that were wastelands of soil erosion.

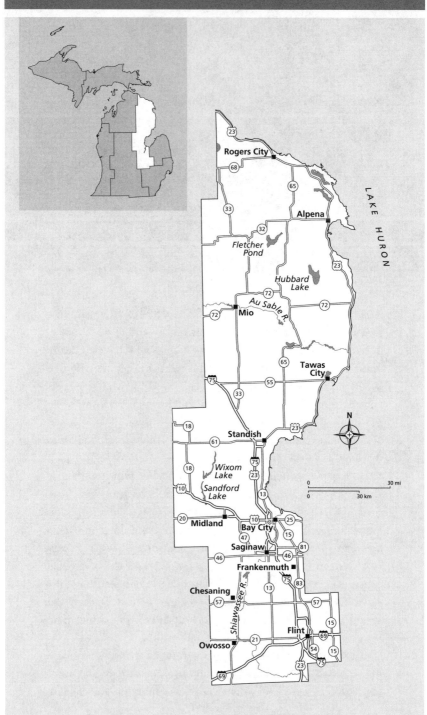

The Huron National Forest was established in 1909 along the Au Sable River, the first of many such preserves, in an effort to repair and manage the land. Lake Huron entered a new era in which terms such as reforestation, conservation, and renewable resources replaced the lumber lingo of log drives, river rats, and clear-cuts.

Almost a century later the northeastern portion of the Lower Peninsula is once again a forested region. The trees are of a different generation and often a different species, but the effect on visitors is the same as when the first Europeans wandered through. To walk quietly among the towering pines in a forest padded by needles while listening to the gentle rustling of a cold-water trout stream is as much an attraction in this part of the state as sandy beaches or a cottage on the lake.

Shiawassee County

In the early 1900s a young writer was tracking a grizzly bear he had shot in British Columbia when suddenly the wounded animal appeared and trapped the man on a narrow mountain ledge. As the author would write later, "Sudden death seemed the hunter's inevitable fate. Then the huge bruin turned away, leaving the hunter unharmed. But not unchanged—the man packed away his guns and never hunted for sport again."

AUTHOR'S TOP TEN PICKS

Curwood Castle,
Owosso;
(989) 725–0597

Dow Gardens,
Midland;
(989) 631–2677

Elk Viewing Sleigh Ride Dinner,
Hillman;
(800) 729–9375

Frankenmuth (the entire town);
(800) 386–8696

Hall of Ideas,
Midland;
(989) 631–5930

Kirtland's Warbler Tour,
Mio;
(989) 826–3252

Lumbermen's Monument,
Oscoda;
(989) 739–0728

Negwegon State Park,
Harrisville;
(989) 724–5126

Ocqueoc Falls,
Onaway;
(989) 739–7322

Shiawassee National Wildlife Refuge,
Saginaw;
(989) 777–5930

TOP ANNUAL EVENTS

Perchville USA,
Tawas City, February;
(800) 558–2927

Brown Trout Festival,
Alpena, July;
(800) 425–7362

Kirtland's Warbler Festival,
Mio, May;
(800) 800–6133

Chesaning Showboat Festival,
Chesaning, July;
(800) 844–3056

Mushroom Festival,
Lewiston, May;
(517) 786–2293

Nautical City Festival,
Rogers City, August;
(989) 734–2535

Bavarian Festival,
Frankenmuth, June;
(800) 386–8696

Great Lakes Lighthouse Festival,
Alpena, October;
(800) 425–7362

Instead James Oliver Curwood used the experience in his best-selling novel *The Grizzly King*, which was published in 1916. In 1989, when the book served as the basis of the movie *The Bear*, Owosso's favorite son—and one of its best-kept secrets—was finally exposed to the rest of the country. Curwood was born in the Shiawassee County town of Owosso in 1878 and returned with his family in 1891. After attending the University of Michigan for two years and working on a newspaper in Detroit, Curwood resigned to pursue literary work entirely in 1907.

He wrote thirty-three novels, most of them fast-paced tales set predominantly in northwest Canada, or "God's country," as the author called it. They were best-sellers worldwide and, between royalties and movie deals, made Curwood a millionaire and allowed him to build **Curwood Castle** along the banks of the Shiawassee River in Owosso in 1922. Built solely as a writing studio, the castle features a great room on the first floor, where the author entertained guests; a twisting staircase leads to his work area upstairs. Today the castle is a museum devoted to the author, featuring memorabilia from Curwood's life, including his original writing desk, which is used in the reception center.

The castle, a replica of a French chateau, is part of the city's historical area, which also includes the first cabin built in Owosso. The museum (989–725–0597) is at 224 Curwood Castle Drive, which is reached from M 52 south of the Shiawassee River. The castle is open from 1:00 to 5:00 P.M. daily except Monday. There is a small admission fee.

At the turn of the twentieth century, Durand was what Detroit's Metro Airport or Chicago's O'Hare is today—the transportation hub of the Midwest. The first railroad, the Detroit-Milwaukee Line, arrived at the small town in 1865 because of Durand's central location, and by 1907 there were seven lines, promoting the construction of **Union Station,** a massive depot 239 feet long and costing $60,000 to build. It burned down two years later but was quickly rebuilt by Grand Trunk Railroad as the age of railroading and the town of Durand entered their golden eras. Almost half of the town's population of 2,500 worked for Grand Trunk, and more people changed trains in Durand than there were residents living there!

Union Station (989–288–3561), often called the "most photographed depot in the country," was designated the Michigan Railroad History Museum and Information Center. Visitors can wander through the station and view a gallery of railroading artifacts, including handcars, engine lights, rolltop desks, and other furnishings of a 1900-era depot.

Durand can be reached from I–69 by heading south at exit 116. Union Station is on the south side of Main Street and is open Tuesday through Sunday, 1:00 to 5:00 P.M.

Genesee County

The heart of Genesee County is Flint, Michigan's fourth-largest city and the home of the Buick Division of General Motors.

The automobile industry and cars are a major part of Flint's livelihood, and both have been well preserved in the city's **Sloan Museum.** The most dramatic chapter in Flint's history is the Great Sit-Down Strike of 1937, which is retold in the museum's permanent 10,000-square-foot exhibit entitled *Flint and the American Dream*. The forty-four-day ordeal ended when General Motors agreed to sign its first contract with the United Auto Workers. It was a bitter struggle that led to the unionization of all American autoworkers and changed the course of history in Michigan, if not the entire country.

Sloan Museum, however, is probably best known for its classic car collection. More than sixty cars are on display in two buildings and range from the oldest production-model Chevrolet in existence and a 1910 Buick "Bug" raced by Louis Chevrolet to prototype vehicles that never made it into production.

The museum (810–237–3450) is in the Flint Cultural Central and is reached from I–475 by taking exit 8A. Head east on Longway Boulevard and follow the signs to the Cultural Central at 1221 East Kearsley Street. Hours are 10:00 A.M. to 5:00 P.M. Monday through Friday and noon to 5:00 P.M. Saturday and Sunday. Admission is $5.00 for adults and $3.00 for children.

Flint also has many interesting nonautomotive attractions, including its delightful **Children's Museum.** Described by its staff as a "touchable discovery center," the museum was proposed in 1980, and after six years of collecting donated materials, the center opened in 1986. Unlike other hands-on museums in Ann Arbor and Lansing, the exhibits here are not complex demonstrations in science or physics. They're simply everyday items that children can touch, ride, climb, and make believe with.

The television studio is probably the most popular area. The news desk, weather map, and talk show set were actually used by Saginaw's WNEM-TV from 1981 to 1987 and then donated to the museum. The set is complete with real television cameras, control board, and monitors, so children can not only give you the straight scoop on current events or weather but watch themselves doing it as well.

If they'd rather play doctor, they'll find a hospital room with an elevated bed, patient gowns, doctors' coats, bandages, crutches, an instrument to check your blood pressure, and another to check your reflexes. Kids can also try their hands in the judge's chambers, appear on stage in costumes, or jump into a role as a bus driver, firefighter, or captain of a full-size boat, where even the life jackets are provided for a safe cruise on the imaginary Seven Seas.

The museum (810–767–5437) is located at 1602 West Third Avenue. Take I–75 to I–475 and then exit 8A to head west on Robert T. Longway Road, which turns into Fifth Avenue. Turn south on Grand Traverse Street and then west on Third Avenue. The center is open year-round from 10:00 A.M. to 5:00 P.M. Monday through Saturday and noon to 5:00 P.M. on Sunday. There is a small admission fee.

There are only two natural waterfalls in the Lower Peninsula, so many cities have created their own, including Flint. **Stepping Stone Falls** is an artificially created cascade of water over an intricate patchwork of steps and levels and one of the most picturesque spots in Genesee County. A scenic, winding path leads visitors to an overlook of the falls, and in the evening underwater lighting creates multicolored patterns on the rushing waters.

Stepping Stone Falls (810–736–7100) is located at the foot of Mott Lake at 5161 Branch Road, across from the historic attraction of Crossroads Village. Hours are 8:00 A.M. to 11:00 P.M. Monday through Thursday and 8:00 A.M. to midnight Friday, Saturday, and Sunday from Memorial Day through Labor Day. Admission is free.

Saginaw County

The only Michigan county without a natural lake, Saginaw County still has plenty of water, as the Saginaw, Tittabawassee, Bad, Cass, Shiawassee, and Flint Rivers make it the largest river basin in the state, with 160 miles of waterway. It was these natural avenues and the vast forests bordering them that allowed the area to boom with loggers and sawmills in the mid-1800s. By the early 1900s the trees and loggers were gone, but reminders of the immense wealth they produced are seen throughout the county in magnificent Victorian-era homes, especially along the Boulevard in Chesaning, a major lumbering center on the Shiawassee River in the southwest corner of the county.

The Boulevard (part of M 57) and its historic homes were developed into the **Old Home Shoppes,** seven of the houses that are now gift and antiques shops. At the beginning and the heart of it is the **Chesaning Heritage House,** one of the finest restaurants in Saginaw County. The house was built in 1908 by George Nanson as a monument to his family's lumbering business. Nanson's father, Robert, was born in England but arrived in 1852 in Chesaning, where he began as a farmer but ended up building a sawmill and, true to the American dream, became one of the wealthiest people in the lumber town. The Georgian Revival–style house reflects all this with stately Ionic columns outside and its grand rotunda opening between the first and second floors.

The house changed hands a few times and was even vacant for ten years before Howard and Bonnie Ebenhoeh purchased it and opened the restaurant in 1980. Dining is a leisurely affair in one of seven rooms on the first or second floor. Four of the rooms have fireplaces that are lit during the winter; another room is the original sunporch, now a glass-enclosed terrace that holds a half dozen tables. The Heritage House prides itself on its preparation of Michigan beef, and one of its specialties is baked tenderloin for two, which arrives with a crown of mushrooms. The dessert tray is also deliciously tempting and always includes an ice-cream sundae pie.

The Heritage House (989–845–7700) is open Monday through Thursday from 11:00 A.M. to 8:00 P.M., Friday and Saturday from 11:00 A.M. to 9:00 P.M., and Sunday from 10:00 A.M. to 8:00 P.M. Dinners range from $12 to $25. Behind the restaurant, the original carriage house has been turned into an antiques and gift shop with two floors of furniture, crafts, and dolls, and a 1908 horse carriage on display upstairs.

Practically across the street from the Heritage House is the **Bonnymill Inn.** The country inn is along the railroad tracks and overlooks a grain elevator.

But what did you expect?

Chesaning Showboat

In 1937, after local businessman Harley Peet provided a $400 loan, the city of Chesaning launched its first "Showboat." At the time it was little more than a local talent show performed on the Shiawassee River with residents sitting in borrowed bleachers. Today the six-day event, called the Chesaning Showboat Festival, is one of the top entertainment venues in the state. Each evening show still arrives on the showboat to a packed house but is now headlined by a nationally known entertainer. Artists appearing there have ranged from Steve Allen and Donny and Marie Osmond to Roy Clark and Louise Mandrell. It's normally standing room only for the shows, which attract more than 40,000 visitors before the showboat takes its final trip back up the river. For dates and ticket information, call the Chesaning Showboat Ticket Office at (800) 844–3056.

The Bonnymill was originally the Chesaning Farmers Coop Elevator, built in the 1920s to replace one that had just burned down. For more than half a century, it stored the corn and soybeans of local farmers and loaded the grain into railroad cars until it was closed down in the fall of 1987.

Then it was renovated into a delightful inn that features twenty-nine guest rooms, including eleven suites featuring king-size beds, fireplaces, and in-room Jacuzzis; some even have wet bars. The center of the inn is a large atrium that includes a winding oak staircase, a spacious lounge complete with a piano and fireplace, and an eating area where a hot breakfast buffet is served in the morning and tea in the afternoon. Outside is a long rambling porch that owners claim is "the biggest porch in mainland Michigan." (The longest porch in the state is at the Grand Hotel on Mackinac Island.)

Rooms at the Bonnymill Inn (989–845–7780) range from $69 to $149 per couple. Special midweek packages include a voucher for dinner at the Heritage House.

Generally recognized as Michigan's number-one attraction is the German town of Frankenmuth. "Little Bavaria" is famous for home-style chicken dinners served at one of two huge restaurants, **Zehnder's** and the **Bavarian Inn,** which face each other on Main Street. The restaurants were founded by the Zehnder brothers, whose family arrived in Frankenmuth from Bavaria in 1846. Each restaurant is a sprawling complex of a dozen German-themed dining rooms, gift shops, bakeries, and candy shops. More than 700 tons of chicken are served annually in the restaurants along with buttery noodles, savory dressing, giblet gravy, salads, and homemade breads in an all-you-can-eat affair.

Chicken dinners are $16 per person at the restaurants, which stop seating at 9:30 P.M. daily. The Bavarian Inn (989–652–9941) is at 713 South Main Street, and Zehnder's (800–863–7999) is at 730 South Main Street.

What could be better with a chicken dinner than a mug of dark German beer? Frankenmuth is the home of the state's oldest brewery, ***Frankenmuth Brewery,*** which is located near the corner of Tuscola and Main Streets. It began making beer in 1862 as the Cass River Brewery and then became Geyer Brewing in 1874. The company was temporarily shut down in 1976 before reopening the following year under its present name with a German brewmaster arriving to direct the operation. A state historic site, Frankenmuth Brewery (989–652–6183) offers tours of its plant year-round. Visitors meet in the Hospitality Center for a brief history of the company, a video of the beer-making operation, and a tour of the facility from brew kettles to bottling. They end up back at the Hospitality Center to sample the finished product (soda is available for kids). The tours are offered daily from April through December from 1:15 to 6:15 P.M. every hour. There is a small fee for the tours.

You can enjoy a stein of the local brew in almost every restaurant and bar in town, but the most intriguing place is the ***Tiffany Biergarten*** just north of Zehnder's Restaurant on South Main Street. The lumbermen's saloon is located on the first floor of the Hotel Goetz, which was built in 1895, when Frankenmuth was one of the leading logging communities in the Saginaw Valley. The tavern picks up its name from its eighteen Tiffany chandeliers, made in the 1930s. It is also adorned by a beautiful wooden bar, the original tin ceiling, inlaid tile floor, and leaded stained glass. Tiffany Biergarten (989–652–6881) is open from 11:00 A.M. to 1:00 A.M. on Friday and Saturday, when there is live entertainment, and from 11:00 A.M. to 11:00 P.M. the rest of the week.

Shopping at Birch Run

In the early 1980s, Birch Run was a sleepy little village at the Frankenmuth exit of I–75. Today it's the discount shopping capital of Michigan, thanks to Prime Outlets at Birch Run (989–624–4868). The 170 stores form the largest manufacturers' mall in the state and include everything from Ann Taylor to Anne Klein and Eddie Bauer to Bugle Boy. The mall is right off I–75, exit 136, and most shops are open from 10:00 A.M. to 9:00 P.M. Monday through Saturday and 11:00 A.M. to 6:00 P.M. Sunday. This place can be unbearably crowded on the weekends with travelers dropping in for a little shopping on their way up north. The best time to shop is the middle of the week from 3:00 to 6:00 P.M.

Shiawassee National Wildlife Refuge

When the fall migration peaks in late October or early November, more than 25,000 Canada geese and 30,000 ducks are often at the Shiawassee National Wildlife Refuge. The sight of so many birds gathered at one time is nothing short of spectacular, making this one of the great wildlife sightings in Michigan.

One of two federal wildlife refuges in Michigan, Shiawassee encompasses 9,042 acres on the doorstep of Saginaw and includes the confluence of four major rivers, the Flint, Cass, Shiawassee, and Tittabawassee. When combined with the Shiawassee River State Game Area, which borders it to the west, this goose management area exceeds 20,000 acres and is larger than any state park in the Lower Peninsula.

The Ferguson Bayou Trail, a 5-mile loop from the Curtis Road parking area, is the best trail to see birds any time of the year but especially during the fall migration. The trail is a network of gravel roads, two-tracks, and paths along the dikes that leads to an observation tower in the heart of the refuge. Most visitors walk to the tower, but the easiest way to explore the park is on a hybrid or mountain bike.

From the tower in the fall, small flocks of geese can be seen arriving by late afternoon. By evening it's practically pandemonium with hundreds of birds coming and going. Stick around for the sunset and your day will end with the most memorable sight at the refuge: flights of geese silhouetted against a red-orange sky.

The Shiawassee National Wildlife Refuge is 7 miles south of M 46 in Saginaw and reached from M 13 by turning west on Curtis Road. Within a mile is the refuge headquarters (989– 777–5930) where trail maps and bird checklists are available. The Ferguson Bayou Trail is 3 miles beyond the headquarters near the end of Curtis Road.

Christmas in July? Only in Frankenmuth, where ***Bronner's Christmas Wonderland*** is home of the world's largest year-round display of holiday ornaments, decorations, trimmings, and gifts. More than 50,000 items are stocked in the 230,000-square-foot building that houses the store's showroom, warehouse, and offices. The business can be traced back to 1945, when Wally Bronner operated Bronner's Displays and Signs out of his parents' home and was approached by Bay City officials to decorate the city streets for the upcoming holiday.

Bronner created and built lamppost panels for the city, leading to more requests by other towns and eventually to his present business providing Christmas decorations to businesses, communities, and private homes. The store is an amazing trip into the spirit of the holiday, especially its religious aspect. Inside you will find more than 500 kinds of nativity scenes, figures from 1 inch tall to life-size; 260 Christmas trees decorated in such themes as sports and wildlife; and more than 6,000 ornaments from around the world. There are music boxes, every model of Hummel figurine ever produced, and, in the store's Nutcracker Suite, 200 styles of wooden characters imported from Austria, Switzerland, and Germany.

You can't miss the store—outside it is surrounded by fifteen acres of painted snowflakes, twinkling lights, and the same kind of lamppost Bronner designed more than forty-five years ago for Bay City. Bronner's Christmas Wonderland (989–652–9931) is at the south end of town just off Main Street (M 83). It is open from June through December from 9:00 A.M. to 9:00 P.M. Monday through Saturday and noon to 7:00 P.M. Sunday. From January through May, hours are 9:00 A.M. to 5:30 P.M. Monday through Thursday and Saturday, 9:00 A.M. to 9:00 P.M. Friday, and noon to 5:30 P.M. Sunday.

In Saginaw, near the Anderson Water Slide, an American creation, is the city's *Japanese Cultural Center and Tea House.* The house was actually built by Japanese artisans, who used no nails, only intricate traditional hand tools. Today the center is the only facility in the country where visitors can observe the classic formal tea ceremony.

The house is open from noon to 4:00 P.M. Tuesday through Saturday. The symbolic tea ritual is performed and interpreted on the second Saturday of each month beginning at 2:00 P.M. There is a $3.00 fee. The house (989–759–1648) and its tranquil gardens are located in Saginaw's Celebration Square, just north of M 46 at South Washington Boulevard and Ezra Rust Drive.

Midland County

To most people the city of Midland is Dow Chemical Corporation, the place where Herbert Dow founded the company in 1897 that today gives us everything from Ziploc sandwich bags and Saran Wrap to much of the aspirin used in the country. The *H. H. Dow Museum* tells the story of the young chemist and features replicas of the gristmill and brine well that he built to launch his famous company as well as the 1890 lab where he perfected his bromine-extracting process. The *Dow Visitors Center* features more than 500 products that are made in Midland, along with exhibits on the company's history. You can also tour the huge chemical facility that includes close-up views of such areas as the Saran Wrap plant.

The H. H. Dow Museum (989–832–5319) is reached from downtown Midland by heading west on Main Street for 1.2 miles and then turning north on Cook Road. Hours are 10:00 A.M. to 4:00 P.M. Wednesday through Saturday and 1:00 to 5:00 P.M. Sunday. There is a small admission fee. The Dow Visitors

Center (989–636–6590) is reached from Business US 10 by turning south on Bayliss Street. The center is at Bayliss and Lyon Road and is open from 7:30 A.M. to 5:00 P.M. Monday through Friday.

Another interesting museum is the ***Hall of Ideas*** in the Midland Center of the Arts. The science, history, and art museum reopened in 1994 after a $3-million face-lift and is four floors of hands-on displays and exhibits. Staff members estimate that 340 topics are covered in the new exhibits and that a person who pushed every button, viewed every screen, and took part in every interactive display would spend more than twenty hours in the hall.

A 500-pound life-size mastodon skeleton greets visitors, and from there the topics range from how an Olympic skater does a triple axel to viewing a replica of Midland's famed Frolic Theater (complete with the aroma of popcorn). The hall (989–631–5930) is at Eastman Avenue and West Street and is open 10:00 A.M. to 6:00 P.M. Tuesday through Saturday and noon to 6:00 P.M. Sunday. Admission is $4.00 for adults and $2.00 for children twelve and under.

Midland is also a city of parks, with 2,700 acres in seventy-four parks scattered throughout the community. The most famous of these is ***Dow Gardens,*** a hundred acres of streams, waterfalls, small bridges, and beautifully manicured landscaping next to Discovery Square, home of the Midland Center for the Arts.

What began as Herbert Dow's backyard in 1899 was eventually extended and shaped in the 1970s by his son, Alden Dow, a noted architect and a student

Père Marquette Rail-Trail

Departing from the Tridge is the Père Marquette Rail-Trail, a perfectly paved path without so much as a ripple, much less a hill. Originally a line for the Flint and Père Marquette Railroad, the rail-trail extends from Midland to Clare, 30 miles.

It's open to a variety of nonmotorized users, including runners, walkers, and cyclists. But in the first 3 miles, from the Tridge to Dublin Road, the most popular form of transportation is in-line skates. The Père Marquette is well designed for that. At the street crossings are locator maps, benches, and, most important, large red posts to stop skaters from flying across the intersections.

This stretch is also very scenic. From the Tridge you skirt the Tittabawassee River for more than a mile, passing fishing docks, the historic Upper Bridge, and one of the original cement mile markers that told railroad engineers how far it was to Saginaw. The trail also passes the H. H. Dow Museum, which has installed interpretive displays along the way.

For more information call the Midland County Parks and Recreation Commission at (989) 832–6870.

of Frank Lloyd Wright. It was the younger Dow who installed the "jungle walk" through a thicket, the sensory trail, and various waterfalls.

The gardens (989–631–2677) are just northwest of downtown Midland off Business US 10 (Eastman Road), next to the *Midland Center for the Arts.* Hours are 9:00 A.M. to sunset daily. Admission is $5.00 for adults and $1.00 for children.

Another intriguing park is Chippewassee, site of the *Tridge,* the only three-way footbridge in the world, city officials proudly claim. The unusual bridge was built in 1981 over the confluence of the Titta-bawassee and Chippewa Rivers, and its wooden spans connect three shorelines. In the middle they form a hub where benches overlook the merging currents of two rivers. The Tridge and the nearby riverfront area form the center of activity in downtown Midland. The Midland Music Society hosts free outdoor concerts in the park Thursdays at noon in June and July, which have unofficially become known as "Brown Bag-It Days," as office workers stream to the area to enjoy their lunch break.

sugarbeets

Bay and Saginaw Counties are the heart of Michigan's sugar beet industry and the home of Pioneer Sugar. The state's first sugar beet factory opened in Bay City in 1889 after Dr. Robert Kedzie of Michigan Agricultural College (now Michigan State University) encouraged local farmers to grow the crop the year before. Within a few short years, Saginaw Valley became the sugar bowl of Michigan.

Also located near the Tridge is the Midland Farmers' Market and its 4-H Club petting zoo for children (open Sundays in July from 1:00 to 4:00 P.M.) as well as a city-operated canoe livery for a leisurely paddle up the river of your choice. The canoes can be rented Saturday and Sunday from 10:00 A.M. to 7:00 P.M. in April and May and during the week from 2:00 to 7:00 P.M. from June through September. The zoo is free, but there is a rental fee for the canoes.

Bay County

The shoreline of Saginaw Bay was the final destination for much of the lumber from the valley, with thirty-two sawmills clustered on the waterfront of Bay City. The city flourished on money from timber and shipbuilding, and a drive down Center Avenue shows where much of it went. The lumber barons seemed infatuated with building the most elaborate homes they could afford, and the restored mansions in this historic district overwhelm visitors. In the middle of this Victorian-era street is the *Historical Museum of Bay County* (989–893–5733), which spins the story of Bay City's golden era through three-dimensional exhibits. The museum is open from 10:00 A.M. to 5:00 P.M. Monday through Friday and noon to 4:00 P.M. Saturday and Sunday. There is no admission charge, but donations are welcomed.

More impressive than the grand homes, however, is the ***Bay City City Hall.*** Built in 1894, the Romanesque-style stone building dominates the city skyline with its 125-foot clock tower at the southeast corner. It was listed in the National Register of Historic Places, and in 1976 the building underwent major renovation that preserved the original woodwork and distinctive metal pillars in the huge lobby. Visitors are welcome to stroll throughout the massive structure and view the 31-foot Chmielewska Tapestry that hangs in the council chambers. Woven with hand-dyed yarns of 500 colors by a young artist from Poland, the tapestry depicts the historic buildings of the community. A climb of sixty-eight steps up the clock tower brings you to a most impressive view of Bay City, the Saginaw River, and the surrounding countryside.

The city hall (989–895–9423) is located downtown at 301 Washington Avenue and is open from 8:00 A.M. to 5:00 P.M. Monday through Friday. Inquire at the personnel office in room 308 for a trip up to the clock tower. There is no admission fee.

The newest attraction in Bay City is the ***Delta College Planetarium and Learning Center.*** Opened in 1997 with funding from NASA, the center is a striking red-domed building that looks like a spaceship in the middle of Bay City. The planetarium uses state-of-the-art equipment to take visitors on simulated outer-space journeys, while the exhibit hall features displays on astronomy and space travel.

The center is at Center Avenue and Water Street and stages two to six shows daily. Call the planetarium (989–667–2260) for the times. There is a small admission fee.

Bay City City Hall

Iosco County

Perhaps the most famous river of the logging era was the Au Sable, which begins west of Grayling and ends at Lake Huron between the towns of Oscoda and Au Sable. In the 1890s it was assumed that forests were meant to be cut, and "driving the Au Sable" was a group of men known as "river rats" and "bank beavers," who floated logs down the Au Sable to sawmills on Lake Huron. A century later it's "downstaters," "flatlanders," and "fudgies" driving the river. Now, however, they're following the Lumbermen's Monument Auto Tour, an especially popular fall trip in Iosco County when tourists come to admire the color of the leaves rather than the size of the trunks.

Many begin the 68-mile loop at the Tawas Area Chamber of Commerce (800–558–2927), where they pick up a free copy of the Lumbermen's Monument Auto Tour brochure. From Tawas City you head west on M 55 for a mile, then turn north (right) onto Wilber Road to reach Monument Road, which ends at River Road. A half mile to the east (right) is the entrance to the **Lumbermen's Monument.**

The impressive bronze statue of three loggers was erected in 1931 and is now surrounded by trees very much like those they made a living cutting down. Even more impressive to many is the nearby interpretive area and museum, which give a good account of the logging era with displays and hands-on exhibits. They put the logger into perspective, a man viewed by many today as a colorful, Paul Bunyan-–like character who ate apple pie and fry cakes for breakfast. In reality he provided cheap labor. In the middle of the winter, he made $2.00 for a twelve-hour day spent pulling a saw while cold water sloshed in his boots. Little wonder that by the time most loggers turned thirty-five years old, they were too worn out or too sick to

paddlewheeltours

The best way to enjoy the fall colors in Iosco County is aboard the *River Queen*, a full-size paddlewheel riverboat that began operating on the Au Sable River in 1966. The *River Queen* departs from a dock on the Au Sable River 6 miles west of Oscoda and offers its two-hour tours daily at noon and 3:00 P.M. from late June through late August and then at 1:00 P.M. through late September.

The tours most in demand are the weekend color tours from late September through mid-October at 10:30 A.M., 1:00 P.M., and 3:30 P.M. These are relaxing cruises along the Au Sable in which passengers enjoy the spectacular fall colors, beautiful scenery, and possibly even a few wildlife sightings such as bald eagles. Most trips are $10 per adult, but the color tours are $13. Reservations are a must in the fall and can be made by calling the *River Queen* office at (989) 739–7351.

continue their trade. The museum and interpretive area is open from 10:00 A.M. to 7:00 P.M. daily from Memorial Day to Labor Day and on weekends through fall colors in mid-October.

The auto tour continues west along River Road and in 1.5 miles comes to *Canoe Race Monument.* The stone monument, topped off by a pair of paddles, was originally built as a memorial to Jerry Curley, who died practicing for the annual Au Sable River Canoe Marathon. Today it stands in honor of all racers who attempt the annual 150-mile event from Grayling to Oscoda, often cited as the toughest canoe race in the country. From the monument site there is another fine overview of the Au Sable River Valley, and for those who keep one eye on the sky, bald eagles can often be seen in this area.

funfacts

One of the few remaining one-room log schools left in Michigan is the Old Bailey School along County Road F30 (Mikado-Glennie Road) near the hamlet of Mikado. Built in 1894, the school remained in use until 1941 and today is used by area residents for a strawberry shortcake social on the Fourth of July.

Still heading west on River Road, you reach *Iargo Springs* in another mile. Iargo is the Chippewa Indian word for "many waters," and this was a favorite spot for members of the tribe traveling along the Saginaw-Mackinac Trail. It's almost 300 steps and eight rest stops down to the springs but well worth the exertion of the climb back up. The area below is pleasant and tranquil as the springs gurgle out of the moss-laden bluffs into the Au Sable River under a canopy of towering pine trees.

Alcona County

At Harrisville, US 23 swings away from Lake Huron and remains inland well into Alpena County. Taking its place along the water in northern Alcona County is Lakeshore Drive, the route to two interesting attractions. The first is *Cedar Brook Trout Farm,* reached 2.5 miles north of Harrisville immediately after turning off US 23. Because of the almost perfect conditions for raising rainbow and brook trout, Cedar Brook was established in the early 1950s as the first licensed trout farm in Michigan. The key to the farm's success is the cold-water springs that flow from the nearby sandy bluffs. The water is funneled into the thirteen ponds and rearing tanks, and its year-round constant temperature (47 degrees) and high level of oxygen are ideal for trout. The constant flow allows owner Jerry Kahn to manage without pumps. He begins with eggs and raises the trout from frylings to rainbows that will measure well over 16 inches.

The bulk of Kahn's business is shipping thousands of trout in a tank truck to individuals and sportsmen's organizations for stocking their own lakes and rivers. He also lets travelers stop by and catch their own in two ponds, one stocked with rainbows, the other with brook trout. The water in the ponds is cold and clear, and below the surface you can easily see hundreds of fish swimming around. Throw some feed in the ponds (available from a coin-operated dispenser), and dozens of large fish rise to the surface in a feeding frenzy. Anglers are provided with cane poles, tackle, bait, and a warning that catching the trout is not as easy as it looks. No fishing license is needed.

Cedar Brook (989–724–5241), one of the few farms in the state that raises brook trout, is open for anglers daily from 9:00 A.M. until 6:00 P.M. from Memorial Day to Labor Day. The cost depends on the size of trout caught, but for $3.00 or $4.00 and a little fishing luck, you can depart with a hefty rainbow.

From the trout farm Lakeshore Drive continues north and in less than a half mile passes the marked side road to ***Sturgeon Point Lifesaving Station*** (989–724–6297) and the preserved lighthouse, built in 1869. The last lightkeeper left in 1941, but the U.S. Coast Guard continues to maintain the light. In 1982 the Alcona County Historical Society began renovating the attached lightkeeper's house and soon opened it to the public. The structure is a classic Michigan lighthouse, but the unique feature is that you can climb to the top of the tower (eighty-five steps) and not only be greeted by a panorama of Lake Huron but still view a working prism as well. Amazingly, all that is needed to throw a light miles out on the Great Lake is this huge work of cut glass and an electric light no larger than your smallest finger.

The lightkeeper's house is now a museum, with the five rooms downstairs furnished as a turn-of-the-century residence for those who maintained the attached tower. The four rooms upstairs are also open, and each showcases a different aspect of the county's history: shipwrecks, fishermen, the original lightkeepers, and, perhaps the most interesting, the ice-collecting industry that boomed in the area during the winter so iceboxes could be kept cold in the summer.

The lighthouse is operated by a volunteer staff that keeps it open daily 10:00 A.M. to 4:00 P.M. Memorial Day through

Lighthouse at Sturgeon Point
Lifesaving Station

Labor Day, and Saturday and Sunday until mid-October. There is no admission fee, but donations are accepted to maintain the lighthouse.

Alpena County

Lumbering turned Alpena from a handful of hardy settlers in 1850 into a booming town of 9,000 in 1884, and when the white pine ran out, the community sustained itself by becoming Cement City, utilizing its huge supply of limestone. From the cement factories emerged Besser Manufacturing Company, the world leader in concrete block-making equipment. Today Alpena is a manufacturing center that can boast the largest population (12,000) and the only enclosed shopping mall in northeast Michigan. The residents of this modern community also value their past and have begun restoring the historic downtown area as Old Town Alpena.

Negwegon State Park

The only development **Negwegon State Park** has ever experienced since the state picked up the tract in 1962 is the construction of a parking area and a 10-mile trail system. What has never been improved is Sand Hill Road. This sandy, deeply rutted county road provides the only access to Negwegon and, in effect, has made it the most remote state park in the Lower Peninsula. Four-wheel-drive vehicles are recommended, and during extended dry spells, spinning tires in shifting mounds of sugary sand is not an uncommon occurrence.

After an agonizing 2.5-mile drive along the Alcona County road, most first-time visitors are stunned to arrive at a huge park sign and a wide, graveled entrance drive in the middle of nowhere. From the parking area at the end, they head into the woods and suddenly emerge at a crescent-moon bay framed by towering red pines on one side and the turquoise waters of Lake Huron on the other. In between is a sweeping shoreline of golden sand unmarred by beach blankets and beer coolers.

Paradise.

This is as far as most people get in the 1,775-acre park. If you can tear yourself away from the beach, Negwegon's trail system offers some interesting hikes. Departing south from the parking lot is the Potawatomi Trail, a 3.3-mile loop that hugs Lake Huron for more than a mile. To the north is the Algonquin Trail, which in 2 miles reaches the spectacular views at the tip of South Point.

To reach the park from US 23, head east on Black River Road and north on Sand Hill Road. Follow the two-track for 2.5 miles to the park entrance. It is best to first stop at Harrisville State Park (989–724–5126) on US 23 for a map and current road conditions before trying to reach Negwegon.

The original shopping area is clustered around North Second Street and features small and specialized shops that could have been found here as early as the 1920s. One of the most unusual stores is the **Country Cupboard.** This antiques and general store is located in the old Sepull's Pharmacy, a landmark in Alpena from its opening in 1920 until Hutton Sepull retired in 1986. Outside, its aluminum facing looks plain, but inside it has the character of an old-time pharmacy, which catches unsuspecting visitors by surprise. There are the tin ceiling and the wraparound balcony on the second floor and the traveling ladders that lead up to the ceiling-high shelves stocked with old medicine containers, apothecary bottles, and boxes of tonic. On the ground floor the walls are lined with hundreds of wooden drawers, each holding some herb, tin of pills, or other merchandise left from pharmacy days.

When the store went on the market, Rita and Al Hess couldn't think of a better place to relocate their antiques business down the street. They filled the shop with collectibles, baskets, stained glass, and country gifts but kept the old pharmacy atmosphere intact and even began to restore much of the original woodwork. They still sell several of Sepull's more unusual or popular products, including Iceland moss (an herb for folk medicine) and the custom-blended Wellington tobacco.

The Country Cupboard (989–356–6020) is located at 102 North Second Street and is open year-round, Monday through Friday from 10:00 A.M. to 5:30 P.M. and Saturday from 10:00 A.M. to 5:00 P.M.

Another Old Town favorite is the **_John A. Lau Saloon._** The restaurant dates to the 1880s when it was a rough-and-tumble waterhole for lumberjacks with a reputation that reached far into the woods. Part of the reason is that Lau always had three bartenders on staff, one who could speak German, one French, and the other Polish, so any logger, no matter where he came from, could order a beer-and-whiskey.

The restaurant still maintains that lumberman's decor with its thick plank floors, tin ceiling, crosscut saws on the walls, and historic photos of the original

lonegoldmine

Alcona County is the site of the only gold mine to operate in the Lower Peninsula. Prospectors went to the vicinity of Harrisville looking for silver or copper after hearing reports of Indians finding large quantities of the minerals in the area. What the miners found in 1912 wasn't copper or silver but gold nuggets. To avoid a gold rush, they kept the discovery secret for several months until a stock company was formed and a mine shaft sunk. Tons of Alcona black dirt was processed for gold, but the venture ended in disaster when the steam-operated equipment blew up.

saloon. Dinners range from $11 to $22. The John A. Lau Saloon (989–354–6898) is at 414 North Second Avenue.

Alpena's *Jesse Besser Museum* is the only accredited museum in northern Michigan and boasts one of the finest collections of Great Lakes Indian artifacts in the country.

The museum also features a sky theater planetarium and a small historic village outside. Hours are 10:00 A.M. to 5:00 P.M. Tuesday through Saturday, and noon to 4:00 P.M. Sunday. The museum (989–356–2202) is a block east of US 23 at 491 Johnson Street. Admission is $3.00 for adults and $2.00 for children.

Presque Isle County

Jesse Besser, founder of the massive concrete block corporation, was also a humanitarian, and in Alpena the Besser Museum is named after him. But Besser also was responsible for leaving something in Presque Isle County—a small tract of land on Lake Huron whose towering white pines somehow escaped the swinging axes of lumbermen.

The industrial genius, realizing the rarity of the uncut pines and the beauty of the undeveloped Lake Huron shoreline, gave the area to the people of Michigan in 1966. Today it is the *Besser Natural Area,* managed by the Department of Natural Resources. The remote preserve, reached from US 23 by taking County Road 405 to the south end of Grand Lake, offers a small niche of beauty and a little history in a quiet setting. Looping through the Besser Natural Area is a sandy 1-mile foot trail, which takes you past a small lagoon that once was part of Lake Huron. Look carefully at the bottom of the lagoon (you need polarizing sunglasses on sunny days) and you'll spot the hull of an old ship. The vessel served the community of Bell, which was located here in the 1880s and consisted of one hundred residents, several homes, a sawmill, a saloon, a store, and a school.

Limestone Capital of the World

The world's largest limestone quarry is operated on the edge of Rogers City by Michigan Limestone. Millions of tons are removed annually and loaded into Great Lakes freighters to be used in the production of steel, cement, chemicals, and construction materials. There are two viewing points of the quarry operations. The Quarry View is an observation deck off Business US 23 where you can look into the 6,000-acre open-pit quarry. From the Harbor View off Calcite Road southeast of town, you can watch freighters entering the harbor and leaving after being loaded.

The most noticeable remains of Bell are the rock pier along Lake Huron, a towering stone chimney, and the collapsed walls of a building whose steel safe and icebox counter indicate it might have been the saloon. Toward the end of the walk, you pass through some of the oldest and largest white pines remaining in a state once covered with the trees. There is no fee to enter the preserve, nor is there a visitor center or any other facility. Descriptive brochures that coincide with the footpath are available from a small box near the trailhead.

Visitors who exit US 23 for the east side of Grand Lake, the state's nineteenth-largest lake, with more than 5,000 acres of water, usually want to view lighthouses. They take in the beautifully renovated **Old Presque Isle Lighthouse** near the end of County Road 405 (Grand Lake Road). Built in 1840, this squat, stone lighthouse is open to the public and features an interesting museum crammed with artifacts and exhibits. The lighthouse is open daily from 9:00 A.M. to 7:00 P.M. from June 15 through October 15. There is a small admission charge. Just a mile north of it is **New Presque Isle Lighthouse Park** with nature trails, picnic area, and a small museum of its own. Built in 1870, the New Presque Isle Lighthouse is one of the tallest on the Great Lakes, standing 109 feet tall.

The **Fireside Inn** is yet another reason to come to this part of the country, especially for anyone whose idea of a vacation in northern Michigan is renting a quaint log cabin on the edge of a lake. The Fireside Inn began its long history as a resort when the original lodge was built in 1908, and the first few authentic log cabins soon began to appear around it. Little has

sceniclake hurondrive

The 56-mile stretch of US 23 between Mackinaw City and Rogers City is one of the most scenic drives in the Lower Peninsula, featuring a dozen parks and scenic turnouts overlooking Lake Huron.

Many of them are clustered around Rogers City. Five miles north of the town is Forty Mile Point Lighthouse Park. The small but delightful park is crowned by the towering lighthouse and includes a picnic area and beach. On the north side of Rogers City is Seagull Point Park, a mix of Lake Huron shoreline, low dunes, and woods that are best enjoyed in the fall by walking a 2-mile interpretive trail.

funfacts

Posen, a village of 350 residents, is the agricultural heart of Presque Isle County with its farmers ranking third in the state as producers of packed and graded table potatoes. The best time to visit the community is during the Posen Potato Festival held the first weekend after Labor Day.

strangeasit sounds

Though it sounds like a tacky road-side attraction, Dinosaur Gardens is actually an interesting, even eerie, place to visit. The forty-acre park was the creation of the late Paul Domke, a self-taught artist and sculptor. In the 1930s Domke built twenty-seven life-size dinosaurs from concrete, wire, and deer hair within the tangled branches of a cedar swamp forest. A winding path leads through the dark woods where a dino lies waiting for you around every bend.

Eeek!

Dinosaur Gardens (877–823–2408) is right on US 23, 10 miles south of Alpena. It's open daily from 9:00 A.M. to 6:00 P.M. from Memorial Day through Labor Day and 10:00 A.M. to 4:00 P.M. in May before Memorial Day and in September. Admission is $5.00 for adults and $4.00 for children.

changed about the lodge or the dining room inside with its rustic wooden beams, plank floor, and large windows looking over Grand Lake. They still ring a dinner bell to signal supper time and serve only one entree family-style; afterward guests still wander out to the rambling porch, an immense sitting area 215 feet long, to claim a favorite wicker chair or rocker.

You can rent one of the cabins with a wood interior and stone fire-place or just a room (shared bath) in the lodge itself. Daily rates range from $40 to $60 per adult for the large cabins with three or four bedrooms. Or you can stop in just for dinner, a delightful experience in itself. Dinner prices range from $8.00 to $12.00, depending on what is being served that night, and you should call ahead if possible. The Fireside Inn (989–595–6369) is located off County Road 405 at the end of the spur, Fireside Highway.

Presque Isle County is home to another unique inn, **Nettie Bay Lodge.** Located 14 miles west of Rogers City, the lodge is on the shores of Lake Nettie and surrounded by 2,000 private acres. Originally developed as a hunting and fishing camp, Nettie Bay Lodge has since be-come known as a wildlife-viewing destination, offering not only accommodations but also the use of photography and observation blinds that overlook marshes and other prime spots to sight wildlife.

Because of the area's diverse habitat, it is not unusual to sight one hundred different birds in a single weekend. Loons nest on a small island right in front of the lodge, bald eagles and ospreys often feed in the shallow waters of the lake, flocks of wild turkeys can be spotted in the woods. Several times in May the Nettie Bay School of Birding is held at the lodge and includes two nights' lodging, some meals, and bird identification workshops and field trips with professional ornithologists.

Nettie Bay Lodge (989–734–4688; www.nettiebay.com) is west of Hawks on County Road 638 and offers eight cottages and two rooms in the lodge. The birding school is $225 per person.

Montmorency County

One of the most popular attractions in Montmorency County isn't a museum or a scenic overlook but a 700-pound elk. Almost 1,500 elk thrive on state forest land between Gaylord and Hillman, making it the largest herd east of the Mississippi River. A unique way to view the animals is an ***Elk Viewing Sleigh Ride Dinner*** arranged through the Best Western Thunder Bay Resort in Hillman. The popular wildlife-viewing adventure began in 1993 when Jack and Jan Matthias started offering sleigh rides to their 1940-vintage hunting cabin. But the high point for most guests was not the gourmet dinner at the cabin but seeing an elk along the way, including bulls whose antlers often exceeded a span of 4 feet.

The Matthiases eventually built a larger cabin to accommodate more people but still cook the five-course meal—crown roast of pork, pear and apple crepes, and homemade soup, among other dishes—over a 1915 wood-burning stove. If you anticipate joining a sleigh ride, bundle up and grab one of the blankets that are provided. The ride through the snowy woods is a forty-five-minute trip each way.

The sleigh ride is offered each winter from Christmas through the third week of March. A two-night weekend package including accommodations at the Thunder Bay Resort, breakfasts, and the sleigh ride is $215 per person, while the one-night, midweek package is $138. When there is available space, you can also book just the dinner and sleigh at $75 per person. For more information or reservations, call the Best Western Thunder Bay Resort at (800) 729–9375.

ocqueocfalls

Located 11 miles inland from Rogers City along M 68 is Ocqueoc Falls, one of only two waterfalls in the Lower Peninsula. This cascade is a series of ledges that drops 6 feet in the Ocqueoc River. Ocqueoc is not the thundering waterfall that you experience throughout the Upper Peninsula, but it's still a beautiful spot, especially in the fall. The day-use area includes picnic tables and foot trails that follow the east bank of the river, while on the south side of M 68 is a rustic state forest campground.

Oscoda County

The state bird of Michigan is the robin, but many argue that it should be the Kirtland's warbler. This small bird, the size of a sparrow, with a distinctive yellow breast, is an endangered species that breeds only in the jack pines of Michigan. It spends its winters in obscurity in the Bahamas and then migrates to areas between Mio and Grayling, arriving in mid-May and departing by early July. Only in these preserved nesting areas do birders and wildlife watchers have the opportunity to observe this rare bird, with fewer than 300 breeding pairs remaining.

The nesting areas are closed to the public, but you can join a **Kirtland's Warbler Tour,** which is sponsored by the U.S. Forest Service. The tour, which lasts from an hour and a half to two hours, includes a movie and a discussion by a Forest Service naturalist and then a short trip to the nesting area. The guided group hikes through the jack pines, usually covering 1 to 2 miles, until the warblers are spotted. Seeing a Kirtland's warbler is not guaranteed, but most tours do, especially in late May through June.

This tour is famous among birders, who come from all over the country for their only glimpse of the warbler, but it is also an interesting spot for anybody intrigued by Michigan's wildlife. The Forest Service office (989–826–3252), north of Mio on M 33, offers the tours daily at 7:00 A.M. There is a $5.00 per-person fee.

Places to Stay in Michigan's Lake Huron Region

ALPENA

Days Inn,
1496 M 32 West,
(800) 582–9050

AUGRES

Pinewood Lodge,
510 West US 23,
(989) 876–4060

BAY CITY

Americ Inn,
3915 Three Mile Road,
(989) 671–0071

Clements Inn Bed-and-Breakfast,
1712 Center Road,
(800) 442–4605

CHESANING

Bonnymill Inn,
710 Broad Boulevard,
(989) 845–7780

FLINT

Red Roof Inn,
G–3219 Miller Road,
(810) 733–1660

Wingate Inn,
1359 Grand Pointe Court,
(810) 694–9900

FRANKENMUTH

Bavarian Inn Lodge,
1 Covered Bridge Lane,
(888) 775–6343

Drury Inn,
260 South Main Street,
(989) 652–2800

Fairfield Inn,
430 South Main Street,
(800) 228–2800

HARRISVILLE

Alcona Beach Resort
700 North Lake Huron Shore,
(989) 724–5471

HAWKS

Nettie Bay Lodge,
9011 West Highway 638,
(989) 734–4688

LEWISTON

Garland Resort,
County Road 489,
(800) 968–0042

MIDLAND

Sleep Inn,
2100 West Wackerly Street,
(989) 837–1010

Valley Plaza Resort,
5221 Bay City Road,
(989) 496–2700

ROGERS CITY

Driftwood Motel,
540 North Third Street,
(989) 734–4777

Manitou Shores Resort,
7995 US 23,
(989) 734–7233

SAGINAW
Fairfield Inn,
5200 Fashion Square
Boulevard,
(800) 228–2800

Hampton Inn,
2222 Tittabawassee Road,
(989) 792–7666

TAWAS CITY
Harbor View Motel,
1008 US 23,
(989) 362–3971

Paradise Beach Resort,
1029 Lake Street,
(800) 472–6518

Places to Eat in Michigan's Lake Huron Region

ALPENA
John A. Lau Saloon
(American),
414 North Second Avenue,
(989) 354–6898

Lud's Hamburgers
(American),
1223 State Avenue,
(989) 356–0339

Mr. D's Steakhouse
(American),
1284 M-32 West,
(989) 358–2050

BAY CITY
Krzysiak's House (Polish),
1605 Michigan Avenue,
(989) 894–5531

The Char House (American),
432 Tuscola Road,
(989) 893–5881

SELECTED TOURISM BUREAUS

**Alpena Area Convention and
Visitors Bureau,**
235 West Chisholm Street,
Alpena 49707;
(800) 425–7362;
www.alpenacvb.com

Bay Area Visitors Bureau,
901 Saginaw Street,
Bay City 48708;
(888) 229–8696;
www.baycityarea.com

**Flint Area Convention and
Visitors Bureau,**
316 Water Street,
Flint 48503;
(800) 253–5468;
www.visitflint.org

**Frankenmuth Convention and
Visitors Bureau,**
635 South Main Street,
Frankenmuth 48734;
(800) 386–8696;
www.frankenmuth.org

Rogers City Chamber of Commerce,
292 South Bradley Highway,
Rogers City 49779;
(800) 622–4148;
www.rogerscitychamber.com

Saginaw Visitors Bureau,
515 North Washington Avenue,
Saginaw 48607;
(800) 444–9979;
www.visitsaginawcounty.com

Tawas City Tourist Bureau,
P.O. Box 10,
Tawas City 48764;
(877) 868–2927;
www.tawasbay.com

FLINT

Bill Thomas' Halo Burger
(hamburgers),
800 South Saginaw Street,
(810) 238–4607

**Makuch's Red Rooster
Restaurant** (American),
3302 Davison Road,
(810) 742–9310

FRANKENMUTH

Bavarian Inn
(German and chicken),
713 South Main Street,
(989) 652–9941

Franken Eck (German),
100 South Main Street,
(989) 652–4586

Frankenmuth Brewery
(brew pub),
425 South Main Street,
(989) 652–6183

Zehnder's
(German and chicken),
730 South Main Street,
(800) 863–7999

MIDLAND

Pi's (Chinese),
1815 North Saginaw Road,
(989) 832–5848

Sweet Onion
(American),
1415 South Saginaw Road,
(989) 631–2062

OSCODA

Wiltse's Brew Pub
(brew pub),
5606 F–41,
(989) 739–2231

ROGERS CITY

Chi Chi's (Mexican
and American),
409 US 23,
(989) 734–4454

SAGINAW

El Farolito (Mexican),
115 North Hamilton,
(989) 799–8959

Levi's Saloon (American),
5212 Bay Road,
(989) 793–6670

Montague Inn (American),
1581 South Washington
Avenue,
(989) 752–3939

TAWAS CITY

Pier 23 Restaurant
(American),
821 US 23,
(989) 362–8856

OTHER ATTRACTIONS

**Crossroads Village
and Huckleberry Railroad,**
Flint

Chippewa Nature Center,
Midland

Junction Valley Railroad,
Bridgeport

Saginaw Historical Museum

Saginaw Children's Zoo

Lake Michigan

The Lake Michigan shoreline may be the Lower Peninsula's western edge, but many will argue that its heart lies in Chicago. The shoreline is now connected to the city by an interstate highway, but that has only cemented what was already a long and enduring relationship between the Windy City and this watery edge of Michigan.

It began with the Great Chicago Fire of 1871, which left the city smoldering in ashes. Chicago was rebuilt with Michigan white pine, and the mill towns along the Great Lake, communities like Muskegon and Saugatuck, worked around the clock to supply the lumber. Maybe it was during these excursions to the sawmills that Chicagoans discovered that this region of Michigan possessed more than towering trees and two-by-fours.

They discovered the sand, the surf, and the incredibly beautiful sunsets of the Lake Michigan shoreline. By the 1880s, the tourist boom was on, and it was being fed by vacationers from cities outside Michigan, places like St. Louis, and South Bend, Indiana, but most of all from Chicago. They arrived by steamships, trains, and eventually automobiles. They caused luxurious resorts and lakeside cottages to mushroom, beginning in New Buffalo on the edge of the Indiana-Michigan border and

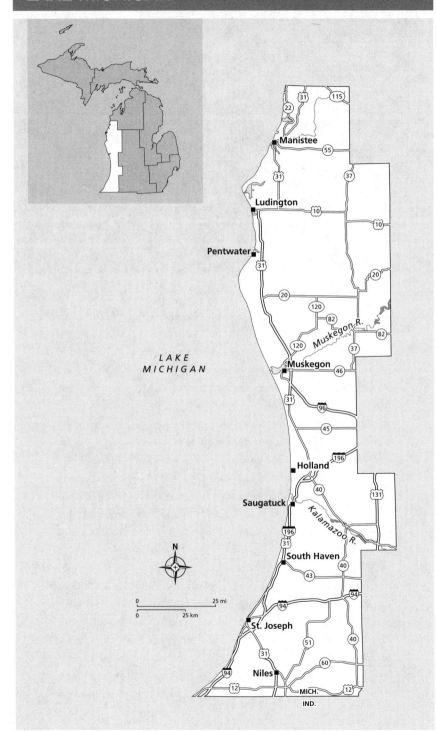

continuing right up the coast: St. Joseph, South Haven, Saugatuck, Grand Haven, and Muskegon.

They call it the Michigan Riviera, and even Richard J. Daley, Chicago's famed political boss and mayor, had a summer home on the strip. With the completion of I–94, the two regions were linked by a four-lane belt of concrete. Many Chicagoans, eager to escape the city heat, were less than two hours from the cool breezes of their favorite resort.

The Lake Michigan shoreline is still the heart of Michigan tourism. This incredibly beautiful region is characterized by great dunes and watery sunsets, but it's also known for its bustling resorts, streets full of quaint shops, and attractive beachfront hotels. The region lies on the western edge of Michigan, but Chicago's influence is unmistakably clear.

Just go to the beach and look at the license plates of the cars, listen to the baseball games the radios are tuned to, or see what city's newspaper someone is snoozing under. You're in Chicago's playland.

Berrien County

You barely cross the state border from Indiana before the first lakeshore communities appear on the horizon with their hotels and motels clustered near the

AUTHOR'S TOP TEN PICKS

Gillette Nature Center,
Hoffmaster State Park;
(231) 798–3711

Hackley and Hume Historic Site,
Muskegon;
(231) 722–0278

Loda Lake Wildflower Sanctuary,
White Cloud;
(231) 745–4631

Ludington State Park,
Ludington;
(231) 843–8671

Mac Wood's Dune Rides,
Silver Lake State Park;
(231) 873–2817

Picking apples at Tree-Mendus Fruit,
Eau Claire;
(877) 863–3276

Saugatuck Chain Ferry and Mount Baldhead Park,
Saugatuck;
(269) 857–4243

Shrine of the Pines,
Baldwin;
(231) 745–7892

Three Oaks Spokes Bicycle Museum,
Three Oaks;
(269) 756–3361

Windmill Island,
Holland;
(616) 355–1030

water. Many are new, each with features little different from the one next door. But if you search a little, you can find an old inn from another era unique in its appearance and half-hidden in a quiet neighborhood near the lake. If you search harder, you might even find the *Inn at Union Pier.*

Union Pier is a cluster of well-shaded streets and nineteenth-century summer homes about 10 miles north of the border. Locate Berrien Street and you'll pass the inn, three nautical buildings painted light blue with white railings.

The inn began in 1918 as a single building called the Karonsky Resort, but business was so good that by 1929 two more structures had been added. An easy journey from Chicago (today it is only ninety minutes by car), the inn thrived in the golden age of the Lake Michigan resorts but by the 1960s was abandoned and closed up. In 1983, Bill and Madeleine Reinke purchased the place, gutted it, and after two years of renovation, opened for business.

From the outside the inn's most striking feature is the wraparound porch on one of the smaller lodges and the matching balcony above it, the ideal place to unwind after a day on the beach. Walkway decks connect the buildings; one has a large hot tub, and tables for breakfast outdoors are on another. Most of the rooms are furnished in light pine and include a Swedish ceramic woodstove. The heart of the main lodge is a spacious common area with a grand piano, overstuffed chairs and sofas, and lots to read. Guests begin each day with a full breakfast of local fruit and fresh baked goods on the deck and then head across the street to the beach, check out one of the inn's bicycles, or take to nearby roads for a winery tour or antiques excursion.

The Inn at Union Pier (269–469–4700) has sixteen rooms priced for double occupancy from $170 to $225 per night, including breakfast. Write ahead for reservations to P.O. Box 222, Union Pier 49129.

In downtown Three Oaks, in the southwest corner of Berrien County, is the *Three Oaks Spokes Bicycle Museum,* where twenty-two bicycles are displayed on the walls, ranging from the Companion, a side-by-side two-seater, to an 1860 velocipede, one of the earliest bicycles ever made, featuring two wheels, handlebars, and a seat—but no rubber tires, inflated inner tubes, or anything resembling a spring or wire spoke. Thus its nickname: the Boneshaker.

The museum is much more than old bicycles and exhibits. What it really showcases is the southwest corner of the state, a pedaler's paradise called Michiana. Promoting recreational cycling in Michiana was the aim of the Three Oaks Spokes Bicycle Club when it was formed in 1974. The club developed the **Backroads Bikeway,** a selection of 12 tours throughout the region that have been posted with color-coded bike route signs. The tours range from 8 miles to more than 50, and wind past sand dunes, wineries, cider mills, and one of the last stands of virgin hardwoods left in southern Michigan.

The developed bike routes brought an increasing number of cyclists passing through town and prompted the club to move its museum from a cramped storefront on Main Street to the historical Michigan Central Railroad Depot in 1994. The century-old depot, featuring tin ceilings, beveled, leaded glass windows, and handcrafted copper light fixtures, was called "the finest depot between Niles and Chicago" in its heyday. Along with two exhibit rooms displaying the twenty-two classic bicycles, the museum also serves as an information center, promoting Michiana tourist attractions as well as cycling events and trails throughout the state. You can even rent a bike here.

The Bicycle Museum (269–756–3361) is located in the historic Michigan Central Railroad Depot at 1 Oak Street, 16 miles west of Niles on US 12 or 71 miles southwest of Kalamazoo. It is open daily year-round from 9:00 A.M. to 5:00 P.M., and there is no admission charge.

The Lake Michigan dunes, the most spectacular natural feature of the region, begin in Indiana and hug the shoreline almost to the Straits of Mackinac.

TOP ANNUAL EVENTS

Trillium Festival,
Muskegon, May;
(800) 250–9283

Tulip Time Festival,
Holland, May;
(800) 822–2770

National Asparagus Festival,
Hart, June;
(800) 874–3982

Harbor Days/Venetian Nights,
Saugatuck, July;
(269) 857–1701

Manistee National Forest Festival,
Manistee, July;
(877) 626–4783

National Blueberry Festival,
South Haven, August;
(800) 764–2836

Apple Cider Century,
Three Oaks, September;
(269) 756–3361

Goose Festival,
Fennville, October;
(269) 561–5013

The largest preserve of dunes in Berrien County is at **_Warren Dunes State Park,_** located on the lake 12 miles north of the state border. The park has more than 2 miles of fine sandy beaches and dunes that rise 240 feet above Lake Michigan. The dunes are a popular place in the summer for sunbathers and swimmers during the day and campers at night. What many people don't realize is that Warren Dunes is the only state park that permits hang gliding, and it is considered by most gliders to be one of the best places in the Midwest, if not the country, for soaring.

Gliders are drawn to the park because of Tower Hill, which looms over the beach parking lot. They trudge up the hill carrying their gliders and then soar into the winds from the top, flying over the sandy park or even above Lake Michigan. When the sport enjoyed its heyday in the mid-1970s, there would be almost a hundred gliders on Tower Hill on a windy weekend, with as many as twenty in the air at one time. The park rangers were so burdened with accidents caused by unqualified fliers that they instituted a certification system and stricter regulations for gliders.

What makes the park so attractive for these soaring adventurers, especially those just learning the sport, are the smooth winds that come off the lake and the soft and relatively forgiving sand below. Gliding takes place year-round, but the best time to watch it is a weekend in the fall or spring with a wind out of the north-northwest. Arrive then and you'll see a half dozen or so colorful gliders. Or, better yet, sign up for a one-day lesson from one of the glider instructors who set up school in the park. For an up-to-date list of the instructors, call Warren Dunes State Park (269–426–4013).

Strange As It Sounds

Tree-Mendus Fruit is like many U-pick fruit farms in western Michigan. The Eau Claire farm has 250 acres of apple orchards to pick, hayrides, a petting area with goats, chickens, and rabbits for children, a country store and gift shop featuring baked goods, jugs of cider, and apple and cherry products, and a picnic area.

But in some ways Tree-Mendus Fruit is the only farm of its kind. Take its International Cherry Pit Spitting Championship held annually on the first Saturday in July. In 1998 the farm celebrated the event's twenty-fifth anniversary with the champion spitting a cherry pit 72 feet, 11 inches, a record effort at the farm.

Tree-Mendus Fruit (877–863–3276) is 2 miles north of Eau Claire and east of M 140 on East Eureka Road. The farm is open from July through October. Hours are 10:00 A.M. to 6:00 P.M. daily except Tuesday through Labor Day, and Friday through Monday in the fall.

Lake Michigan does more than provide water for the beaches or a view from the top of sand dunes. It also tempers the winter storms that roll in from the Great Plains and moderates the sweltering summer heat felt elsewhere in the Midwest. These effects, combined with the light soil of the region, have turned the lakeshore strip into a cornucopia of orchards, berry farms, and especially vineyards. Michigan is the third leading wine-producing state in the country after California and New York. Paw Paw in Van Buren County is the unofficial center for the state's wine makers, with the largest vineyards, St. Julian Wine Company and Warner Vineyards, located right off I–94.

Smaller wineries are also found throughout the region, including a frequent winner in national competition, *Tabor Hill Winery,* in the center of Berrien County. The winery began when two Chicago salesmen who sold steel but loved wine brought a selection of hybrid grapevines back from France in 1968. They chose their vineyard site in the rolling hills of the county, hoping the conditions there were similar enough to those in France to bring success. They were. The transplanted vines thrived, and the winery produced its first bottle in 1970. Seven years later a bottle of its 1974 Baco won a gold medal in the American Wine Competition, and since then both the vineyard and Leonard Olson, steel-salesman-turned-wine maker, have won numerous awards. The winery remains small, producing 40,000 gallons (or about 15,000 cases) of wine annually in almost two dozen types of whites, reds, and blends.

The best way to view Tabor Hill is on a walking tour that begins where workers bottle the wine and then heads out into the rows of trellised vines for a history of the grapes. You also descend into the wine cellar for a look at the huge vats and hand-carved oak casks that age the wine, and then finish the tour in the tasting room for some tips on how to "judge" wine. The twenty-five-minute tour ends with everybody age twenty-one or older sampling some of Tabor Hill's finest wines (kids can sample grape juice).

The winery also includes an excellent restaurant with tables that overlook the rolling vineyard and a huge deck outside. A favorite activity of many, especially during fall, is to pack a picnic lunch and enjoy it on the open deck with a bottle of Tabor Hill wine.

funfacts

Bear Cave near Buchanan is one of the few caverns in Michigan. Formed in rare "tura rock," the cave is estimated to be 25,000 years old. In 1875, bank robbers hid their loot in the cave, an event that inspired the movie *The Great Train Robbery,* in which the cave was featured.

Bear Cave (269–695–3050) is 6 miles north of Buchanan on Red Bud Trail. Tours of the cave are available during the summer.

Tabor Hill (269–422–1161 or 800–283–3363) is on Mount Tabor Road and can be reached from I–94 by taking exit 16 and heading north on Red Arrow Highway to Bridgman. From Bridgman head east along Shawnee Road and keep an eye out for the signs. This vineyard is definitely off by itself. The free tours go from noon to 4:30 P.M. every day in summer.

In between the sand dunes, the orchards, and the wineries of Berrien County is a lot of history. Niles, the community of four flags, was the first settlement in the Lower Peninsula and claimed one of the first museums in the country when a private one opened here in 1842. Eventually it became the **Fort St. Joseph Museum,** and today it houses more than 10,000 historical items on two floors. Much of the museum's collection relates to its namesake fort, for which the French built the stockade in 1691. The British took it over in 1761, and the Spanish captured it twenty years later. In 1783, the Americans arrived and raised the fourth and final flag over Fort St. Joseph.

The museum's most noted displays, however, are devoted to the Sioux Indians of the Great Plains, not to the residents of Fort St. Joseph. Many of the Indian artifacts were obtained by Captain Horace Baxter Quimby, whose daughter moved to Niles. While the U.S. Army captain was based in the Dakota Territory in 1881 and 1882, he became friendly with Sitting Bull, the most famous Sioux chief. Among the gifts Quimby received from Sitting Bull were thirteen pictographs of the chief's greatest battles. The set of pictures is one of only three known collections of the Sioux chief.

The museum (269–683–4702) is right behind the Niles City Hall at 508 East Main Street. Niles can be reached from US 12, 23 miles east of I–94 or 33 miles west of US 131. Hours are 10:00 A.M. to 4:00 P.M. Wednesday to Saturday.

More history can be seen at Berrien Springs' **1839 Courthouse.** The building, which at various times was a militia drill hall, a college, and even a church, was repurchased by the county in 1967 and restored as the nineteenth-century courtroom where law was interpreted and justice dispensed in Michigan's early years of statehood. The classic Greek Revival–style structure is the centerpiece of the Berrien County Courthouse Square, a complex of five buildings that is listed on the National Register of Historic Places. It gives visitors a glimpse of the machinery of old-fashioned government.

You can climb the wooden stairs to the second-floor courtroom where former Michigan Supreme Court Justice Epaphroditus Ransom presided over the first session in April 1839. Little in the building has changed since then. The wooden floors still creak as you approach the bench, and floor-to-ceiling windows still illuminate the courtroom furnishings of pewlike benches, wood-burning stoves, and the curved railing that separated the participants from the gallery.

The historic complex (269–471–1202) is located in Berrien Springs at US 31 and Union Street. Berrien Springs is 11 miles southeast of exit 27 off I–94. Hours for the buildings are 9:00 A.M. to 4:00 P.M. Tuesday through Friday and 1:00 to 5:00 P.M. Saturday and Sunday. Admission is free.

Van Buren County

South Haven has a long and colorful history spiced with Great Lakes vessels and shipbuilding, and much of it is explained at the ***Michigan Maritime Museum,*** which is dedicated to the boats that were built and used on the Great Lakes. Founded in 1976, the museum includes a 600-foot outdoor boardwalk around a historical fish tug and a vessel used in the U.S. Life-Saving Service. Inside the museum hall the exhibits range from collections of small vessel motors and tools used by local shipbuilders to personal belongings of Great Lakes mariners.

Michigan Maritime Museum (269–637–8078) is on Dyckman Avenue where it crosses the Black River and is reached from I–196 by taking exit 20 and heading west on Phoenix Street. Turn north on Broadway Street and then west on Dyckman Street. Hours are 10:00 A.M. to 5:00 P.M. Monday and Wednesday through Saturday and noon to 5:00 P.M. Sunday. Admission is $2.50 for adults and $1.50 for children.

The good life on the lakes can also be enjoyed at dinnertime aboard the *Idler* at the ***Magnolia Grille,*** a restaurant floating in the Black River downtown in Old Harbor Village. The *Idler* was built in Clinton, Iowa, in 1897 for Lafayette Lamb, a lumber baron who used the 120-foot houseboat for his own personal enjoyment on the Mississippi. He never installed an engine in the *Idler* because he didn't want to be disturbed by the vibrations, so the vessel was always pushed up and down the river by a small tug.

The *Idler* appeared at the 1904 World's Fair in St. Louis, but in 1910 it burned to the waterline. It was immediately rebuilt and eventually captured the fancy of actor Vincent Price's father. He owned it for fifty-eight years, and in a letter now framed and hanging in the restaurant, Price said that what his father liked most about the riverboat was playing the piano on board. Eventually the boat was purchased, and it was brought to South Haven in 1979. Today it has been beautifully restored, and topside is the Bayou Beach Club, an open-air bar with sweeping views of the town and the Black River from every table. In the Magnolia Grille, located below, you can dine on white linen in either the original dining quarters or one of four staterooms. Each accommodates a party of six for a private gastronomic evening. The menu lists more than twenty entrees priced from $12 to $22, and every day six new entrees are featured. Many local people know the restaurant best for its Cajun dishes—blackened fish and steak, barbecued shrimp, and Louisiana steak salad—and its sinfully rich cheesecakes.

Magnolia Grille (269–637–8435) is open daily from 11:00 A.M. to 10:00 P.M. Monday through Thursday, 11:00 A.M. to 11:00 P.M. Friday and Saturday, and 11:00 A.M. to 8:00 P.M. Sunday. Reservations are accepted, and dress is casual on the riverboat.

Sportfishing fans throughout Michigan head for the streams, inland lakes, and Great Lakes to fill their creels with a variety of catch. If they are passing through Van Buren County on M 43, they should also head for the **Wolf Lake State Fish Hatchery,** one of the main reasons fishing is so good in Michigan. The hatchery dates to 1928 and by 1935 was the largest in the world. Construction of the present facility began in 1980, and three years and $7.2 million later, the technological upgrading had made Wolf Lake the finest complex in the country for producing both warm-water and cold-water species. No other hatchery in Michigan raises as many species as Wolf Lake, which hatches steelhead, brown trout, Chinook salmon, and grayling along with the warm-water species of tiger musky, northern pike, walleye, bass, and bluegill.

Hatchery tours should begin at the interpretive center, which will fascinate anybody who dabbles in sportfishing. In the lobby is a wall with plaques of Michigan's record fish—sort of a fishing hall of fame—plus displays of trout fishing on the state's renowned Au Sable River. Off to one side is the "Michigan

Caruso's Candy Kitchen

Since the Roaring Twenties, vacationing families have been stepping up to the Italian marble soda fountain bar at Caruso's Candy Kitchen in Dowagiac to sip a creamy soda or indulge in an ice-cream concoction served in a tall glass sundae dish. They're still doing it today because little has changed at this venerable ice-cream parlor.

Founded in 1822 by Antonio Caruso, who had just sailed to the United States from Italy with his wife, Caruso's still features pedestal stools, a wavy mirror behind the counter, lime green Hamilton Beach malt mixers, and high wooden booths. This is where you come for a real milk shake, made with hand-dipped ice cream in a metal malt glass. The specialty of the shop is the Green River: lime phosphate syrup on the bottom of a sundae dish, two scoops of vanilla ice cream, and topped off with crushed cherries, pineapple, mixed nuts, and real whipped cream. It is based on the green, white, and red flag of Italy and was Antonio Caruso's way of saluting his native country.

Caruso's (269–782–6001) is in downtown Dowagiac at 130 South Front Street and is open from 8:00 A.M. to 5:30 P.M. Monday through Saturday.

Room," a walk-through exhibit area that begins with an interesting series of habitat dioramas, cross sections of every type of water you might drop a line into, from trout streams to the Great Lakes. Each diorama shows the species that will be found, the habitat they like, and the lure of a frustrated angler trying to land the lunkers that lie below. There are also exhibits on fish anatomy, slide presentations of Michigan's commercial fisheries, and an area devoted to sportfishing gear, including a delightful display of more than a hundred historic lures, plugs, and other tackle.

After viewing the exhibits and a short slide presentation in the auditorium, visitors are encouraged to wander through the hatchery itself to view millions of fish in the ponds. If you want to see something bigger, ask for some fish feed at the interpretive center and walk out on the small pier at the visitors' pond. The small lake was developed so that people, especially children, could actually see some large fish. Among the species in it are sturgeon, including one that is 5 feet long and weighs fifty-five pounds. Imagine that at the end of your line!

The center (269–668–2876) is open Tuesday through Saturday from 10:00 A.M. to 6:00 P.M. and Sunday from noon to 5:00 P.M. during the summer. There is no admission fee to visit Wolf Lake, which is reached from I–94 by heading north on US 131 for 4 miles and then west on M 43 for 6 miles.

Michigan has no short supply of vineyards and wine-tasting rooms to visit, but few have the old-world character of *Warner Vineyards* in Paw Paw. The building itself is a Michigan Historical Site, constructed in 1898 as the town's first waterworks station. The vineyard purchased it in 1967 and proceeded to renovate the structure using lumber from old wine casks to transform it into a wine haus and bistro.

Today the brick and stone building is reached by crossing a footbridge over the east branch of the Paw Paw River, which gurgles its way through the shaded grounds and around an outdoor deck. The whole setting is one of idyllic enjoyment. You can go on a wine tour or simply stop for a little wine tasting.

Warner Vineyards (800–756–5357) is reached from I–94 by taking exit 60 and heading north on M 40 into Paw Paw. The winery is at 706 South Kalamazoo and open from 10:00 A.M. to 5:00 P.M. Monday through Saturday and noon to 5:00 P.M. Sunday.

Just down the road in Paw Paw is the ***St. Julian Winery,*** the state's oldest and largest vineyard. Founded in 1921, St. Julian (800–732–6002) produces forty types of wines and also offers tours and tasting as well.

Allegan County

On the map Saugatuck looks like just the next beachfront community along the lake, but in reality it is a trendy resort whose streets are lined with fine restaurants, quaint shops, and lots of tourists. Perhaps the most striking sight in Saugatuck is the docks along the Kalamazoo River, where moored at the edge of the shopping district is an armada of cabin cruisers and sailboats 30, 40, or 50 feet in length or even longer. You can pick up the boardwalk that winds past the boats anywhere along Water Street, and if you follow it north, eventually you'll come to the most unusual vessel afloat, the ***Saugatuck Chain Ferry.*** It's the only chain-powered ferry in the state and has been carrying passengers across the Kalamazoo River since 1838. An operator hand-cranks a 380-foot chain attached at each shore, pulling the small white ferry through the water.

It's only $1.00 for the five-minute ride, and it is your escape from the bustling downtown shopping district to one of the most beautiful beaches on the lake. Once on the other side, you walk north for a few hundred yards until you reach ***Mount Baldhead Park,*** with tables, shelter, and a dock on the river. There is also a stairway that takes you (after a little huffing and puffing) to the top of the 200-foot dune, where you are greeted with a glorious panorama of Saugatuck, Kalamazoo Lake to the southeast, and Lake Michigan to the west. On the other side you have a choice. You can descend to ***Oval Beach*** along the Northwoods Trail, an easy walk that includes a view of the lake and beach along the way. Or you can dash madly down the steep and

The Saugatuck Chain Ferry

sandy Beach Trail, right off the towering dune, across the beach, and into the lake for a cool dip.

Moving inland, another interesting attraction is the old Allegan County Jail in Allegan. Seriously. The imposing redbrick building was built in 1906 and features Greek Revival architecture with a peaked roof and columns along the porch. It has bars on the windows, a hexagonal turret in the corner, and a three-story grandeur that is lacking in its newer counterpart across the street.

But most unusual is the small red sign on Walnut Street that says ***Allegan County Historical Museum.*** Go to jail and get a history lesson in penitentiary punishment. Within the museum are a variety of exhibits, including a country store loaded with nineteenth-century merchandise, a display devoted to Allegan's General Benjamin Pritchard, whose men captured Confederate President Jefferson Davis during the Civil War, and a historical laundry room.

But coat hangers and wringers are not what draw more than 1,000 visitors to the museum every year. It's a macabre fascination with slammers and pokeys. To that end, a guide leads you through the sheriff's living quarters and the large kitchen, where his wife would prepare meals for up to thirty prisoners a night and then pass plates through a small door in the wall. On the second floor are rows of 6-by-8-foot cells, complete with the graffiti that disheartened convicts scratched on the walls in the 1930s. You can even walk through the maximum-security cells, now filled with a historical toy collection, view the old padded cell, and examine the holding pen for "ladies."

The jail is open on Friday from 2:00 to 5:00 P.M. from June through Labor Day or by appointment by calling Marguerite Miller at (616) 673–4853. To reach the museum, take M 222 (exit 55) off US 131 and head west into Allegan. The old jail is at 113 Walnut Street, between Hubbard and Trowbridge.

funfacts

Beneath the sand near the mouth of the Kalamazoo River on Lake Michigan lies the site of Singapore, one of Michigan's most famous ghost towns. The town was founded in the 1830s by New York land speculators who hoped it would rival Chicago or Milwaukee as a lake port. Singapore bustled as a lumbering town for almost forty years, but once the trees were gone by the 1870s, the residents fled.

Ottawa County

Every spring Holland bursts into a rainbow of colors thanks to the millions of tulips that residents plant seemingly everywhere. The event climaxes during the Tulip Time Festival in mid-May, when the flowers are in full bloom and the Dutch-founded city hosts more than a half-million visitors, who book hotel rooms months in advance.

But historical Holland can be an interesting trip the rest of the year as well. Founded in 1847 by Dutch religious dissenters, Holland celebrated its sesquicentennial in 1997 and today is the undisputed center of Dutch culture in Michigan. For a dose of old Holland, visit ***Dutch Village.*** This fifteen-acre theme park is a re-created nineteenth-century Dutch village complete with canals, tulip gardens, and historical displays along with some kitschy attractions like a wooden-shoe slide to keep the kids happy. Among the many buildings are a wooden-shoe factory and Queen's Inn, Holland's only restaurant serving Dutch food.

Dutch Village (616–396–1475; www.dutchvillage.com) is along US 31, 2 miles northeast of downtown Holland. From April through mid-October the grounds are open from 9:00 A.M. to 6:00 P.M. daily. Admission is $8.00 for adults and $5.00 for children.

Windmill Island is a city park that features De Zwaan, the only working Dutch windmill allowed to be shipped out of the Netherlands. The five-story-high windmill is still operating as it grinds whole wheat flour that is sold in shops nearby. Also at Windmill Island are the Posthouse Museum, Little Netherlands Museum, and an 1895 carousel. The park (616–355–1030) is just northeast of downtown Holland at Seventh and Lincoln Streets and open in the summer from 9:00 A.M. to 6:00 P.M. Monday through Saturday and 11:30 A.M. to 6:00 P.M. Sunday. There are reduced hours of operation in the spring and fall. Admission is $6.50 for adults and $3.50 for children ages five to twelve.

Holland also has two wooden-shoe factories where you can buy the oaken loafers or simply see a demonstration of how they are made. The best is the **Wooden Shoe Factory,** which also includes a display on the many kinds of wooden shoes worn in Europe. The Wooden Shoe Factory (616–399–1900) is off US 31 just south of Sixteenth Street. Hours are 8:00 A.M. to 6:00 P.M. Monday through Friday and 9:00 A.M. to 5:00 P.M. Saturday and Sunday from May through October.

Grand Haven has developed its waterfront along the Grand River and includes a riverwalk that extends several miles from downtown to the picturesque Grand Haven Lighthouse out in Lake Michigan. But by far the most noted aspect of the river is the city's **Musical Fountain,** the world's largest, which performs nightly during the summer with electronically controlled and synchronized music. Performances begin around dusk (9:00 to 9:30 P.M.), and most people enjoy the free concerts by assembling in the Waterfront Stadium.

Muskegon County

In the late 1800s this county was the heart of lumbering on Michigan's western side, and the city of Muskegon grew during the prosperous era to be known as the Lumber Queen of the World. A drive down West Webster Avenue shows how much money was made and where much of it went: The Victorian mansions are fabulous. The most elaborate houses were built by the two men who prospered most of all from Michigan white pine, Charles H. Hackley and his partner, Thomas Hume. They built their homes next to each other, and it reportedly took 200 artisans and craftsmen two years to complete the houses. Behind the homes the men shared the same carriage house. The **Hackley House** and **Hume House** are listed on the National Register of Historic Places and have been called two of the nation's most outstanding examples of Victorian architecture.

Although restoration continues, the homes are open for tours. The Hackley House is especially impressive, a virtual museum of carved woodwork that strikes you from the moment you walk into the home and are greeted by unusual figures along the walls. Almost every aspect of the house is overwhelming, from its original furnishings and stained-glass windows to the hand-stenciled walls and the eleven fireplaces, each made unique with imported ceramic tiles. If you see only one restored home in Michigan, it should be the Hackley House, where it's hard to imagine living in such style.

The Hackley and Hume Historic Site (231–722–0278) is at 484 West Webster Avenue. Tours are offered mid-May through September, Wednesday through Sunday from noon to 4:00 P.M. They are also offered the same hours on weekends in December. There is a small admission fee.

Another interesting museum in Muskegon is actually underwater. The **USS Silversides** is a U.S. Navy submarine that was commissioned just eight days after the Japanese attacked Pearl Harbor on December 7, 1941. It went on to serve in the Pacific Fleet during World War II and ranked third among all U.S. submarines for enemy ships sunk.

Today *Silversides* is docked at the Muskegon Channel Wall in Père Marquette Park at 1346 Bluff Street and open to the public. Guides lead you down the gangplank so you can view torpedo rooms, crew quarters, the galley, and many other sections of the 312-foot-long submarine. Tours of the USS *Silversides* (231–755–1230) are given daily June through August from 10:00 A.M. to 5:30 P.M. In May and September hours are 1:00 to 5:00 P.M. on weekdays and 10:00 A.M. to 5:30 P.M. on weekends. Admission is $7.00 for adults, $6.00 for students ages twelve to eighteen, and $5.00 for children five to eleven. Children four and under are free.

The towering dunes along the eastern side of Lake Michigan are the world's largest accumulation of dunes bordering a body of freshwater and are

strange as it sounds

The world's largest weather vane is located in Montague. Erected in 1884 by the Whiteall Metal Studios across the street, the vane is 48 feet tall and weighs 3,500 pounds. It has a 26-foot-long arrow and directional letters that are 3 feet, 6 inches tall, and is topped off by a 14-foot-long schooner. The vane is right off Business US 31 in a park overlooking the town harbor.

renowned throughout the country. One of the best places for learning how dunes develop and change is the **Gillette Nature Center** within P. J. Hoffmaster State Park. The center is, in fact, overshadowed by a huge dune best viewed from the lobby's glass wall to the west. The center features an exhibit hall entitled *From a Grain of Sand,* which guides you through the natural history of the dunes, and an eighty-two-seat theater that uses a nine-projector, multi-image slide show to further explain their delicate nature. On the ground floor is a gallery that offers hands-on exhibits to help children understand the environment of the park.

Most visitors view the exhibits and then hike up to the Dune Platform Overlook. The trail begins next to the center and includes a wooden walkway of 165 steps. It puts you 190 feet above the lake, with spectacular views of the surrounding dune country. There is a vehicle permit fee to enter the state park (231–798–3711), which is reached by heading south of Muskegon on US 31, exiting at Pontaluna Road, and heading west. The Gillette Nature Center is open during summer from 10:00 A.M. to 4:30 P.M. Tuesday through Saturday and noon to 4:30 P.M. Sunday; the rest of the year, hours are Tuesday through Friday 1:00 to 5:00 P.M. and Saturday and Sunday 10:00 A.M. to 5:00 P.M.

Newaygo County

The most distinctive structure in the southern Newaygo County town of Grant is its wooden water tower. Built in 1891, it's the classic *Petticoat Junction* water tower, the last one standing in the state. Driving down Main Street, you half expect to see Uncle Joe and the rest of the cast from that zany old sitcom.

Drive through the town to see the water tower, but stop because of its train depot. Chuck Zobel has transformed the once bustling passenger station into the **Grant Depot Restaurant,** one of the county's best eateries—unless you're a railroad enthusiast, then it's a fascinating train museum that serves a very good Mile High Lemon (meringue) Pie.

After purchasing the empty depot in 1979, Zobel spent a year renovating it, and in the process of tearing down walls and replacing floors, he turned up a variety of artifacts from the era of the iron horse: tickets and train orders from 1903, bottles, telegrams, signs, even the remains of a copper sulfate battery that powered the telegraph before the age of electricity. Today you can sit at a table in what a century ago was the passenger waiting room, or in a bay window overlooking the tracks, where a station agent once worked a telegraph. What was the baggage room is now the kitchen, and the dining room walls are covered with memorabilia—from lanterns and oilcans to warning lights, tickets, and an engineer's manual on how to operate a locomotive.

The Grant Depot Restaurant (231–834–7361) is open from 7:00 A.M. to 8:00 P.M. Monday through Thursday, 7:00 A.M. to 9:00 P.M. Friday and Saturday, and 8:00 A.M. to 5:00 P.M. Sunday. From I–96 in Grand Rapids, head north on M 37 (exit 30). Grant is reached in 24 miles, and the depot is right off M 37.

Wildflower lovers ought to stay on M 37 in Newaygo County to reach the **Loda Lake Wildflower Sanctuary.** In 1938, Forest Service rangers invited the Federated Garden Clubs of Michigan to help them create a sanctuary for native plants, including endangered and protected species, to ensure their survival. Although part of the Manistee National Forest, the preserve is still managed by the Federated Garden Clubs, and over the years it has evolved into a unique haven for botanists, wildflower enthusiasts, and families who just want to know the difference between Michigan holly and Holly, Michigan.

blessingof thebikes

One of the most unusual festivals in Michigan is the Blessing of the Bikes, which is held the third weekend in May in Baldwin. Hundreds of motorcyclists, many of them riding classic Harley-Davidsons, arrive in town for the weekend and gather on Sunday at the local airstrip to have their bikes blessed by a priest.

The self-guiding trail is a mile loop of easy hiking where you encounter the first numbered post in less than 20 feet, and before you return to the picnic area, you'll pass thirty-eight others. The interpretive posts mark the locations of trillium, blueberries, swamp rose, insect-eating sundew plants, and fragrant water lily, among other plants, and they correspond to a trail guide available near the parking area.

From White Cloud head north on M 37 and then left on Five Mile Road, where the directional sign to Loda Lake is posted on the corner. Head a mile west and turn right on Fletcher Road. The entrance to the sanctuary is a mile to the north. For a trail guide, call or stop at the U.S. Forest Service Ranger Station (231–745–4631) at 650 North Michigan Avenue in Baldwin.

Lake County

When you look at a stump, what do you see? A stump? Is a tree root just a tree root? Not to Ray Overholzer. This hunting guide-turned-craftsman would stroll along the Père Marquette River, find a stump left over from Michigan's logging era, and see a table or maybe a piece of a rocking chair. Then he would spend months fashioning it by hand until his unique vision became reality. This is woodworking as an art, and it's preserved today at the **Shrine of the Pines,** a small but—to those of us who struggled in shop class just to build that bird-house—intriguing museum.

Overholzer constructed a rocking chair from roots that is so perfectly balanced it rocks fifty-five times with a single push. His gun rack holds twelve hunting rifles and rotates on hand-carved wooden balls like ball bearings—not a screw or a hinge in the elaborate cabinet. A stump became a bootlegger's table with a hidden compartment for the whiskey bottle and another for the shot glasses. Perhaps most amazing is the dining room table that began as a 700-pound stump of a giant white pine. By the time Overholzer was done working with the piece of discarded wood, it was a 300-pound table with roots carved into legs and storage bins hollowed out of the sides. In 1940 and 1941 Overholzer built a huge lodge on the banks of the Père Marquette and originally intended to operate it as a hunting lodge. But his furniture was too dear to him by then and, fearing it would get scratched, he changed his mind. The intended lodge became a museum of more than 200 pieces, the world's only collection of handcrafted white pine furniture.

The Shrine of the Pines (231–745–7892) is located on M 37, 2 miles south of Baldwin. The museum is open May through September from 10:00 A.M. to 5:30 P.M. Monday through Saturday, and 11:00 A.M. to 5:30 P.M. Sunday. There is a small fee.

Oceana County

County Road B–15 turns off from US 31 north of Whitehall and swings west toward Lake Michigan before returning to the highway at Pentwater, the bustling resort community at the northwest corner of Oceana County. Along the way the county road passes Silver Lake, an impressive sight that slows most cars bearing sightseers to a crawl. The lake is bordered to the west by a huge dune that towers over it, and from the car window you see beach and sunbathers, crystal clear lake and sailboats, the mountain of sand and dune climbers. Much of what you see, including the strip of dunes between the inland lake and Lake Michigan, is part of *Silver Lake State Park.*

Silver Lake is different from other state parks along Lake Michigan because the dunes have been divided into three areas for three types of users. The section in the middle is the pedestrian area, where people scramble up the huge dunes and hike across them to Lake Michigan.

The region to the south is one of only two places in the state where dune rides are offered in large open-air jeeps that hold up to twelve passengers. *Mac Wood's Dune Rides* date back to the 1930s, and today thousands enjoy the popular rides every year from mid-May through mid-October. The scenic

Nickerson Inn

In northern Oceana County is the resort town of Pentwater, which was no more than a few settlers at the mouth of the Pentwater River until Charles Mears showed up in 1859. The timber magnate turned the town into a major shipping port by building mills, hotels, and docks. He even straightened out the end of the Pentwater River to assist ships carrying his lumber. Today there is a state park in the city named after Mears, while on a wooded dune overlooking the park's Lake Michigan beach is the Nickerson Inn, built in 1914.

The inn's trademark is its long veranda, where in the summer you can sit and watch families stream toward the beach. Upstairs are ten rooms, including two Jacuzzi suites with gas log fireplaces and balconies. The inn's restaurant is renowned. Its enclosed porch overlooking Lake Michigan is a stunning place to watch the sunset during dinner, and a favorite of former governor James Blanchard.

Summer room rates begin on Memorial Day weekend and range from $150 to $250 for the suites, including breakfast. Call (800) 742–1288 for reservations.

thirty-five-minute ride takes passengers through the heart of the Silver Lake dune country from the top of the tallest dunes to the edge of Lake Michigan. It's a wild ride down sandy hills and through the surf of Lake Michigan, but never too scary for small children to handle. The tour is even more spectacular near sunset on a clear summer evening.

Mac Wood's Dune Rides (231–873–2817) is on Sixteenth Avenue at Scenic Drive just south of the state park campground. Hours are 9:30 A.M. to sunset daily from mid-May to mid-October. The cost is $13.50 for adults, $9.00 for children.

The northern area of the park is most unusual, as it is designated for off-road vehicles. This is the ORV capital of the Midwest, the only public dunes in Michigan where people can drive their three- and four-wheelers, dirt bikes, trail jeeps, or any other vehicle built for the soft sand and steep terrain. On almost any day of the summer, the ORV parking lot at the end of Hazel Road will be filled with a wide assortment of vehicles, their drivers, and the trailers and vans they arrived in. They come from Indiana, Illinois, Ohio, and Wisconsin to ride here, as well as from all over Michigan. Pedestrians don't venture into the motorized area, but there is a wooden viewing platform overlooking the ORV entry point. Here you can view all the daredevil drivers and their machines as they climb the first dune.

Tiny Hart, population 1,900, is known for two things: asparagus and rail trails. Hart hosts the ***National Asparagus Festival*** (800–874–3982) in the first week of June because Oceana County grows more of the green stuff per capita than anywhere else in the world. The four-day event includes parades, farm tours, fun runs, and the opportunity to feast on the asparagus that has been prepared every which way, from dip to cakes.

Not into vegetables? Then arrive with your bicycle. Hart is the northern end of the **Hart-Montague Trail.** The 22.5-mile paved path became one of the first rail trails in Michigan when an abandoned track of the Chesapeake and Ohio Railroad was converted into recreational use in 1987. A trailhead with maps and parking is located in Hart's John Gurney Park. The northern 8 miles of the trail, from Hart to Shelby, is by far the most scenic section.

Mason County

Continue on South Lakeshore Drive, pass the huge Ludington Power Plant, and then after a few miles keep an eye on the east side of the road for **Bortell's Fisheries.** From the outside the fish market is not glamorous, but it has been in business since 1937 and gradually has evolved into western Michigan's finest shop for fish and seafood. It carries a variety of frozen seafood, makes delicious marinated herring in cream and wine, and smokes one of the best selections of fish in the state, including trout, chub, salmon, sturgeon, blind robin, and menominee. Want something fresher? When in season, its cases are filled with fresh perch, pike, walleye, trout, and even smelt in the spring, all half buried in ice.

Still not fresh enough? Then you can wander around back with a pole and catch a rainbow trout out of one of its stocked ponds. Bortell's will cook any fresh fish right there in the market and serve it with french fries and homemade potato salad or coleslaw. You can enjoy your meal outside at one of a half dozen picnic tables next to the market, or better yet, cross the street to Summit Park, where you have a view of Lake Michigan from your table. The freshest fish, good food, and beautiful scenery at a little out-of-the-way county park—it doesn't get much better than that.

Bortell's Fisheries (231–843–3337) is 7 miles south of Ludington on South Lakeshore Drive between Meisenhiemer and Deren Roads. From May through September the store is open daily from 11:00 A.M. to 8:00 P.M.

The first frame house in Mason County was built by Aaron Burr Caswell in 1849. Six years later the two-story home was still the only frame building in an area that was trying to organize itself into Michigan's newest county. So that year Caswell offered the front half of his home as the first courthouse and county seat of Mason. Today the preserved building is a state historic site and the centerpiece of **White Pine Village,** a museum complex operated by the Mason County Historical Society.

Trapper's Cabin in White Pine Village

The village is composed of some twenty preserved buildings or replicas, all from the surrounding county and set up along streets on a bluff overlooking Lake Michigan. Each of the buildings, which range from an 1840s trapper's log cabin to a hardware store of the early 1900s, is completely renovated inside and can be viewed on a leisurely self-guided walk. Throughout the village people in traditional dress ply their trades, everything from a blacksmith to a turn-of-the-century housewife cooking on a woodstove to a violin maker.

What makes White Pine Village an enjoyable experience is the active visitor participation in the exhibits. A documented trial that was held in the Caswell home in the 1860s is reenacted today with visitors filling in as the jury, and nine out of ten times handing down the same verdict as the first time. A log chapel on the rise overlooking the area still holds a Sunday service, and afterward people are encouraged to help the village cooks and enjoy their fresh-baked treats.

Death of Father Jacques Marquette

Located on Lakeshore Drive just north of White Pine Village is a memorial to Father Jacques Marquette, a 45-foot-tall metal cross set in stone. The seventeenth-century missionary explorer is famous for founding St. Ignace and Sault Ste. Marie and for joining Louis Jolliet on a 3,000-mile paddle in discovering the Mississippi River. Realizing he was losing his health, Marquette tried to return to his beloved St. Ignace mission in 1675 but never made it. Instead he died on the banks of Lake Michigan in Buttersville at the site of the cross. He was buried here, but his remains were later exhumed and taken to St. Ignace for final burial.

White Pine Village (231–843–4808) is open from late April until mid-October Tuesday through Saturday from 10:00 A.M. to 5:00 P.M. The museum complex is located off US 31, 3 miles south of Ludington, and is reached by exiting west onto Iris Road and then turning north at South Lakeshore Drive for a quarter of a mile. Admission is $6.00 for adults and $4.00 for children.

From Ludington the famous dunes of Lake Michigan continue to the north, and the area immediately adjacent to the city has been preserved as **Ludington State Park.** It's a popular place where visitors enjoy miles of beach, rolling dunes, and modern campgrounds, or a hike to historic Point Sable Lighthouse. Along with a 300-site campground, the state park (231–843–8671) also features the Great Lakes Interpretive Center and an unusual nature trail in Hamlin Lake for canoers.

Where Ludington State Park ends, the **Nordhouse Dunes** begin, a 1,900-acre preserve in Manistee National Forest that is not as well known or as frequently visited as the state park but is equally beautiful.

A Michigan governor called the Nordhouse Dunes "one of the most outstanding scenic resources" in the state, and in 1987 they were given a federal wilderness designation. What makes these dunes unique is that the area is entirely undeveloped. Travel through the dunes is only on foot either along 10 miles of easy-to-follow trails or by simply making your way across the open hills of sand. The area is the only place in Michigan where you can hike in and camp among the dunes. Because of its inaccessibility to motorized traffic, the

Lake Michigan Carferry

In 1897 the *Père Marquette* departed Ludington, offering the first ferry transportation across Lake Michigan between Michigan and Wisconsin. A century later you can still hop on a ferry for a trip to Manitowoc, Wisconsin, thanks to the SS *Badger,* the only steam-powered auto passenger ship on the Great Lakes.

Launched in 1952, the 410-foot ferry was extensively refurbished in 1991 and now includes staterooms, a maritime museum, food and beverage service, theater and bingo hall, an outdoor deck, and live entertainment. The 60-mile crossing takes four hours but saves you the 450-mile drive around the lake between the two cities. The cruise, a throwback to when luxurious steamers sailed the Great Lakes in the 1920s, is so popular that the company offers a single-day ticket. The round-trip fare for an adult without a vehicle is $78 and $36 per child.

In the summer the ferry departs Ludington at 8:00 A.M. and 7:55 P.M. and Manitowoc at 1:15 P.M. and 12:30 A.M. For tickets or reservations call the SS *Badger* at (800) 227–7447.

Skyline Trail

Anyone who loves boardwalk paths with benches will savor the Skyline Trail, a short but spectacularly scenic hike in Ludington State Park. The path follows the crest of a wooded dune, and erosion of the original trail prompted the park staff to replace it with a boardwalk path in 1981. The two-year project included use of Air National Guard helicopters to airlift much of the lumber to the top of the dune.

The sweeping views of Lake Michigan and the park's open dune country are so good that numerous benches were built into the boardwalk. Sure, the trail is only a half mile long, but if you sat on every bench and admired the scene, it would take you most of the afternoon to hike it. The view from the bench at Post Number 11 is especially scenic as you gaze south at the miles of open dunes stretched out to the Lake Michigan shoreline, the Ludington Harbor Lighthouse, and, on a clear day, even the Silver Lakes dunes 25 miles away.

Beside the benches are thirteen numbered posts along the boardwalk that correspond to information in a brochure available from map boxes at the foot of each staircase. They identify the three common evergreens in Michigan, explain dune country succession, and point out stumps and other remnants of the loggers who arrived in 1851 to cut down the white pine.

dunes area also offers those willing to hike in the opportunity of having a beach to themselves along its 4 miles of sandy lakeshore.

Access into Nordhouse Dunes is through the Lake Michigan Recreation Area, a semiprimitive campground on the northern end of the preserve that is maintained by the national forest's Manistee Ranger District (231–723–2211). Trails into the dunes begin from the recreation area, which also contains one hundred camping sites, a beach, and observation towers overlooking the lake. To reach the recreational area, take US 31 to Lake Michigan Road (also known as Forest Road 5629) located 10 miles south of Manistee. Follow Lake Michigan Road 8 miles west to the area. There is no fee for exploring the dunes or for day use of the recreational area. There is a $13 nightly fee for camping.

Manistee County

Manistee is another lakeshore town that boomed during the lumbering era; at one time in the late 1800s, it boasted thirty-two sawmills and seventeen millionaire lumber barons among its residents. Almost the entire town was destroyed in the Great Fire of 1871 on the same day Chicago experienced its famous blaze. One of the first buildings erected after the fiery mishap was the

Lyman Building, which was a place of business throughout its existence until the Manistee County Historical Society turned it into the only "storefront museum" in the state.

The Lyman Building Museum is not just another county museum displaying local artifacts. The many fixtures, walk-in vault, and wraparound balcony have been preserved, and part of the first floor has been restored as an early drugstore with brass apothecary scales, pill makers, an impressive selection of antique medicines and balms, and fading posters on the walls selling Pe-Ru-Na, which "cures catarrh." The other half of the first floor is set up as a general store, while in the back is an old newspaper office with original Linotype machines. Upstairs are ten more rooms, including a dentist's office, a bank, and the living room of an early 1900s home. The hallway between the rooms is filled with Victor talking machines and Victrolas. The Lyman Building Museum (231–723–5531), at 425 River Street in downtown Manistee, is open year-round from 10:00 A.M. to 5:00 P.M. Monday through Saturday from June through September, and Tuesday through Friday the rest of the year. There is a small admission charge.

thegreatfire of1871

A historical marker in Orchard Beach State Park 2 miles north of Manistee commemorates the Great Fire of 1871. On October 8, the day the famous Chicago fire began, fires also broke out in Michigan after an exceptionally long, hot summer. Most of Holland and Manistee was ruined within hours, with the flames sweeping east across the state and eventually reaching Port Huron.

Another impressive building left over from the town's golden lumbering era is the ***Ramsdell Theatre,*** built in 1903 by Thomas Jefferson Ramsdell and today listed on the National Register of Historic Places. Ramsdell, a local lawyer and later a state legislator, wanted to add some culture to the rough-and-tumble logging town and built one of the most elaborate opera houses in the state. It featured a double balcony upstairs and private viewing boxes along the main floor. It was proclaimed "acoustically perfect," and famed theatrical artist Walter Burridge painted the main curtain, which is still used today. Other paintings adorn the dome and archways of the lobby.

Local residents saved the theater from demolition in the 1920s, and the city finally purchased the structure in 1943. Today the Manistee Civic Players operates the facility and uses it to stage a summer series of plays. Stop in when the box office is open (a week before each show, Monday through Saturday from noon to 6:00 P.M.) and you can view the interior. Or call (231–723–7188) for a tour of the opera house. The Ramsdell Theatre is at First and Maple Streets.

Places to Stay in the Lake Michigan Area

DOUGLAS

Sherwood Forest Bed & Breakfast,
99 Center Street,
(800) 838–1246

GRAND HAVEN

Fountain Inn,
1010 South Beacon Road,
(800) 745–8660

Harbor House Inn,
114 South Harbor Drive,
(800) 841–0610

LUDINGTON

Pier House,
805 Ludington Avenue,
(800) 968–3677

Viking Arms Inn,
903 East Ludington Avenue,
(231) 843–3441

MANISTEE

Lakeshore Motel,
101 South Lakeshore Drive,
(231) 723–2667

Ramsdell Inn,
399 River Street,
(888) 823–8310

Riverside Motel,
520 Water Street,
(231) 723–3554

NEW BUFFALO

Harbor Grand Hotel,
111 West Water Street,
(888) 605–5900

ONEKAMA

Portage Point Inn,
8567 South Portage Point Drive,
(231) 889–4222

PENTWATER

Nickerson Inn,
262 West Lowell Street,
(800) 742–1288

Pentwater Inn Bed & Breakfast,
180 East Lowell Street,
(231) 869–5909

SAUGATUCK

Maplewood Hotel,
428 Butler Street,
(800) 650–9790

Rosemont Inn,
83 Lakeshore Drive,
(800) 721–2637

Twin Gables Country Inn,
900 Lake Street,
(269) 857–4346

SOUTH HAVEN

Inn at the Park,
233 Dyckman Avenue,
(877) 739–1776

Old Harbor Inn,
515 Williams Street,
(269) 637–8480

Yelton Manor Bed & Breakfast,
140 North Shore Drive,
(269) 637–5220

ST. JOSEPH

Boulevard Hotel,
521 Lake Boulevard,
(800) 875–6600

South Cliff Inn,
1900 Lakeshore Drive,
(269) 983–4881

UNION PIER

Gordan Beach Inn,
16220 Lakeshore Road,
(269) 469–0800

Inn at Union Pier,
9708 Berrien Street,
(269) 469–4700

WHITE CLOUD

The Shack,
2263 West Fourteenth Street,
(231) 924–6683

WHITEHALL

Michillinda Beach Lodge,
5207 Scenic Drive,
(231) 893–1895

Places to Eat in the Lake Michigan Area

BRIDGMAN

Hyerdall's (American),
9673 Red Arrow Highway,
(269) 465–5546

BUCHANAN

B&W Olde Village Inn
(Greek and American),
116 Main Street,
(269) 695–5871

Tabor Hill Winery
(fine dining),
185 Mt. Tabor Hill Road,
(800) 283–3363

GRANT

Grant Depot Restaurant
(American),
22 West Main Street,
(231) 834–7361

HOLLAND

Alpen Rose (Austrian),
4 East Eighth Street,
(616) 393–2111

Piper (American),
2225 South Shore Drive,
(616) 335–5866

Queen's Inn (Dutch),
Dutch Village at US 31
and James Street,
(616) 396–1475

LUDINGTON

Old Hamlin Restaurant
(American),
122 West Ludington Avenue,
(231) 843–4251

P. M. Steamers (American),
502 West Loomis,
(231) 843–9555

MANISTEE

Four Forty West (waterfront
dining),
440 River Street,
(231) 723–7902

MONTAGUE

Dog 'n Suds,
4454 Dowling Street,
(231) 894–4991

NEW BUFFALO

Casey's Bar & Grill,
136 North Whittaker,
(269) 469–5800

PENTWATER

Nickerson Inn (American),
262 West Lowell Street,
(231) 869–6731

SELECTED CHAMBERS OF COMMERCE AND TOURISM BUREAUS

**Holland Area Convention and
Visitors Bureau,**
76 East Eighth Street,
Holland 49423;
(800) 506–1299;
www.holland.org

**Ludington Convention and
Visitors Bureau,**
5300 West US 10,
Ludington 49431;
(877) 420–6618;
www.ludingtoncvb.com

**Manistee Convention and
Visitors Bureau,**
P.O. Box 13,
Manistee 49660;
(877) 626–4783;
www.visitmanistee.com

**Muskegon Convention and
Visitors Bureau,**
610 Western Avenue,
Muskegon 49440;
(800) 250–9283;
www.visitmuskegon.org

**South Haven Convention and
Visitors Bureau,**
415 Phoenix Street,
South Haven 49090;
(800) 764–2836;
www.southhaven.org

**Southwestern Michigan
Tourist Council,**
2300 Pipestone Road,
Benton Harbor 49022;
(269) 925–6301;
www.swmichigan.org

**Spring Lake Area
Convention and Visitors Bureau,**
One South Harbor Drive,
Grand Haven 49417;
(800) 303–4094;
www.grandhavenchamber.org

OTHER ATTRACTIONS

Curious Kids Museum,
St. Joseph

Fernwood Botanic Gardens,
Buchanan

Pearl Mill Museum,
Buchanan

Manistee Fire Hall,
Manistee

**Southwestern Michigan
College Museum,**
Dowagiac

SS *Keewatin* Museum,
Saugatuck

Trillium Ravine,
Niles

SAUGATUCK

Mermaid Grill (seafood),
360 Water Street,
(269) 857–8208

SOUTH HAVEN

The Idler (Cajun),
Old Harbor Village on the
Black River,
(269) 637–8435

Three Pelicans (Caribbean),
38 North Shore Drive,
(269) 637–5123

STEVENSVILLE

Tosi's (Italian),
4337 Ridge Road,
(269) 429–3689

ST. JOSEPH

Clementine's Too
(American),
1235 Broad St.,
(269) 983–0990

Boulevard Bistro
(fine dining),
521 Lake Boulevard,
(269) 983–3882

THREE OAKS

Froehlich's
(bakery and cafe),
26 North Elm Street,
(269) 756–6002

UNION PIER

Miller's Country House
(American),
16409 Red Arrow Highway,
(269) 469–5950

Red Arrow Roadhouse
(American),
15710 Red Arrow Highway,
(269) 469–3939

Northwest Michigan

In many ways Northwest Michigan is a continuation of the region stretching along Lake Michigan. It's accented by vast tracts of dunes, miles of beaches, and a handful of well-developed resort towns whose specialty shops bustle in the summer and winter. But it is also distinctly different.

This is "the land of many little bays," with scenic Grand Traverse Bay dominating the center of the region, Little Traverse Bay farther up the shoreline, and remote Sturgeon Bay at its northern tip. For many tourists this is Mackinaw City, a tour of Fort Michilimackinac, and a ferry ride to Mackinac Island, the summer resort island known throughout the country for its horse-and-carriage transportation and the Grand Hotel.

Most of all, this is Michigan's Cherry Country. Moderate weather from the Great Lakes and light soils help this region produce 80 to 85 percent of the state's total cherry crop. Drive along US 31 from Traverse City to Charlevoix in spring, and you'll pass rolling hills of trees in full bloom and air scented by cherry blossoms.

Arrive in July and you can enjoy the bountiful harvest these fruit farms produce. Along this 50-mile stretch of road, you'll pass dozens of farms and will undoubtedly see harvesting crews

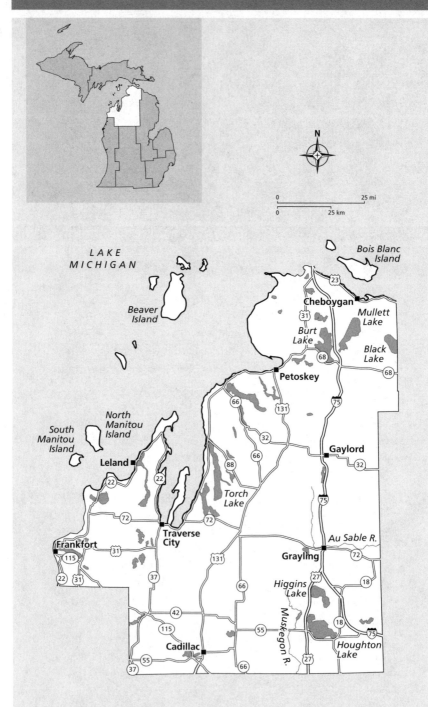

"shaking" one tree after another, with the cherries ending up in a large metal tank of water.

You'll also see numerous roadside fruit stands that will be hard to pass up, and you shouldn't even try. The most common sweet cherries sold are Bing and Schmidt; tourists often call them black cherries, though if they are, the fruit is overripe. Look for cherries that are firm and dark maroon, and be prepared when you bite into your first one. The juice will explode from the cherry, dribble down your chin, and send your taste buds into a state of ecstasy. There are few things as wonderful in this state as a northern Michigan cherry in July.

Benzie County

One of the smallest counties in the state, Benzie is also one of the most scenic. It features rolling forested hills, spring-fed trout streams, towering sandy bluffs, and endless beaches along Lake Michigan and Crystal Lake, a body of water whose clarity lives up to its name. In the natural beauty of this north woods setting, Gwen Frostic emerged as one of Michigan's most noted poets and publishers from her background as an artist and a conservationist. Her love of nature has always been with her, but she began writing and carving blocks for prints in the mid-1940s in the blue-collar community of Wyandotte, south of Detroit.

AUTHOR'S TOP TEN PICKS

Avalanche Peak,
Boyne City;
(231) 582–6222

Beaver Island,
Charlevoix;
(888) 446–4095

Dennos Museum Center,
Traverse City;
(231) 995–1055

Grass River Natural Area,
Bellaire;
(231) 533–8576

Gwen Frostic Prints,
Frankfort;
(231) 882–5505

Michigan Forest Visitor Center,
Hartwick Pines State Park;
(989) 348–7068

Mill Creek Historical State Park,
Mackinaw City;
(231) 436–7301

Pierce Stocking Scenic Drive,
Empire;
(231) 326–5134

South Manitou Island,
Leland;
(231) 256–9061

Tunnel of Trees Drive and Legs Inn,
Cross Village;
(231) 526–2281

In the early 1960s she moved to a wooded spot 2 miles west of Benzonia and set up *Gwen Frostic Prints* on a personal wildlife sanctuary of 285 acres.

Her large gallery is housed in a building of native stone, glass, and old wood, which seeks to "bring the outdoors in" while blending into the natural surroundings. She accomplished that surprisingly well. Inside you'll walk below rough-cut beams past huge stone fireplaces and view the tumbling water of natural fountains. You'll be surrounded by Frostic's woodblock prints, tables covered with books of her poetry, and bird carvings by some of the country's leading wildlife carvers. There is a small library overlooking a pond where waterfowl usually are feeding, and another room displays all the honors she has received, including a Michigan governor's proclamation of an official "Gwen Frostic Day."

funfacts

In 1873 a canal was built to Lake Michigan that drained the water out of inland Crystal Lake. The level of Crystal Lake dropped 25 feet, creating the beautiful beaches that make it such a popular resort area today. The canal, on the other hand, eventually became a swamp.

Most impressive, perhaps, is the publishing aspect of the gallery. From a balcony above, visitors can view fifteen original Heidelberg presses clanking away as workers print a wide selection of cards, notepaper, wall prints, and books, all using block designs carved by Frostic, featuring natural subjects and sold in the gallery.

Gwen Frostic Prints (231–882–5505) is at 5140 River Road, 2 miles west of US 31 and 6 miles east of M 22 in Frankfort. The gallery is open from 9:00 A.M. to 4:30 P.M. daily from May through September and Monday through Saturday the rest of the year. The presses are in operation only Monday through Friday.

Back in the 1930s a small group of Frankfort residents discovered the thrill of soaring in gliders. They would take off from the high bluffs overlooking Lake Michigan and fly through the air, sometimes for hours, before landing on the beach. What emerged was the *Northwest Soaring Club of Frankfort*, which at one time hosted a national soaring championship in this small town.

The art of soaring has changed over the years, but the club is still around, offering lessons and, for visitors passing through on vacation, introductory rides. Passengers join a certified pilot in a two-seat glider 25 to 35 feet long, with a wingspan of about 50 feet. The glider is towed to a height of 2,000 to 3,000 feet by a small plane and then released. What follows is a spectacular ride along the Lake Michigan shoreline with extensive views of the lake, sand dunes, and beautiful Crystal Lake. The length of the ride depends on the wind and thermal conditions, but it ranges from thirty minutes to sometimes several hours.

Introductory rides are offered from May through October and cost $50 per person for a 2,000-foot tow and $60 for a 3,000-foot tow. The higher the tow, the longer the flight. Interested persons should call ahead to the Northwest Soaring Club at (231) 352–9160. Club rides take off from Frankfort Airport, located on Airport Road south of M 115.

Of all the dunes along Lake Michigan, the best known are those in **Sleeping Bear National Lakeshore,** administered by the National Park Service. Thousands of people visit the area every year, and many head straight to the **"Dune Climb,"** a 150-foot-steep hill of sand located right off M 109 in Leelanau County. This is the park's most famous feature, a knee-bending climb up the towering dune and a wild run down through the soft sand. In addition, there are other aspects of the park, many having nothing to do with dunes and often overlooked by visitors who rush through the area in an afternoon.

The national lakeshore begins in Benzie County and includes one of the most scenic beaches on Lake Michigan. **Platte River Point** is a long, sandy spit divided from the mainland by the crystal clear Platte River. It's pure sand, this narrow strip, with endless Lake Michigan on one side, the knee-deep salmon and trout river on the other, and panoramas of towering dunes off in the distance. To reach it, sunbathers turn west from M 22 onto the marked Lake Michigan Road and follow it to the end. Then it's a quick wade through the rippling waters of the Platte River with Dad holding a young one or the picnic lunch high on his shoulder. There is no bridge.

People at Platte River Point swim, build sand castles, and beachcomb as on any other beach, but the favorite activity here is floating. They bring out an old inner tube or an air mattress, hike a few hundred yards up the point, and then let

funfacts

Michigan has a total of 275,000 acres of sand dune formations on three Great Lakes, with almost half of them in public ownership.

the Platte River give them a free ride right out to Lake Michigan if they wish. It's debatable who enjoys it more, the kids or the parents. If you don't have an inner tube, you can rent one from **Riverside Canoe Trips** (231–325–5622) located on M 22 right before you turn off for the beach. Tubes for one to four people can be rented, and there are drop-off and pickup services for those who want to spend an afternoon "tubing" the Platte River from the Platte Lake to the Great Lake. Rental rates depend on the length of your float and the size of your tube.

The sign out front says all you need to know about the **Homestead Sugar House.** It's attached to a wooden scaffold just below a large noose, and reads HANG THE DIET! Don't even think about "that four-letter word" when you stumble

Best Cherry Pie in Northern Michigan

A sure way to start an argument in northern Michigan is to ask who bakes the best cherry pie in this land of cherries. You're bound to get a wide range of opinions, and one of them will surely be the Cherry Hut.

Located in Beulah, right on US 31, the *Cherry Hut Restaurant* has been around since 1922 and has been run by the Case family since 1959. Locals know it's a good place to go for turkey dinners or giant cinnamon rolls.

But it's a thick slice of cherry pie, made with locally grown tart cherries and wrapped in a golden flaky crust, that is the Cherry Hut's claim to fame and why the readers of AAA's Michigan Living magazine voted it the best in the state.

The Cherry Hut (231–882–4431) is open from Memorial Day weekend through October from 10:00 A.M. to 10:00 P.M., serving lunch and dinner. During the summer the restaurant also serves breakfast and opens at 7:30 A.M. A slice of cherry pie is $2.75, and a whole pie is $5.95.

Might as well buy a whole pie—they're that good.

upon the maple bush (a farm on which sugar maples grow) of Jean and Russell Morstadt, home of Benzie County's oldest candy-making shop. Don't worry about counting calories or losing that 2-inch pinch at the waist. Just enjoy the aroma that greets you as soon as you pull in; let your eyes feast on the hand-dipped, long-stemmed chocolate cherries and maple creams displayed in the glass case inside; and when Jean Morstadt, dressed in a Grandma Moses style, offers you something sweet, don't be bashful.

The Morstadts were living in Chicago in 1948 when they decided they had had enough of city life, and they moved to northern Michigan. They bought a 300-acre maple bush in the rolling hills east of Beulah and began farming. After years of "harvesting nothing but bills," the couple began making candy in the shack outside their home in 1963. They are approaching their fortieth anniversary as candy makers, and among their loyal customers is singer Linda Ronstadt.

From US 31 turn onto Homestead Road in downtown Benzonia and head east for 4.5 miles to the farm with a scaffold outside. The shop (231–882–7712) is open from 9:00 A.M. to 4:30 P.M. daily from May through October.

Leelanau County

For a view of spectacular dune terrain, take a ride along the *Pierce Stocking Scenic Drive* at Sleeping Bear National Lakeshore. Often called "the slowest, shortest, but most scenic stretch of pavement in the state," the drive is only a

7.4-mile loop but passes three stunning overlooks of the national lakeshore's perched dunes. Pierce Stocking, the self-taught naturalist who built the road in the early 1960s and operated it until his death in 1976, charged each car $2.00. The next year the National Park Service took over the road and changed its name to honor the man who'd built it.

The speed limit is only 15 miles per hour, but even that seems fast at times. Along with the scenic viewing points of the dunes and the sweeping shoreline, there are also twelve interpretive stops that correspond with information in a brochure provided at the fee station. From the Dune Overlook you can also walk the Cottonwood Trail, a short nature trail that leads you to within view of the Dune Climb. Feel energetic? There is also a bicycle lane along the road, but keep in mind that it's a very hilly bike ride. Above all, pack a lunch and plan to picnic at the Lake Michigan Overlook.

The entrance to Pierce Stocking Scenic Drive is on M 109, 3 miles north of the Sleeping Bear National Lakeshore visitor center (231–326–5134) in Empire. A weekly or annual vehicle pass is required to enter the drive.

The dunes are one of the main attractions of the area today. At the turn of the twentieth century, however, the noted feature was the Manitou Passage,

TOP ANNUAL EVENTS

Winter Fest,
Gaylord, February;
(800) 345–8621

North American Snowmobile Festival,
Cadillac, February;
(800) 225–2537

Mesick Mushroom Festival,
Mesick, May;
(231) 885–2679

**National Morel Mushroom
Hunting Festival,**
Boyne City, May;
(231) 582–6222

**Au Sable River Canoe
Marathon and River Festival,**
Grayling, July;
(800) 937–8837

National Cherry Festival,
Traverse City, July;
(231) 947–4230

Venetian Festival,
Charlevoix, July;
(800) 367–8557

Buckley Old Engine Show,
Buckley, August;
(231) 269–3750

Harbor Days,
Elk Rapids, August;
(231) 264–8202

Suttons Bay Art Fair,
Suttons Bay, August;
(231) 271–3050

Harbor Springs Cycling Classic,
Harbor Springs, September;
(800) 530–9955

between the Manitou Islands and the mainland. During the heyday of Great Lakes shipping from the 1860s to 1920, when a hundred vessels might pass through on a single day, this was a shoal-lined shortcut they all took. The narrow Manitou Passage's shallow, reeflike shoals, and often violent weather produced more than their share of shipwrecks, and eventually several lighthouses and lifesaving stations were built on the mainland and the islands.

One of them has been preserved by the National Park Service as **_Sleeping Bear Point Coast Guard Station Maritime Museum._** The facility began its service in 1901 as a U.S. Life-Saving Station and was actually situated on Sleeping Bear Point. When a migrating sand dune threatened to bury it in 1930, the U.S. Coast Guard (having replaced the U.S. Life-Saving Service) moved the buildings 1.5 miles toward Glen Haven. The station ended its duty in 1942 and now is a well-restored museum that tells the story of the U.S. Life-Saving Service, which monitored the coastline all around the country.

funfacts

The Dune Climb in Sleeping Bear National Lakeshore is the most popular dune to climb in Michigan and possibly the country. Park officials estimate that more than 300,000 people climb it annually.

Anywhere from six to ten men would live at the remote station, and their former living quarters, a huge two-story building, is now the main exhibit area. It allows visitors a glimpse of the regimented work they performed and the isolated life they lived. Nearby the boathouse contains the lifesaving boats, complete with tracks down to the beach for a quick launch, and other equipment, including the beachcart. When ships ran aground within 400 yards of shore, the lifesavers would pull out the beachcart and use the small cannon on it to shoot a guideline to the distressed vessel. That rope was used to string more lines across the water, and a breeches buoy was sent to the ship on a pulley. Then, one by one, sailors would step into the buoy's breeches and ride the line to the shore and safety.

The museum is open daily from 10:30 A.M. to 5:00 P.M. from Memorial Day to Labor Day. A vehicle permit is required to enter. Check with the park headquarters (231–326–5134) in Empire for time and day of the museum's "Heroes of the Storm" program, in which rangers demonstrate a turn-of-the-twentieth century shipwreck rescue using the beachcart, the breeches buoy, and volunteers from the audience who fill in for sailors and lifesavers. Only the cannon is missing.

The village of Leland's trademark is a row of weathered dockside shacks along the Leland River that at one time housed commercial fishermen and today is a historic district known as Fishtown. All the commercial fishermen except Carlson Fisheries have disappeared from the strip, but their buildings have been preserved and now house specialty shops and stores. With its unique setting and atmosphere, Fishtown is the proper place to begin a nautical adventure to **South Manitou Island,** a portion of the Sleeping Bear National Lakeshore located 17 miles from Leland in Lake Michigan.

Island visitors board a ferry at the end of Fishtown and begin with a ninety-minute cruise to South Manitou that passes a lighthouse and the scenic shoreline of Sleeping Bear Dunes. The island, with its hardwood forests and natural harbor, attracted settlers, a lighthouse, and a lifesaving station as early as 1840, and it has an interesting history. The ferry has a four-hour layover at the national park dock, more than enough time to view the small museum at the visitor center, climb the 116 steps to the top of the lighthouse, and enjoy a lunch on a nearby beach.

For the more energetic, there are trails and old farm roads across the island, and it's possible to hike the 6-mile round-trip to the **Francisco Morazan** and return to the mainland the same day. The *Morazan* was a Liberian freighter that ran aground in November 1960 at the southwest corner of the island, and a large portion of the battered vessel is still visible above the waterline today. For the best adventure on South Manitou, camp for a night or two at Weather Station Campground, a national park facility that is free. The campground is a 1.5-mile hike in from the dock, and you can explore the tract of sand dunes on the west side of the island. The dunes, perched on bluffs high above Lake Michigan, are probably the most remote and least visited ones in the state.

Leelanau Cheese

From the humble beginnings of a converted gas station in Omena comes Michigan's most honored cheesemakers, Anne and John Hoyt of Leelanau Cheese. The couple began producing handcrafted wedges of raclette cheese and containers of fromage blanc in the former gas station in 1995 after learning the cheese-making trade in Switzerland. Raclette is a semihard Swiss melting cheese made from whole cow's milk, with each eight-pound wheel aging ninety days before it is sold.

Eventually the couple was honored as the state's top cheesemakers four out of five years at the Michigan State Fair as well as winning many national honors at cheese competitions throughout the country. In 2000 they moved their operation to Blackstar Farms, an elegant inn and vineyard at 10844 East Revold Road near Sutton's Bay. At the farms you can go horseback riding, sip locally produced wines or watch the Hoyts make their cheese and taste samples. You can even spend the night, as the inn has eight guest rooms that are $200 to $350 a night. For reservations contact Blackstar Farms at (231) 271–4970 or www.blackstarfarms.com.

All visitors must bring their own food to South Manitou, and campers have to be self-sufficient with tent, sleeping bags, and other equipment. Contact Manitou Island Transit (231–256–9061; www.leelanau.com/manitou) about the ferry that sails to the island daily from June through August. The round-trip fare is $25 for adults and $14 for children twelve and under.

The growing conditions in southwest Michigan that made Paw Paw the wine-producing center of the state are also found in Leelanau and Old Missionary, two peninsulas filled with fruit farms and a half dozen vineyards of surprising quality. All the vineyards have a tasting room, and an interesting day can be had visiting each of them. The first bonded wine cellar in the area—and many think the most beautiful one in the state—is **Boskydel Vineyard,** a small winery on the shores of Lake Leelanau. There is no restaurant at Boskydel or even any picnic tables outside, but it is built on the side of a hill, and from the parking lot you have a view of the sloping vineyard leading down to the huge lake, framed by the rolling hills of the Leelanau Peninsula. All this prompted one wine critic to proclaim Boskydel the most beautiful site for a winery in the country.

It was within the family tradition that Bernie Rinke should plant a vineyard. He grew up on an Ohio farm, and his father bootlegged wine during Prohibition. Rinke began planting his vineyard in 1964 and now cultivates twenty-five acres of grapes, producing 6,000 gallons (2,500 cases) annually of several dry and semidry red and white table wines. The tasting room is open daily year-round from 1:00 to 6:00 P.M., and if you want a tour of the winery, Rinke will lead you through a ten-minute look at his facility.

Actually, Rinke would rather stay in the small tasting room, plop a large wineglass in front of you (no plastic cups here), and talk—about his grapes, about wine tasting, about his days as Northwestern Michigan College's first librarian in nearby Traverse City. (Ask him where the name of the winery comes from.) A beautiful vineyard, a most delightful wine maker, and not a bad wine either, Boskydel (231–256–7272) is 3.5 miles southeast of the town of Lake Leelanau at County Road 641 and Otto Road.

At the tip of the Leelanau Peninsula is the 1,350-acre Leelanau State Park. From this park you can enjoy spectacular views along miles of lakeshore, from platforms on top of dunes, and even from the tower of a lighthouse. In addition to a campground, picnic area, and hiking trails, the park also includes the historic **Grand Traverse Lighthouse.**

Built in 1916, the Grand Traverse Lighthouse is the most recent light in a series of lighthouses that have guided ships around the peninsula since 1852. Today it is an interesting maritime museum where visitors can tour the first

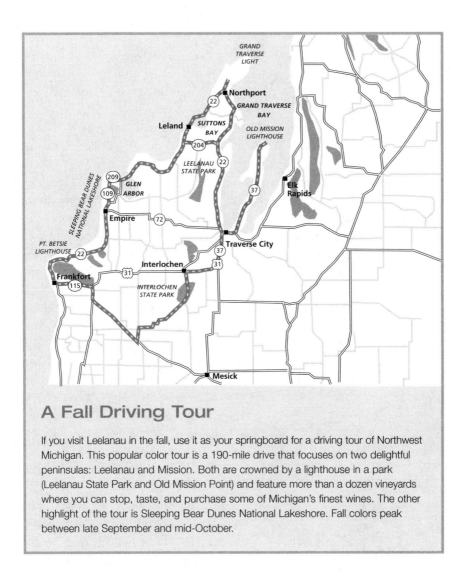

A Fall Driving Tour

If you visit Leelanau in the fall, use it as your springboard for a driving tour of Northwest Michigan. This popular color tour is a 190-mile drive that focuses on two delightful peninsulas: Leelanau and Mission. Both are crowned by a lighthouse in a park (Leelanau State Park and Old Mission Point) and feature more than a dozen vineyards where you can stop, taste, and purchase some of Michigan's finest wines. The other highlight of the tour is Sleeping Bear Dunes National Lakeshore. Fall colors peak between late September and mid-October.

floor, which has been restored as a lightkeeper's home of the 1920s, and then climb the tower for a grand view of Lake Michigan. The foghorn building next door has also been restored and is now a gift shop with a maritime theme.

Leelanau State Park is located 8 miles north of Northport on County Road 629. The Grand Traverse Lighthouse (231–386–7195) is open from 10:00 A.M. to 7:00 P.M. daily in May, September, and October, and from 10:00 A.M. to 7:00 P.M. daily the rest of the summer. A vehicle permit is required to enter the state park, and there is a small admission fee for the lighthouse.

Grand Traverse County

The most noted feature of the county is Grand Traverse Bay, a beautiful body of water with Traverse City at the south end and old Mission Peninsula splitting it up the middle. Its protected waters have become a haven for sailboats, catamarans, and sailboarders, but by far the most impressive vessel afloat during the summer is the **Manitou,** a replica of a two-masted, gaff-rigged, topsail 1800s coasting cargo ship. The 114-foot, 100-ton ship was built in 1983 to look and sail like a traditional schooner, and it's that love for old wooden boats that draws most of its passengers on deck. From May through September the *Manitou* offers three sailings daily, with two-hour cruises at noon and 3:00 P.M. and a two-and-a-half-hour evening sail with picnic meal—the most popular trip, of course—at 6:30 P.M. Passengers who dream about a life on the high seas go a step further and book a cabin on the *Manitou,* which at night becomes Michigan's only floating bed-and-breakfast. The quarters are tiny, with bunks built into the curves and angles of the hull. The head (bathroom) is shared, and the showers are back on land. In the evening guests wander topside to take in Traverse City lights shimmering on the bay or snuggle up in their bunks to be put to sleep by the gentle swells and the creaking of the wooden hull.

The *Manitou* is operated by the Traverse Tall Ship Company (800–678–0383). Its office and dock are at 13390 Southwest Bay Shore Drive. Daily cruises range from $32 to $39 for adults, and overnight accommodations, which include a hearty breakfast with the crew in the galley, range from $105 for singles to $184 for doubles.

You can also enjoy the water from above through ***Grand Traverse Balloon,*** which offers hot-air balloon rides across Grand Traverse Bay, often beginning at the Château Grand Traverse vineyards on Old Mission Peninsula. This may well be the most spectacular view from any hot-air balloon in Michigan, as below you lies the narrow peninsula, the rippling waters of the bay, Traverse City, and the endless rows of the cherry orchards to the northeast. The entire flight takes three hours, with an hour in the air, and flights are always at sunrise or sunset because there's

The *Manitou*

less wind turbulence. They are priced at $195 per person. Jeff Geiger, the Traverse City balloonist who runs Grand Traverse Balloon (231–947–7433), recommends reservations but says he can usually fulfill last-minute urges to float above the bay.

For another unusual view of the bay, head to the highest ridge on the Mission Peninsula just before sunset. At this high point Robert Begin has built the state's newest vineyard, **Château Chantal,** and included a brick terrace that overlooks both the West Arm and East Arm of Grand Traverse Bay. With vineyards and cherry orchards at your feet, you settle back with a glass of Chardonnay or a semidry Riesling and some sharp cheeses or freshly cut fruit and watch the sky melt into a collage of oranges and reds over the bays of northern Michigan.

Begin, a former priest, and his wife have built the unique winery on a former ridgetop cherry farm and named it after their daughter. You can stop by for a tour or a sip in the vineyard's wine-tasting and sales area, a great room that features hardwood floors, a polished granite bar top, and a grand piano in front of a 20-foot-wide bay window overlooking Grand Traverse Bay. Or you can simply stop for the night and unwind. That's because this winery is also a bed-and-breakfast, featuring three rooms with sitting areas and private baths.

Château Chantal (231–223–4110) is located just off M 37 on Mission Peninsula, 12 miles north of Traverse City. Tours are offered daily during summer at 1:00, 2:00, and 3:00 P.M. The tasting room is open year-round from 11:00 A.M. to 8:00 P.M. Monday through Saturday and noon to 5:00 P.M. Sunday. Rooms range from $135 to $185 per night.

One of Michigan's newest art museums is no stuffy gallery with ancient masterpieces in gilded frames. Located on the campus of Northwestern Michigan College, the **Dennos Museum Center** opened in 1991 after more than a decade in the planning.

The jewel of the museum is its permanent Inuit Art Gallery, a collection that began in 1960 and was housed in the college library. Today there are 550

a "chew-chew" train

Romance, adventure, and fine dining are all available with a trip on the Grand Traverse Dinner Train. The restored 1950s dining cars are used for a five-course gourmet dinner served during a three-hour ride along the Boardman River and deep into the Père Marquette State Forest. Entrees range from garlic prime rib to northern Michigan trout with peach salsa.

The trains depart from a depot at 642 Railroad Place in downtown Traverse City and run year-round, with the schedule depending on the season. Dinner is $75 per person. For reservations call Grand Traverse Dinner Train at (231) 933–3768.

pieces of sculptured soapstone and colorful prints depicting the harsh life and fascinating culture of these Arctic people. Carvings and prints depict hunters pulling a walrus out of the ice with a rope, kayaking through the open seas, bedding down in an igloo, and waiting patiently at a breathing hole in the frozen Arctic Ocean for a seal to surface.

But families and kids usually head for the Discovery Gallery, which combines art, science, and technology into an intriguing set of hands-on displays. One of the exhibits is the *Recollections Piece.* With the use of video cameras and computer-generated images, visitors can watch themselves "come alive in color" as they move in front of a room-size screen. The museum staff calls it "painting with your body."

From downtown Traverse City head north on US 31 to the Northwestern Michigan College campus. Dennos Museum Center (231–922–1055) is on the small campus. The center is open Monday through Saturday from 10:00 A.M. to 5:00 P.M. and Sunday from 1:00 to 5:00 P.M. There is a small admission fee.

If you're traveling just north of Traverse City on US 31 and pass a place called the ***Music House,*** turn off the car stereo. Strip the headphones and Walkmans from your kids' ears and toss that huge boom box in the trunk. Then turn around and see how music used to be enjoyed. Housed in an old granary built in 1905, The Music House is a showcase for automatic musical instruments from the 1880s to the 1920s. Visitors are entertained rather than educated, as the hourlong tour is a musical journey with toe-tapping demonstrations ranging from small music boxes to one of the largest ballroom dance organs ever made.

Tours begin in the phonograph gallery, where a huge model of Nipper, the famous RCA Victor dog, greets you. There are rows of "talking machines"

A Singer Named Jewel

In the mid-1990s, regulars at Ray's Coffeehouse in Traverse City remember, they would hear a young singer with a distinctly sweet and high voice. By 1997 they knew her well, though she had been gone for years. Her name—the only name she goes by—was Jewel. Jewel was a student at the Interlochen Fine Arts Camp that summer and playing for tips in local coffeehouses. In time she would become one of the hottest singers on the pop music scene.

You can catch other possible future stars at the internationally acclaimed music camp that overlooks Green Lake near the town of Interlochen. The camp hosts more than 750 performances each year by faculty members, students, and big-name entertainers, with many of them taking place in its open-air pavilion overlooking Green Lake. For ticket information call (800) 681-5920.

beginning from 1900 with their wax cylinders instead of records and colorful morning glory horns instead of speakers. In the main portion of the barn are larger musical machines set up in the environments in which they were enjoyed. The most impressive sight for many visitors is upstairs in the loft, which is home to the 30-foot facade of the Amaryllis dance organ. Built in 1922 for a palace ballroom in Belgium, the instrument plays a folded perforated cardboard book using hundreds of wooden and metal pipes along with percussion instruments.

The Music House (231–938–9300) is located on a 180-acre cherry farm off US 31, 1.5 miles north of the highway's junction with M 72 or 8 miles north of Traverse City. It is open daily from "cherry blossoms through fall colors," or, to be more exact, May 1 through October 30, 10:00 A.M. to 4:00 P.M. Monday through Saturday and noon to 4:00 P.M. Sunday. From mid-November through December, it is open Friday through Sunday. Admission is $8.00 for adults and $2.50 for children.

Continue north on US 31 for a few more miles and you'll come to **Amon Orchards,** offering guided tours and the best view of a working cherry farm. Visitors ride in an open tractor trolley, and in July you can watch workers mechanically harvest cherries and even pick a few of your own. Tours at Amon Orchards (231–938–1644) in July are offered at 10:00 A.M. and 2:00 P.M. daily. There is a $5.00 fee for the ninety-minute tour.

Antrim County

Speeding along US 131 in the middle of Antrim County, you pass one of the most spectacular inland viewing points in the Lower Peninsula, though you would never know it from this road. The side road to **Deadman's Hill** is 7 miles north of Mancelona, but there is little fanfare about the scenic overlook: Only a small brown sign points the way. Follow Deadman's Hill Road for 1.5 miles until it dead-ends at a pair of Department of Natural Resources pit toilets and a wood-chip path. Some 15 yards up the path is a spectacular panorama from a high point of more than 1,200 feet. You take in a 180-degree view of the Jordan River valley stretching 15 miles to rugged hills that fill the horizon. During October the view from this spot is priceless, as the entire valley with the river winding through it is on fire with autumn reds and oranges.

Deadman's Hill earned its name from the logging era at the turn of the twentieth century. The steep hills made the Jordan River valley a treacherous place to log, and numerous accidents occurred. But people grieved the most in 1910 when "Big Sam" Graczyk, twenty-one years old and soon to be married, was killed while driving a team of horses and a big wheel of logs. The name for the ridge stuck. You can admire the view and have a picnic while sitting on the edge, and the more adventurous can hike the Jordan River Pathway, which begins at this point. Part of the trail is a 3-mile loop down to the river and back, or it can be turned into an 18-mile overnight walk to a hike-in campground for backpackers.

Where there is a boardwalk or similar planking along a trail, there is usually a swamp, marsh, or bog surrounding it. At the **Grass River Natural Area,** there are an awful lot of boardwalks. Some trails are nothing but boardwalks, because a good slice of this 1,037-acre Antrim County park is sedge meadow, marsh, and cedar swamp.

Grass River itself is only 2.5 miles long and just chest deep. It's a crystal clear waterway that connects Lake Bellaire to Clam Lake as part of Antrim County's "Chain of Lakes." But the extensive floating sedge mats and other wetlands that surround the river are so intriguing that they prompted a fundraising effort to buy the land and dedicate it as a natural area in 1976.

They've been building boardwalks ever since. Along with an interpretive center, which features several rooms of displays and a small bookstore, Grass River has a 5-mile trail system that is marked with interpretive posts and winds through a variety of habitats.

The Woodland/Wildfire Trail is the longest at 2.2 miles; the quarter-mile Tamarack Trail is designed to be accessible for people with disabilities. But to many the Sedge Meadow Trail is the most enjoyable. It's one long boardwalk—almost every step of it is on wood—that passes through a variety of wetlands where plants have been identified and numbered posts correspond with information in a trail guide. Eventually the trail emerges at the edge of Grass Lake where observation platforms and towers have been built on the boardwalk along with a series of benches.

From US 131 in Mancelona, head west on M 88 toward Bellaire and within 2 miles continue on Alden Highway (County Road 618). The entrance road to Grass River Natural Area (231–533–8314) is off CR 618 before you reach Alden. The trails are open from dawn to dusk. The interpretive center is open daily from 9:00 A.M. to 5:00 P.M. June through August.

Charlevoix County

South of Charlevoix off US 31 is yet another state park along Lake Michigan. **Fisherman's Island State Park** possesses many of the same features as the other parks: 3 miles of sandy shoreline, excellent swimming areas, scenic views of the Great Lake. But Fisherman's Island also has a couple of unique features.

Not nearly as popular or crowded as some other locales, the park offers fifteen rustic campsites right on Lake Michigan. Each one is tucked away in the trees with a table and a spot to pitch a tent only a few feet from the lapping waters of the lake. These are some of the most beautiful campsites in the Lower Peninsula, and naturally they are the first to be chosen in the campground. Be prepared to camp at an inland site the first night and then claim a lakeside one first thing the next morning.

The other noted feature of the state park is the **Petoskey stones.** The state stone is actually petrified coral, a leftover fragment of the many coral reefs that existed in the warm-water seas from Charlevoix to Alpena some 300 million years ago. Today the stones are collected by rock hounds, and many of them end up polished and used in jewelry, paperweights, and other decorative items. Dry stones are silvery with no apparent markings to the untrained eye, but when the rocks are wet, it's easy to see the ringlike pattern that covers them. Rock hounds searching for the stones are usually seen closely inspecting the waterline or washing off handfuls of rocks in the lake.

The 2.5-mile park road begins at the ranger station and ends at the sandy beaches of the state park but along the way passes an extended rocky shoreline. Many gem enthusiasts say this is one of the best places in northern Michigan to find Petoskey stones. Stop at the ranger station for a park map and information on the famous stones. There is a vehicle fee to enter Fisherman's Island State Park (231–547–6641) and an additional charge to camp overnight.

The Great Lakes, which have blessed Michigan with miles of magnificent shoreline, also have given it many islands that have become unique destinations for visitors. The most popular is Mackinac Island, a nonmotorized resort (no cars or buses) that tourists flock to each summer, taking ferries out of Mackinaw City on the Lower Peninsula or St. Ignace across the Mackinac Bridge on the Upper Peninsula. There are also many islands without the crowds, commercialization, and fudge shops of Mackinac that make for an interesting side trip. One of the largest is **Beaver Island,** reached by a ferry from Charlevoix.

Known as Emerald Isle for its strong Irish heritage, Beaver Island lies 32 miles northwest of Charlevoix and is fifty-five square miles of forests, inland lakes, and farms. Its recorded history dates to 1832, when Bishop Frederic Baraga, the "Snowshoe Priest," brought Christianity to a small Indian settlement here. The island's most bizarre period began in 1847 after James Jesse Strang arrived. Strang and his band of Mormon followers had just broken away from the leadership of Brigham Young and established St. James, the island's only village. Eventually Strang would crown himself "king of Beaver Island" and rule the island and its religious sect with an iron hand before being shot in

The Escape from Rush-Hour Madness

Rumbling along in his Suburban on Beaver Island, Keith Pintler slowed down when he approached East Side Drive, glanced up the dirt road for oncoming traffic, and then resumed his 30-mile-an-hour speed.

"I don't know why I bother to look," said the president of the Beaver Island Chamber of Commerce. "In nine years of living here, I've never seen anybody come that way. Never, ever."

Peaceful, tranquil, trafficless Beaver Island, the true escape from the rush-hour madness of mainland Michigan.

If you've ever visited this 37,385-acre island in the summer and liked the slow pace of life, you'll be enchanted with it in the fall. After Labor Day most of the 3,000 people who maintain summer cottages on the island are gone. So are their cars. So are the majority of the 30,000 visitors who step ashore at St. James annually.

What you'll find on the island in September and October are 488 year-round residents, stunning fall colors, and more than 50 miles of beaches where the only footprints in the sand are yours.

Sure, most of the shops and a few of the restaurants will be closed, but what price tranquillity?

1856 by a disgruntled subject. Irish immigrants followed in the 1870s to fish the waters of northern Lake Michigan, and today many of the 350 people who live year-round in or near St. James have roots back in Ireland.

Beaver Island has an assortment of lodge and hotel accommodations and restaurants for overnight visitors, but on Saturdays in July and August, it also makes an ideal day trip. You can depart from Charlevoix at 8:30 A.M. on the ferry and reach the island by 10:30 A.M. for a six-hour visit before catching the last ferry back to the mainland at 5:30 P.M. In St. James there are several museums, including the **Old Mormon Print Shop** (231–448–2254, which was built by King Strang in 1850, and the **Marine and Harbor Museum,** a 1906 net shed dedicated to the time when the area bustled with fishermen.

The museums are open from June through August. Hours are 11:00 A.M. to 5:00 P.M. Monday through Saturday and noon to 3:00 P.M. Sunday. There is a small admission charge.

Another interesting attraction in St. James is the **Toy Museum and Store** (231–448–2480). Once known as "the last nickel toy store in the U.S.," the Toy Museum is still affordable to anybody on a weekly allowance: Chinese fans three for a dollar, a disappearing dagger for 75 cents, and green army men at a nickel apiece. Suspended from the high-peaked ceiling is the "museum," an interesting collection of antique toys that range from foot-pedal Roadsters and "rocket cars" from the 1930s to clay marbles and dolls that predate the 1900s.

You can also rent a mountain bike or a Jeep and tour the island, which has more than 100 miles of roads, most of them dirt and gravel. On a pleasant summer day, this is a most delightful adventure and a great way to see the old farmhouses, inland lakes, remote shoreline, and lighthouse located outside St. James. Pack a picnic lunch and plan on driving three to four hours to circle Beaver Island.

The Beaver Island Boat Co. (888–446–4095) operates the ferry and charges $31 for a round-trip adult ticket. You can rent a vehicle for $55 a day from Gordon's Auto Clinic (231–448–2438) or a mountain bike from Lakesports Rentals (231–448–2166). For a complete list of island businesses, lodging, and sites, contact the Beaver Island Chamber of Commerce, P.O. Box 5, Beaver Island, St. James 49781, (231) 448–2505 or check out the Web site www.beaverisland.net.

A number of writers have ties to Northwest Michigan but none as famous as Ernest Hemingway, who spent the summers of his youth at his family's cottage on Walloon Lake. Hemingway buffs often tour the area to see artifacts and places that made their way into his writing. Most begin in Petoskey's Little Traverse Historical Museum (see Emmet County) and then head down US 141 past Walloon Lake. Some go to **Hemingway Point** on the south shore of Lake Charlevoix, to which the young author once fled (it was owned by his uncle) when being pursued by a game warden.

Of course, almost all eventually stop at the **Horton Bay General Store,** located across the lake on Boyne City Road. Built in 1876 with a high false front, the store's most prominent feature is its large front porch with benches and stairs at either end. Hemingway idled away some youthful summers on that porch and fished nearby Horton Creek for rainbow and brook trout. He also celebrated his first marriage in Horton Bay's Congregational Church, and eventually the general store appeared in the opening of his short story "Up in Michigan." The Horton Bay General Store has had a string of owners, but remarkably little has changed about its appearance. It is still the classic general store; only the bright red benches outside receive a new coat of paint every now and then.

You enter through a flimsy screen door with a bell above it, and inside you find the worn wooden floors and shelves stacked with canned goods and other merchandise. There is an old wooden tub filled with ice and cold drinks, a small freezer that holds four or five flavors of ice cream, and the lunch counter where the morning coffee drinkers gather. Then as your eyes wander toward the ceiling, you realize this is more a preserved shrine to Hemingway than a store for the local residents. On one wall hang guns, old traps, mounted deer heads, and a panel of photographs of the author during his days in Northwest

Michigan. Horton Bay General Store is open from 7:00 A.M. to 6:00 P.M. Monday through Thursday, 7:00 A.M. to 8:00 P.M. Friday and Saturday, and 7:00 A.M. to 4:00 P.M. Sunday.

From Horton Bay you can continue around Lake Charlevoix in a scenic drive that will take you past Young State Park, through the historic downtown

An Anniversary on Avalanche Peak

For a quick getaway to celebrate our anniversary, my wife and I spent a weekend near Boyne City, and on Saturday we were blessed with one of those priceless Michigan autumn days. Set against a deep blue sky, the fall colors were more vivid than ever, and on such a clear, crisp afternoon, there is only one thing to do. "Overlooks," I announced.

We stopped at the Boyne City Brewing Company and picked up some sandwiches and a couple of bottles of its Lake Trout Stout. From there we drove to Avalanche Peak, a city park at the end of Lake Street, threw the lunch in a daypack, and began hiking toward the base of this towering hill.

I don't think there's ever been an avalanche in Boyne City, but the hill is incredibly steep—so steep that in the 1950s, it was a downhill ski area with rope tows and even a chairlift. We had only reached the steps for the climb up when my wife said, "Okay, I'm tired, let's eat lunch."

"Um, honey, we have to climb to the top."

"Why?"

I turned to her and said what I'd been waiting to say to somebody my entire life: "Because it's there." After a long pause, I added, "Besides, the view is nicer from the top."

Some 200 steps up I heard a familiar voice from behind say, "That view better be good." Another 100 steps and I had to retreat and use a chocolate chip cookie to coax her off a bench. At 400 steps I was sure that on the fifteenth anniversary of my marriage, I was headed for a divorce.

Finally, after 473 steps, we arrived at the top, where the city has thoughtfully built an observation deck with several benches. There isn't a better view below the Mackinac Bridge than what greets you from the top of Avalanche Peak. At your feet is Boyne City, while stretching out to the west is Lake Charlevoix dotted with sailboats.

We plopped down on a grassy knoll behind the observation deck and for more than an hour enjoyed our lunch while soaking in that view. Finally I said, in a romantic sort of way, "Think we should come back here for our twenty-fifth anniversary?"

"Only if they put back that chairlift."

You gotta love her.

area of Boyne City, and near Hemingway Point, where Ferry Road abruptly ends at the South Arm of the lake. If you want to continue, you have to take passage on the *Ironton Ferry,* one of Michigan's most delightful boat rides, even though it's only five minutes long.

Ferry service on the South Arm dates back to 1876, when the first barge was pulled back and forth by horses. It was apparently a moneymaker right from the start, as the 1884 rates are still listed on the side of the ferry office. The present ferry was installed in 1926 and is guided by cables 35 feet down on the lake bottom, making it, say officials, one of two cable-operated automobile ferries in the country.

That's only one of the Ironton Ferry's many little oddities, the reason it was once featured in "Ripley's Believe It or Not." Consider its size (so small it holds only four cars), the length of its trip (a mere 575 feet of water), and the fact that it doesn't have a rudder. Perhaps most unusual is that the Ironton Ferry doesn't make regularly scheduled crossings. It's operated on demand because the South Arm is so narrow that passengers can be seen waiting on the other side.

funfacts

By following Michigan's Chain of Lakes (Mullett, Burt, and Crooked Lakes), Native Americans and fur traders had only one short portage in traveling from Lake Huron to Little Traverse Bay on Lake Michigan. Thus they avoided a paddle through the Straits of Mackinac and facing its strong winds and wicked currents.

The ferry operates from mid-April to Thanksgiving Eve, 6:30 A.M. to 10:30 P.M. daily. A trip across is $1.50 per vehicle or 50 cents per walker.

On the shores where Hemingway's family had their cottage are a number of historic buildings, including the Walloon Lake Inn. The century-old inn has a number of rooms upstairs, a fine lakeside restaurant downstairs, where you can arrive by car or boat, and, during the winter, the *Fonds du Cuisine Cooking School.* For four days small groups of students spend their mornings in the restaurant's kitchen working with chef David Beier and their afternoons in the dining room eating lunch. From Tuesday through Friday they are up to their elbows in sauces and batters at a school where textbooks are replaced by mixing bowls and wire whisks.

Classes are held between the countertop and the range, as the students receive their own ducks to truss and rainbow trout to fillet. Class ends with the midday meal, a lavish affair that may last two hours and usually involves a little wine tasting and comparing of each other's creations. Walloon Lake Inn (231–535–2999), in the heart of Walloon Lake Village, is 8 miles south of Petoskey and is reached from US 31 by heading west a quarter of a mile on M 75. The school is offered a dozen times from September through mid-March and costs $440 per person, including four nights of lodging, breakfast, and daily luncheon.

Emmet County

Housed in Petoskey's Chicago and West Michigan railroad depot, which was built in 1892, the **Little Traverse Historical Museum** is the first logical stop on any Hemingway tour. The display case is small but contains photographs, other memorabilia, and some rare first-edition books that Hemingway autographed for his friend Edwin Pailthrorp, whom he visited in Petoskey in 1947. There is also a display case devoted to another famous writer, Bruce Catton, who was born in the Emmet County town and grew up in nearby Benzonia. Later Catton would pen *A Stillness at Appomattox,* for which he won a Pulitzer Prize in 1953. The original manuscript of that book and other personal artifacts are in the museum.

The museum (231–347–2620) is on Dock Street on Petoskey's picturesque waterfront and is open May through October from 10:00 A.M. to 4:00 P.M. Monday through Friday and 1:00 to 4:00 P.M. Saturday and Sunday. There is a small admission fee.

passenger pigeons

At one time Michigan was a favorite nesting ground for the passenger pigeon. Vast quantities of beechnuts attracted them, and each spring immense flocks arrived, literally darkening the skies for hours at a time as they flew over.

At Crooked Lake in Emmet County, a nesting in 1878 covered ninety square miles, drawing the attention of thousands of hunters who quickly converged on the area. Millions of birds were killed, packed in barrels, and shipped to Petoskey. Such wanton slaughter led to the extinction of the passenger pigeon by 1914.

From the well-developed resort town of Harbor Springs, M 119 heads north and hugs the coastline for 31 miles until it ends at Cross Village. The drive is often cited as a scenic one, but not for the views of Lake Michigan you might expect when tracing it on a map. This is the **Tunnel of Trees Shore Drive,** a narrow road that climbs, drops, and curves its way through the thick forests along the rugged coast. At times the branches from trees at each side of the road merge overhead to form a complete tunnel, shading travelers even when the sun is beaming down at midday. You finally emerge from the thick forest at Cross Village, a small hamlet and home of **Legs Inn.**

The inn is the creation of one man, Stanley Smolak, a Polish immigrant who fell in love with this part of Michigan and moved here from Chicago in

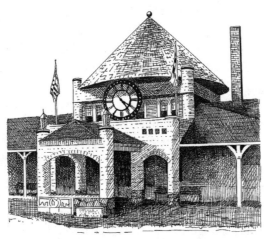

Little Traverse Historical Museum

1921. Smolak quickly made friends with the local Ottawa Indians, who inducted him into their tribe as Chief White Cloud. Then in 1930, with a Polish past, a love for northern Michigan, and his new Indian heritage, Smolak began building the inn. He combined the driftwood and stones he found along the shoreline to construct an unusual building on a bluff overlooking Lake Michigan. From the outside the architecture of the Legs Inn is bizarre at best, but the interior is even more fascinating, for Smolak loved to carve the driftwood. He would take a piece, see something in it, and then whittle away. The inn has several rooms, all filled with Smolak's driftwood sculpture.

Naturally, the menu reflects Smolak's homeland and includes entrees of pierogi, *gotabki,* and *bigos,* a hearty Polish stew. The restaurant even serves a beer imported from Poland. The Legs Inn (231–526–2281) is located in the heart of Cross Village (you'll know it when you see it) and is open May through October from 11:00 A.M. to 10:00 P.M. Sunday through Thursday and even later on Friday and Saturday. Dinner entrees on the menu range from $11 to $19.

Cheboygan County

The residents are certainly friendly in Cheboygan. Arrive in this Lake Huron town of 5,100 during the summer or early fall and the first place people want you to go is the jail. Stay as long as you like, they say. Plan to spend a few minutes in each cell, because that's where you'll find the pride and heritage that is Cheboygan—in the ***Cheboygan County Historical Museum*** located in the old county jail. At this museum you not only get to view the history of the area in an interesting series of displays and exhibits, you also have the opportunity to wander through a nineteenth-century jail. It's debatable which is more fascinating.

Built in 1890, the facility served as the area jail until 1970, when the county board of commissioners gave the building to the historical society. You enter the attached brick home where the county sheriff and his family lived, and the first room you walk into is a huge kitchen, where his wife cooked not only for him and his family but for all the prisoners as well. From the home you pass through a metal door, entering the jail. Little has changed about the facility except that the historical society has filled each cell with a display, ranging from the town's first hardware stores to its maritime history to an exhibit on logging. Call it "history behind bars."

The museum is at Huron and Court Streets. From US 23 within town, head south on M 27 and then west on Court Street for 3 blocks. The jail museum (231–627–9597) is open from mid-June through mid-October from 1:00 to 4:00 P.M. Monday through Friday; closed Saturday and Sunday.

Another intriguing historical spot in Cheboygan County is just a few miles north on US 23. **Historical Mill Creek** was opened in 1984 after the site was "rediscovered" in 1972 by a local archaeologist. It dates to the 1780s, when a Scottish trader named Robert Campbell obtained a 640-acre tract of land around the only stream in the area with enough power to operate a mill, making the creek one of the oldest industrial centers in the Midwest. There was a great demand for lumber at the time, since the British were moving their military post from Fort Michilimackinac at the tip of the Lower Peninsula to Mackinac Island. The island's high limestone bluffs made it easier to defend against the Americans, who were thought to be on their way.

strangeas itsounds

You can only drive north on I–75 so many times before the billboard about a "man-eating clam" entices you off the highway at exit 326 and into the parking lot of Sea Shell City.

Inside the huge gift shop, between the rows of rubber tomahawks and other tacky souvenirs for tourists, is a 505-pound Giant Clam (*Tridacna gigas*) from the Philippines. This is reputed to be the largest mollusk in the world and "has the capacity to snuff out a man's life with one sharp snap of its shells." Reality is that the clam is a vegetarian that feasts on algae.

Visitors enter the area through an orientation center that houses a museum and a small auditorium, where a slide show on the mill's history is presented. From the center, trails lead through the 625-acre park to exhibits that include a working reconstructed mill as well as other buildings, nature trails, and scenic overlooks where the straits and Mackinac Island can be viewed through telescopes. The park is reached from I–75 by taking exit 338 and heading south on US 23 for 4 miles. Mill Creek (231–436–7301) is open from mid-May through mid-October from 9:00 A.M. to 5:00 P.M., and daily from mid-June through August. Admission is $7.50 per adult and $4.50 per child.

Otsego County

The eastern elk, once a common sight to Indians in the Lower Peninsula, disappeared from Michigan around 1877. After several unsuccessful attempts to reintroduce the animal in the early 1900s, seven Rocky Mountain elk were released in Cheboygan County in 1918, and today biologists believe Michigan's herd of 1,400 elk descended from those animals. The herd ranges over 600 square miles in Cheboygan, Montmorency, Otsego, and Presque Isle Counties, but its heaviest concentration is in the wilderness areas of the *Pigeon River Country State Forest.*

The 95,000-acre state forest features rustic campgrounds, miles of hiking trails, and fishing opportunities, but come fall most visitors have their hearts set on seeing the elk. As big as the adults are (ranging from 700 to 900 pounds), they're tough to spot during the summer, for they break up into small groups or are solitary and lie low in the thick forest. But in September the bulls begin the "bugling season," when they move into open areas and form harems of fifteen to twenty cows by calling out to them with a high-pitched whistlelike sound. Watchers will see from thirty to a hundred elk gathered in an open field and then hear the most amazing sound—the huge bull making his high-pitched mating call.

To witness one of Michigan's great wildlife scenes, head to the Pigeon River forestry field office, 13 miles east of Vanderbilt, just off Sturgeon River Road. The office is open from 8:00 A.M. to 4:30 P.M. Monday through Friday, and workers can provide maps and suggest open areas to view the elk. The rule of thumb is that two weeks on either side of September 20 is the best time to catch the bugling, or rutting, season. Plan to be at an open area just before dawn or dusk, and sit quietly to await the movement of the herd. One traditional spot to see elk is off Ossmun Road near Clark Bridge Road northeast of the forestry office. Here you will find a large open field, a small parking lot off the road, and a few elk viewers waiting patiently during September.

Crawford County

The best-known attraction in this county is **Hartwick Pines State Park** and its **Michigan Forest Visitor Center,** the new interpretive center dedicated to Michigan's lumber era at the turn of the twentieth century. On the outside the building, decks, and wooden walkways blend naturally into a grove of pines. Inside there are sitting areas with glass walls looking out over the ancient trees, the reason the state park was created.

The hands-on displays, dedicated to Michigan's vast forests, are excellent. There is a mounted wolf that looks so real a sign was needed saying PLEASE DON'T PET THE WOLF. Instead you touch a piece of fur and immediately a pack of wolves begins to howl all around you. The Living Giant is a white pine that talks to you, explaining what heartwood is or how its needles produce food. But the most captivating display is "Reading the Rings." The computerized program displays a cross section of a white pine. Touch one of its rings and the screen flashes to what happened that year, including 1994 when the tree was blown down in a windstorm and cut up for firewood.

From the interpretive center you can walk the Virgin Pines Trail that loops through a forty-nine-acre stand of 300-year-old virgin white pine. Along the way you will pass through a reconstructed loggers' camp with various lumber machines on display, including "Big Wheels" that were used to haul giant logs out of the woods.

The state park (989–348–7068) is north of Grayling and can be reached by exiting I–75 at M 93 and following the park signs. The Michigan Forest Visitor Center is open from 9:00 A.M. to 7:00 P.M. daily except Monday from June until late November, when the center is open only Saturday and Sunday. A vehicle permit is required to enter the park.

By the time the logging of the late nineteenth century was finished, much of the state had been reduced to a stump-ridden wasteland. The Civilian Conservation Corps (CCC) replanted the forests, and its story is also told in Crawford County. The **Civilian Conservation Corps Museum** is located in North Higgins Lake State Park and is dedicated to the program created during President Franklin Roosevelt's administration to help the vast numbers of unemployed people during the Great Depression. It was signed into law as the Emergency Conservation Work Act on March 31, 1933, and by July of that year Michigan had forty-two CCC camps employing 18,400 men. In all, more than 102,000 Michigan men were enrolled in CCC work projects that involved

The Holy Waters

The most revered trout stream east of the Mississippi River is an 8-mile stretch of the Au Sable River east of Grayling that is known among fly fishers as the Holy Waters. It was on the banks of the Holy Waters that Trout Unlimited was founded in the 1950s.

Ironically, trout are not native to the river but were introduced. The original fish of the Au Sable was grayling, the troutlike fish with the distinctively high dorsal fin. These were first classified by biologists in 1864, and within a decade, after railroads had penetrated northern Michigan, anglers from all over the country were arriving in Grayling to fish for grayling.

The fishing was so easy that anglers could often catch three or four grayling at a time by tying multiple hooks to their line. Such heavy fishing pressure and the deforestation caused by the lumber industry made the Michigan grayling rare by the turn of the twentieth century and extinct by 1930.

constructing dams, building hiking trails, stocking lakes, and putting up fire towers. They are best known for planting trees—during the CCC era Michigan led the nation in planting 485 million trees.

The museum consists of several buildings, including an original cone barn, where workers extracted the seeds from pinecones to be planted later. There is also a replica of a CCC barracks with displays inside that examine the spartan camp life of the men and the duties they performed for $30 a month, of which $22 had to be sent home to their families.

North Higgins Lake State Park (989–821–6125) is reached from US 27 by exiting east on Military Road and from I–75 by heading west at exit 244. There is no admission fee for the CCC museum, but there is a vehicle entry fee for the rest of the park. The museum is open from 10:00 A.M. to 4:00 P.M. daily from Memorial Day through Labor Day.

Wexford County

Hunting and fishing have a long tradition in Michigan. How long? In 1994 the state celebrated the one hundredth year in which deer licenses had been issued. There is no better place to see the history of hunters and anglers in Michigan than at the *Carl T. Johnson Hunting and Fishing Center,* a state interpretive site in Cadillac. Located adjacent to Mitchell State Park along M 115, the center features a variety of exhibits and hands-on displays, including a marsh diorama, a wall-size aquarium stocked with native fish, and a full-size stuffed elk, a species reintroduced to the state thanks to the efforts of sportsmen's groups.

The Battle of Sherman

The first settlement and first county seat in Wexford County was Sherman, which was settled in 1863. Several years later Cadillac was founded and immediately wanted to be the seat of government, setting off a ten-year struggle between the two logging towns that became known as the Battle of Sherman.

In 1881 the seat was moved to Manton, but later that year Cadillac residents arrived and took the county records by force. The next year Cadillac was officially designated the county seat while Sherman eventually became a ghost town.

Push a button and you can hear the call of the elk along with the calls of many other Michigan species in the exhibit hall. From the center a trail leads north into the Heritage Nature Study Area, which includes observation platforms and marshes where you have a reasonably good chance of spotting many of Michigan's wild species.

The Carl T. Johnson Hunting and Fishing Center (231–779–1321) is open Tuesday through Sunday from 10:00 A.M. to 6:00 P.M. from May through November and the rest of the year from noon to 5:00 P.M. Friday and 10:00 A.M. to 5:00 P.M. Saturday and Sunday. A state park vehicle pass is required to enter ($4.00 per vehicle to enter any state park).

Places to Stay in Northwest Michigan

BAY VIEW

Stafford's Bay View Inn,
US 31,
(800) 258–1886

Terrace Inn,
1549 Glendale Street,
(800) 530–9898

BEAVER ISLAND

Beaver Island Lodge,
St. James,
(231) 448–2396

Laurain Lodge,
St. James,
(231) 448–2099

BELLAIRE

Grand Victorian Bed & Breakfast,
402 North Bridge Street,
(800) 336–3860

CHARLEVOIX

Inn at Grey Gables,
306 Belvedere,
(231) 547–2251

Pointes North Inn,
101 Michigan Avenue,
(866) 547–0055

Weathervane Terrace Hotel,
111 Pine River Lane,
(800) 552–0025

ELK RAPIDS

Camelot Inn,
10962 U.S. 31,
(800) 761–4667

White Birch Lodge,
571 Meguzee Point Road,
(231) 264–8271

ELLSWORTH

House on the Hill Bed & Breakfast,
9661 Lake Street,
(231) 588–6304

EMPIRE

Maple Lane Resort,
8720 Dorsey Road,
(231) 334–3413

FRANKFORT

Chimney Corners Resort,
1602 Crystal Drive,
(231) 352–7522

GAYLORD

Days Inn,
1201 West Main Street,
(989) 732–2200

Marsh Ridge Resort,
4815 Old US27,
(800) 743–7529

HARBOR SPRINGS

Birchwood Inn,
7077 Lakeshore Drive,
(800) 530–9955

Nick Adams Hotel,
266 East Main Street,
(800) 526–6238

LELAND

Falling Waters Lodge,
200 West Cedar,
(231) 256–9832

Whaleback Inn,
M 22,
(231) 256–9090

MAPLE CITY

Leelanau Country Inn,
149 East Harbor Highway,
(231) 228–5060

OMENA

Omena Sunset Lodge,
12819 Tatch Road,
(231) 386–9080

PETOSKEY

Apple Tree Inn,
915 Spring Street,
(800) 348–2901

Comfort Inn,
1314 US 31,
(231) 347–3220

Stafford's Perry Hotel,
Bay and Lewis Streets,
(800) 737–1899

TRAVERSE CITY

Baymont Inn,
2326 US 31 South,
(231) 933–4454

Beach Haus Resort,
1489 US 31,
(231) 947–3560

Cherry Tree Inn,
2345 US 31,
(800) 439–3093

Grand Beach Resort Hotel,
1683 US 31 North,
(800) 968–1992

Grand Traverse Resort,
100 Grand Traverse Village
Boulevard (Acme),
(800) 748–0303

Park Place Hotel,
300 East State Street,
(800) 748–0133

Places to Eat in Northwest Michigan

BEAVER ISLAND

Dalwhinnoe Bakery (deli),
St. James,
(231) 448–2736

Old Rectory
(American),
Grant's Road,
(231) 448–2318

BEULAH

Cherry Hut (American),
216 US 31,
(231) 882–4431

CHARLEVOIX

Acorn Cafe
(American),
101 Park Avenue,
(231) 547–1835

Grey Gables Inn
(fine dining),
308 Bevedere Avenue,
(231) 547–9261

Whitney's (seafood),
307 Bridge Street,
(231) 547–0818

ELLSWORTH

Tapawingo (fine dining),
9502 Lake Street,
(231) 588–7971

Rowe Inn (fine dining),
6303 East Jordan Road,
(231) 588–7351

ELK RAPIDS

Pearls (Cajun),
617 Ames Street,
(231) 264–0530

FRANKFORT

Chimney Corners Resort
(American),
1602 Crystal Drive,
(231) 352–7522

GAYLORD

Big Buck Brewery
(brew pub),
550 South Wisconsin,
(989) 732–5781

Diana's Delights (American),
143 West Main Street,
(989) 732–6564

Mama Leone's (Italian),
2583 South Old US 27,
(989) 732–4431

GRAYLING

Spike's Keg o' Nails,
301 North James Street,
(989) 348–7113

HARBOR SPRINGS

Juilleret's (whitefish),
130 State Street,
(231) 526–2821

New York Restaurant
(American),
101 State Street,
(231) 526–1904

LAKE LEELANAU

Key to the County
(fine dining),
104 Main Street,
(231) 256–5397

LELAND

Bluebird (fish),
102 East River,
(231) 256–9081

The Cove (outdoor dining),
111 River Street,
(231) 256–9834

SELECTED CHAMBERS OF COMMERCE AND TOURISM BUREAUS

Beaver Island Chamber of Commerce,
P.O. Box 5,
Beaver Island 49782;
(231) 448–2505;
www.beaverisland.net

Boyne Country Convention and Visitors Bureau,
401 East Mitchell Street,
Petoskey 49770;
(800) 845–2828;
www.boynecountry.com

Charlevoix Area Convention and Visitors Bureau,
408 Bridge Street,
Charlevoix 49720;
(800) 367–8557;
www.charlevoix.org

Gaylord Area Convention and Tourism Bureau,
P.O. Box 3069,
Gaylord 49735;
(800) 345–8621;
www.gaylord-mich.com

Mackinaw Area Tourist Bureau,
708 South Huron Avenue,
Mackinaw City 49701;
(800) 666–0160;
www.mackinawcity.com

Sleeping Bear Dunes Visitors Bureau,
P.O. Box 517,
Glen Arbor 49636;
(231) 334–2000;
www.sleepingbeardunes.com

Traverse City Convention and Visitors Bureau,
101 West Grandview Parkway,
Traverse City 49684;
(800) 940–1120;
www.mytraversecity.com

OTHER ATTRACTIONS

Benzie Area Historical Museum,
Benzonia

Clinch Park Zoo,
Traverse City

Colonial Michilimackinac,
Mackinaw City

Empire Area Museum,
Empire

Gaslight Shopping District,
Petoskey

Leelanau Historical Museum,
Leland

Lighthouse Park,
Old Mission Peninsula

Sunset Park,
Petoskey

MISSION PENINSULA

Bowers Harbor Inn
(fine dining),
13512 Peninsula Drive,
(231) 223–4222

Old Mission Tavern
(American),
17015 Center Road,
(231) 223–7280

PETOSKEY

Andante (fine dining),
321 Bay Street,
(231) 348–3321

City Park Grill (pasta),
432 East Lake Street,
(231) 347–0101

Jesperson's (American),
312 Howard Street,
(231) 347–3601

Roast & Toast (American),
309 Lake Street,
(231) 347–7767

Whitecaps,
215 East Lake Street,
(231) 348–7092

TRAVERSE CITY

Blondie's (barbecue),
933 US 31 South,
(231) 943–8019

Don's Drive-In
(hamburgers),
2030 US 31 North,
(231) 938–1860

Mabel's (American),
US 31 North
and Eighth Street,
(231) 947–0252

North Peak Brewing
Company (brew pub),
400 West Front Street,
(231) 941–7325

Omelette Shoppe & Bakery
(American),
1209 East Front Street,
(231) 946–0590

Poppycock's (vegetarian),
128 East Front Street,
(231) 941–7632

Eastern Upper Peninsula

The "Mighty Mac" might sound like a hamburger with the works, but to most Michiganders it's the Mackinac Bridge, the only link between the Lower and Upper Peninsulas and the third-longest bridge in the country. Building a bridge was first considered in 1884, but the 5-mile span wasn't built until 1957, finally uniting a state that for its first 120 years was divided by a stretch of water known as the Straits of Mackinac.

Most travelers view the *Mackinac Bridge* as a very scenic drive. A trip across the Mighty Mac is a 360-degree panorama of shorelines, Great Lakes, and islands scattered everywhere, while below, the straits bustle with ferries, freighters, and fishing boats. The bridge is also the link between two worlds. Unlike industrialized southern Michigan, the Upper Peninsula's economy was based on lumbering and mining. After the majestic white pines were cut and the mines closed, this section of Michigan fell upon hard times, which in some ways continue today. Residents of the north, however, are quick to point out that the first permanent settlement in the state was not Detroit but Sault Ste. Marie and that their endurance proves their long history is not about to end anytime soon. Survival is a way of life in the U.P.

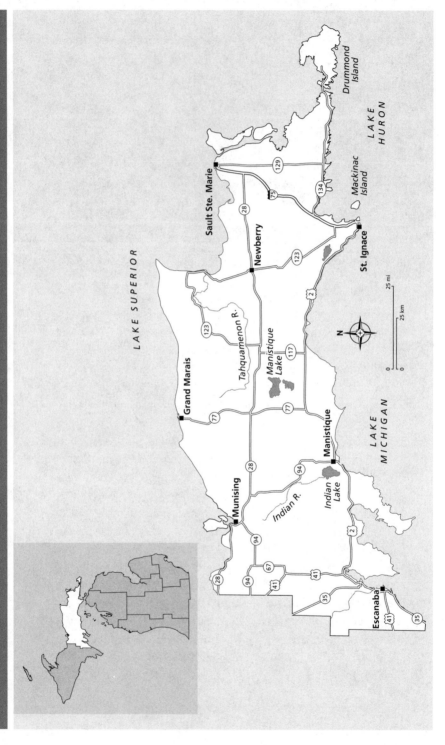

EASTERN UPPER PENINSULA

What travelers will quickly discover upon crossing the bridge is a place of remote beauty and unique character, where interstate highways are almost non-existent, and motel chains and fast-food restaurants are few and far between. Almost every road in the U.P. is "off the beaten path," offering natural beauty, family-run inns and cafes, and outdoor opportunities that will satisfy any lover of pristine forests, lakes, and streams.

Mackinac County

Sometimes in our rush to see one place, we overlook another. Such is often the case of a place like St. Ignace. This historical town, the second oldest settlement in Michigan, has a scenic harbor and a main street full of shops and restaurants. Only who takes the time to look around when we're all racing through to catch the next boat to Mackinac Island?

Slow down. St. Ignace is an intriguing city, and you don't have to go any farther than the **_Museum of Ojibwa Culture_** to discover why. The city-operated museum gives a vivid picture of the Straits of Mackinac in the 1600s and 1700s when the Ojibway, Huron, and Odawa Indians mingled with the French in what is now downtown St. Ignace. The museum is housed in a former Catholic church, and through video presentations and exhibits it focuses

AUTHOR'S TOP TEN PICKS

Fayette State Park,
Garden;
(906) 644–2603

Peninsula Point Lighthouse,
Stonington;
(906) 786–4062

Fort Mackinac,
Mackinac Island;
(906) 847–3328

Pictured Rock Boat Cruises,
Munising;
(906) 387–2379

Grand Hotel,
Mackinac Island;
(800) 334–7263

Seney National Wildlife Refuge,
Germfask;
(906) 586–9851

Great Lakes Shipwreck Museum,
Paradise;
(906) 635–1742

Soo Locks Park,
Sault Ste. Marie;
(906) 253–9101

Kitch-Iti-Kipi,
Manistique;
(906) 341–2355

Tahquamenon Falls,
Paradise;
(906) 492–3415

A Legitimate Tourist Trap

Before there was Mystery Spot and Sea Shell City with its "man-eating clam" or a miniature golf course in the shape of Michigan, there was Castle Rock.

In a region of the state lined with tourist traps and gift shops selling rubber tomahawks and "I-Am-A-Yooper" refrigerator magnets, Castle Rock is the original. It is also one of the most affordable attractions on either side of the Mackinac Bridge and, located right at exit 348 off I-75, a great leg stretcher after the long drive north.

What the heck, let's stop.

There is nothing phony about the rock itself. Castle Rock is a sea stack, one of a handful in and around St. Ignace, the result of limestone caves collapsing and waves eroding the remaining rock into pillars and arches more than 4,000 years ago. The most famous are Sugar Loaf and Arch Rock on Mackinac Island, while in downtown St. Ignace there's St. Anthony's Rock. At 183 feet, Castle Rock is not only the tallest one but also the only one you're allowed to climb.

The slick brochure promoting Castle Rock states that it was used by Indians as a lookout and that Pontiac, the great Ojibway chief, was thought to have stood on it. Of course it also says that the legendary giant Paul Bunyan and his blue ox, Babe, once sat at the base of it. Believe what you want.

What is known is that historical photos show people climbing the rock as early as 1911 and that in 1930 Clarence Eby purchased the rock and 80 acres surrounding it. He built a souvenir stand at the base of it and a stairway to the top of it, and he charged people 10 cents to climb it, enticing them with signs that read STOP AND CLIMB. STILL ONLY A DIME!

on the Woodland Indian culture and how these indigenous people survived the harsh winters of the Upper Peninsula. Outside there is a replica of a Huron longhouse that can be viewed.

The Museum of Ojibwa Culture (906–643–9161) is at 500 North State Street, next door to the St. Ignace Chamber of Commerce office. Hours are 10:00 A.M. to 8:00 P.M. Monday through Saturday and noon to 8:00 P.M. Sunday, from late June to Labor Day. In early June and from September to mid-October, the museum is open until 5:00 P.M. There is a small admission fee.

Next door to the museum is *Marquette Mission Park,* while across State Street is one end of the *Huron Boardwalk.* Together the small park and the 2-mile-long boardwalk take you back more than 300 years into the life of this town.

Marquette Mission Park features Father Marquette's grave and several outdoor exhibits that retrace the significance of this little plot of land. From the park you then cross the street to Huron Boardwalk, which winds south along

That's one of the most amazing things about Castle Rock—its admission fee. It remained 10 cents until 1979, when it was raised to 25 cents. Finally, in 2001 the fee was increased to 50 cents. Still, it's cheaper to climb Castle Rock than to cross the Mackinac Bridge.

To reach the sea stack, you first have to pass through Castle Rock Curios Shop, and this is where you might lose the kids. The large gift shop is stocked with thousands of souvenirs people expect you to bring home from the Upper Peninsula: polished agates, Mackinac Bridge playing cards, Daniel Boone raccoon caps, fake arrowheads, and a bald man's hairbrush (it has no bristles).

From the shop you head outside where there is a giant statue of Paul Bunyan and Babe (life-size?) and the stairway to the top of Castle Rock, a climb of 170 steps.

The climb is worth it as the view is magnificent. Spread out below you is St. Ignace, while offshore is Mackinac Island and in between them a handful of ferries hustling tourists back and forth. You can see Lake Huron, Lake Michigan, even the towers of the Mackinac Bridge.

The view is so expansive that it's easy to envision Indians using Castle Rock as an observation post. But as for Paul Bunyan using it as a backrest . . . that's still a stretch for this flatlander.

Castle Rock (906–643–8268) is open May through October from 8:30 A.M. to 9:30 P.M. daily.

the St. Ignace waterfront. The boardwalk features its own series of historical displays, which cover everything from "Nineteenth-Century St. Ignace" to the "Legacy of White Pine" in text and photos. Between the displays are benches, each with a million-dollar view of Mackinac Island, the ferries making high-speed runs to the resort island and the rest of the bustling waterfront. To reach Marquette Mission Park and Huron Boardwalk from I–75 on the north side of the Mackinac Bridge, take exit 344A and follow Business Loop I–75 to State Street, which parallels the boardwalk.

There are numerous forts to visit in Michigan, but without a doubt the most famous and probably the most beloved is **Fort Mackinac** on Mackinac Island. Built and first occupied by the British in 1779, the fort is part of Mackinac Island State Park and is the scene of cannon firings and other living-history demonstrations throughout the summer. The Officer's Stone Quarters, constructed of limestone in 1781, is the oldest building in Michigan. The scene of the white stockade looming above the island's downtown area is

laborday bridgewalk

Labor Day is the only time of the year that people are allowed to walk across the Mackinac Bridge. More than 70,000 people trek across the 5-mile-long bridge that day, including the governor of Michigan and, in 1992, President George H.W. Bush. Walkers begin on the north side of the bridge and jump on free shuttle buses to return to their cars afterward.

probably one of the most photographed in the state.

The fort is open daily from 9:30 A.M. to 6:30 P.M. from mid-June through August and 9:30 A.M. to 4:30 P.M. from mid-May to mid-June and after Labor Day through mid-October. Admission is $8.25 per adult, $5.25 per child, which also covers six other interesting museums in the downtown area of Mackinac Island including Mission Church, the oldest church in Michigan; Indian Dormitory, with displays and craft demonstrations on Native American cooking and weaving; and Beaumont Memorial.

Mackinac Island State Park actually covers 1,800 acres, or 83 percent of the island, and offers much more than just cannon demonstrations twice a day. There are 140 miles of roads and trails, open to use by hikers, cyclists, and equestrians, but not cars, which are not allowed on the island. The roads and

abattlewithout ashot

Mackinac Island was the site of one of the most celebrated moments in Michigan's history. After Americans took over Fort Mackinac diplomatically, the British recaptured it during the War of 1812 by secretly landing in the middle of the night and dragging a cannon up a bluff overlooking the fort. When the American garrison woke up the next morning and saw what was aimed at them, they gave up without firing a single shot.

trails loop through a surprisingly rugged and wooded terrain, past some of the most interesting natural formations in Michigan, including **Arch Rock,** the almost perfect 50-foot-wide limestone arch. The vast majority of visitors reach these attractions on a bicycle, which can either be brought to the island on the ferry or rented in the downtown area.

For more information on Mackinac Island State Park, call (906) 847–6330, beginning in mid-May. For information on the three ferry companies that provide transportation to the island, call Arnold Transit (800–542–8528), Shepler's Mackinac Island Ferry (800–828–6157), or Star Line (800–638–9892).

Scenic shoreline drives abound in Michigan, but it's hard to argue when someone says the most spectacular of all is the stretch of US 2 from St. Ignace to the hamlet of Naubinway. The views of Lake Michigan, beaches, dunes, and offshore island are rarely interrupted along this 42-mile segment. One of the places to spot for a panoramic view on this drive is *Cut River Gorge Roadside Park* on US 2, 26 miles west of St. Ignace.

Actually there are three parks on both sides of this stunning gorge that are connected by the impressive Cut River Bridge, a steel-arch cantilever structure that was built in 1948 and stands 147 feet above the river. You can walk across the bridge for an impressive view of Lake Michigan or follow one of three foot trails that wind down to the Cut River and then out to a beautiful beach on the Great Lake. By combining the two trails with a walk across the bridge itself, you'll enjoy an interesting loop of between 1 and 1.3 miles.

A much less traveled but equally scenic route is east of the Mackinac Bridge on M 134. The road follows the U.P. shoreline along northern Lake Huron, passing the intriguing Les Cheneaux Islands and ending at De Tour, the departure point for remote Drummond Island, a haven of fishing resorts. The best stretch is the 24 miles from Cedarville in Mackinac County to De Tour in Chippewa County. This segment is one continuous view of the lake, the islands, and long stretches of sand where there are more than a dozen turnoffs and roadside parks, allowing everybody an uncrowded beach for a lazy afternoon in the sun.

Chippewa County

Sault Ste. Marie is synonymous with the Soo Locks, the world's largest and busiest locking system, the crucial link for freighters passing between Lake Superior and Lake Huron. The city of 15,000 is Michigan's oldest and has been an important center since the French Canadian voyagers in the 1700s portaged their long canoes and bales of furs around St. Mary's Rapids.

Most of this colorful history of shipping can be appreciated by walking along Water Street, beginning at its east end, where the *SS Valley Camp* is docked next to the Chamber of Commerce Information Center. The 550-foot freighter was once owned and used by the Republic Steel Corporation and frequently passed through the locks. Today it has been turned into one of the largest Great Lakes marine museums and is listed as a National Historic Site. From the pilothouse and the 1,800-horsepower steam engine to the captain's quarters and the galley, visitors are free to roam the ship

funfacts

More than eighty-two million tons of cargo pass through the Soo Locks annually, with more than half of it iron ore from mines in the Upper Peninsula and Minnesota. Coal being shipped north accounts for fifteen million tons, and Minnesota wheat being shipped east, nine million tons.

Feasting on Mackinac Island

Dinner began downtown, near Huron Street, where daytime visitors, with a rubber tomahawk under one arm and a one-pound box of fudge under the other, were scurrying toward the ferries to get off this historical island before dark. We went in the other direction.

We signaled for a horse-drawn taxi and then settled back in the cushioned carriage seats as it clip-clopped its way past the Grand Hotel, up a steep hill, and finally into the island's wooded interior. Some fifteen minutes later we emerged from the trees at the impressive Stonecliffe Mansion.

Built in 1905, it was once the site of several religious and educational institutions and today houses the Woods Restaurant. The interior is a cross between a hunting lodge and a Bavarian mountain retreat with clunky wooden chairs, a huge stone fireplace, and enough stuffed animals on the walls to make any hunter feel at home.

We feasted on Mackinac whitefish baked in parchment, grilled venison chops with red current glacé, and wild mushroom stew, and then enjoyed a second bottle of wine, not worrying about drinking and driving because, as our waiter pointed out, "there are no cars on the island to drive." We topped off the evening with another carriage ride back to our hotel.

And you thought the only thing to eat on Mackinac Island was fudge.

There is more to dining at this summer retreat than its legendary candy shops. Dozens of restaurants, cafes, and pubs cater to thousands of tourists each summer, satisfying even those with the most finicky taste buds. But the key to a memorable dining experience is to stick around after the last ferry has pulled out, to book a room in a hotel or a bed-and-breakfast, and then indulge in that time-honored tradition of a late and leisurely dinner, enjoyed long after the daytime crowds have vanished.

Reserve a room by first calling the Mackinac Island Chamber of Commerce at (906) 847–6418 for a list of accommodations. Then hop on the first ferry leaving the mainland and take a gastronomic romp around the island:

for a close-up look at life aboard an ore carrier, where a crew of almost thirty worked, slept, and ate. Down below, in its massive cargo holds, are models and displays of Great Lakes vessels, aquariums of the freshwater fish that abound nearby, and a room devoted to wreckage of the *Edmund Fitzgerald*, the ore carrier that sank in raging Lake Superior in 1975, taking its captain and crew of twenty-eight with it.

The SS *Valley Camp* (906–632–3658) is open daily from 10:00 A.M. to 6:00 P.M. mid-May through June, 9:00 A.M. to 9:00 P.M. in July and August, and 10:00 A.M. to 6:00 P.M. from September through October 15. Admission is $8.00 for adults and $4.00 for children ages six to sixteen.

Horn's Gaslight Bar: In the 1920s Ed Horn was working for the Life-Saving Service at the Round Island Lighthouse when he and his wife opened up a pool hall and snack shop on Huron Street. After Prohibition, Horn acquired one of Michigan's first liquor licenses, and his pool hall became Horn's Gaslight Bar in 1933. It still is, and the interior includes the original tin roof, historical photos on the walls, a long polished bar, and, of course, a honky-tonk piano player. Try the tequila prawns, oversize shrimp sautéed in tequila, lime, and garlic.

Grand Hotel Main Dining Room: Everybody knows there is a $10 fee during the day to stroll along the world's longest porch if you're not a guest. Few people realize you can have dinner at the hotel's main dining room without either booking a room or paying that fee. And everybody should, at least once. Dinner at the Grand Hotel is an experience, not a meal. You begin by strolling through the middle of the huge, 760-seat dining room along the carpeted runway affectionally known as "Peacock Alley." Go ahead, strut a little on the way to your table.

An army of fifty-five waiters will tend to your needs as you indulge in such entrees as broiled whitefish and trout scaloppine, sliced veal loin with sweetbreads, or herb-roasted prime rib of beef. Afterward you can enjoy a fine cigar and a snifter of brandy on the porch.

Fort Mackinac Tea Room: There's more to this fort than just the musket and cannon demonstrations. The Tea Room Restaurant in the Officer's Stone Quarters is a string of yellow-canopy tables overlooking the island's bustling harbor, the Mackinac Bridge, the two Great Lakes that meet there, and so on.

Thus at the fort they boast that you can enjoy sandwiches, soups, and salads in the oldest building on Mackinac Island (1781) with the best view in the state.

The newest stop in any tour of the city is the ***River of History Museum,*** which opened in 1993. Through the use of eight exhibit galleries and a state-of-the-art audio system, the museum takes you on an 8,000-year journey along the shores of St. Mary's River. You begin with the sounds of ice melting and the rapids roaring as a glacier carves out the river valley. You move on to the sprawling Indian camp that was once here and then see the first French explorers paddling ashore in 1662.

The River of History Museum (906–632–1999) is at 209 East Portage Avenue. It's open mid-May through mid-October from 10:00 A.M. to 5:00 P.M. Monday through Saturday and noon to 5:00 P.M. Sunday. There is a small admission fee.

To reach the locks to the north, return to and follow Water Street, which in 1982 was renovated into the **Locks Park Walkway,** providing an excellent overview of the city's 350-year past. The walkway is marked by blue symbols of freighters, and interpretive plaques explain the history of various areas and renovated buildings. Along the way you'll pass the Baraga House, the 1864 home of Bishop Frederic Baraga, a missionary and historian known as the "Snowshoe Saint" who was the first bishop of the U.P. Nearby is the Johnston House, which was constructed in 1794 for an Irish fur trader, making it the oldest surviving home in Michigan. The walkway also passes the site of Fort Brady, built by the Americans in 1823 and the spot where in 1820 General Lewis Cass lowered and removed the last British flag to fly over U.S. soil.

funfacts

The only Michigan highway not used by cars or trucks is M 185, the 8-mile blacktopped road that circles Mackinac Island. Except for emergency vehicles—fire trucks and ambulances—travel on M 185 is restricted to pedestrians, bicyclists, and horses.

Water Street ends at **Soo Lock Park** in the heart of downtown Sault Ste. Marie. The U.S. Army Corps of Engineers maintains the park and visitor center, and next to the locks it has built a raised viewing platform that provides an excellent view of ships being raised and lowered to the various lake levels. Your chances of seeing this take place are quite good; some 12,000 vessels pass through the locks annually. During the summer an average of 30 freighters pass through each day.

The interesting visitor center was doubled in size in 1995 and tells the history of the locks, beginning with the construction of the first American lock in 1853. Exhibits include a short video and a working model of a lock. The Soo Locks Information Center (906–253–9101) is open mid-May through mid-November from 8:00 A.M. to 10:00 P.M. There is no admission fee.

You can experience the locks directly through **Soo Locks Boat Tours.** For an admission fee, people take a two-hour cruise up and down St. Mary's River, first passing through an American lock and then returning through the Canadian one. Boats depart daily from May 15 through October 15, beginning at 10:00 A.M. and ending with the last cruise at 6:30 P.M. Soo Locks Boat Tours (800–432–6301) maintains two docks, both on Portage Avenue south of the SS *Valley Camp.* Tickets are $18.50 for adults and $8.50 for children ages four to twelve (three and under free).

As well known to locals as the locks is the **Antlers,** an Irish bar and restaurant on Portage Avenue. The exterior of the simple stone building that houses the seventy-five-year-old eatery is misleading. Inside, the decor is a museum of collectibles (or, some say, junk) including hundreds of mounted animals on the walls, a birch-bark canoe hanging from the ceiling, and a 15-foot boa constrictor overlooking the bar. No wall is left bare. Hockey great Gordie Howe (whose picture also adorns the walls) was a frequent patron of the restaurant, which is known for its steaks and "Paul Bunyan" hamburgers. The Antlers (906–632–3571) is open daily from 11:00 A.M. to 9:00 P.M., and dinner prices range from $7.00 to $16.00.

One of the more interesting drives in the U.P. follows Whitefish Bay, beginning at Brimley (reached from M 28) and ending at desolate Whitefish Point. At Brimley follow Lake Shore Drive to the west as it hugs the shoreline, with frequent views of beaches and Lake Superior. In 7.5 miles, you'll come to the ***Point Iroquois Lightstation.*** The classic lighthouse was built in 1870 and operated until 1963, when sophisticated radar made it obsolete. The Coast Guard turned it over to the U.S. Forestry Service, which worked with local historical societies to open it to the public in 1984. It has since been added to the National Register of Historic Places and features a few displays and artifacts in three rooms of the lightkeeper's house. This lighthouse is mainly popular for its curved staircase of seventy steps that leads to the top of the tower and a view of the surrounding area. The panorama, needless to say, is impressive, as you can see almost the entire coastline of Whitefish Bay and miles out into Lake Superior, including any freighter that happens to be passing by. The lighthouse is open May 15 through October 15 from 9:00 A.M. to 5:00 P.M. daily.

Lake Shore Drive, with its numerous turnoffs and scenic beaches, ends at M 123. The state road is well traveled as it first heads north along Whitefish Bay

Point Iroquois Lightstation

and then swings west at Paradise to head inland to Tahquamenon Falls. Though the popular falls, second in size only to Niagara Falls east of the Mississippi River, is the destination for most travelers, there is a good reason to continue heading north on Whitefish Point Road. At the very end, at the very tip of the remote peninsula that juts out into Lake Superior, is the *Great Lakes Shipwreck Museum.* Whitefish Point is a combination of sandy beach, small dunes, and thunderous Lake Superior waves crashing along the shoreline. It also marks the eastern end of an 80-mile stretch that sailors knew as the Graveyard of the Great Lakes. Raging northwest storms, built up over 200 miles of open water, have caused 300 recorded shipwrecks in which 320 seamen have died along this section of shoreline.

The Great Lakes Shipwreck Historical Society, a group of divers researching the wrecks, opened the museum in 1986 in abandoned buildings of the Coast Guard station, whose light, beaming since 1849, is the oldest active one on Lake Superior. In the main museum, each display is devoted to a different shipwreck. Visitors see a drawing or photograph of the vessel and artifacts that divers have collected, and read the story of its fatal voyage. The ships range from sailing schooners of the early 1800s to the **Edmund Fitzgerald,** the latest and largest shipwreck, which continues to fascinate residents of the U.P. A darkened interior with theatrical lights, soft music, and special sound effects of seagulls and foghorns sends tingles down the spines of most people.

Another building has been turned into a theater where underwater films of the wrecks are shown, and the lightkeeper's house has been recently restored. The museum (888–492–3747) is open from mid-May through mid-October daily from 10:00 A.M. to 6:00 P.M. Admission is $8.50 for adults, $5.50 for children, or $23.00 for a family.

Most of the point is a state wildlife sanctuary, renowned for the variety of birds that pass through. The Michigan Audubon Society has established the *Whitefish Point Bird Observatory,* across from the Point Iroquois Lightstation, where a small information room tells birders the species to be watching for as they hike along the point's network of trails. The point is best known for hawks, as up to 25,000 have been sighted in a season, while in April and May, as many as 7,000 loons will pass by. Other species seen include bald eagles, peregrine falcons, and a variety of songbirds. The observatory is open from 9:00 A.M. to 4:30 P.M. daily from mid-April through mid-October.

Luce County

The county that lies between Chippewa and Alger is probably best known for the Two Hearted River, used by Ernest Hemingway as the setting for one of his stories. Today it remains a favorite for anglers and canoers, who enjoy the solitude of this remote wilderness river that empties into Lake Superior.

The best place to soak in this wilderness setting is Tahquamenon Falls State Park, the second largest state park in the Upper Peninsula. Split between Luce and Chippewa Counties, the 38,496-acre park includes ***Upper Tahquamenon Falls,*** which spans 200 feet across the Tahquamenon River and descends 50 feet into a sea of mist and foam. You can hear the thunder of the falls the minute you step out of the car.

East of the Mississippi River, only Niagara Falls in New York and Cumberland Falls in Kentucky have longer drops than Tahquamenon.

The falls is a day-use area 21 miles from Newberry on M 123. From the parking lot, it's a quarter-mile walk to bluffs overlooking the Upper Falls. The best views, however, are obtained by descending the long staircase into the gorge.

Four miles downriver is ***Lower Tahquamenon Falls.*** While not as impressive as the Upper Falls, this series of cascades is much more fun because

TOP ANNUAL EVENTS

International Bridge Walk,
Sault Ste. Marie, June;
(800) 647–2858

Lilac Festival,
Mackinac Island, June;
(800) 451–5227

Straits Area Antique Auto Show,
St. Ignace, June;
(800) 338–6660

Les Cheneaux Antique Wooden Boat Show,
Hessel, August;
(888) 364–7526

Upper Peninsula State Fair,
Escanaba, August;
(888) 335–8264

Labor Day Bridge Walk,
St. Ignace, September;
(800) 338–6660

Frozen Falls

The Upper Tahquamenon Falls, a stunning sight in the summer, is equally beautiful in the winter when the Upper Peninsula's frigid temperatures turn the tumbling water into sculptured ice. There is no need to pack snowshoes. The falls is such a popular sight with snowmobilers that the park staff plows the parking lot and keeps the short path and stairs to the viewing decks open.

During most winters the river above the falls remains open and flows to the brink of the cascade where the water in the middle tumbles down across large ice formations. Downriver everything is frozen white, and along the rocky bluffs that enclose the falls are gigantic icy stalactites and stalagmites, some of them 10 to 15 feet long.

The walk in is short. Within a quarter mile from the parking lot, you're standing at the first overlook, viewing the falls from a distance. The best view, however, is reached by descending the ninety-four steps into the gorge to a platform right above the cascade where you can lean against the railing for a close-up of the ice formations that grow larger with every splash of water heading downstream.

The formations are so varied and intriguing that you could study them for hours. But most winter visitors are scurrying back up the stairs after ten or fifteen minutes before their toes and fingers turn into stalagmites and stalactites, too.

it is best viewed by combining a short paddle across the river with a walk around a small island.

The adventure begins by renting a rowboat from the park concession and then shoving off into the brown waters, which are stained by tamarack trees, of the Tahquamenon River. At the island there is a large dock at which to tie up your boat while a wooden stairway leads to the start of the trail. Step-for-step this is one of the most beautiful footpaths in the state, only there are not a lot of steps. It's a loop of less than a mile that skirts the outside of the island, passing one display of tumbling water after another. Along the way parents and kids kick their shoes off, wade out onto the ledge of one of the many drops, and let the river cascade across their legs.

Lower Tahquamenon Falls (906–492–3415) is on M 123, 12 miles west of Paradise and 23 miles northeast of Newberry. A vehicle entry permit is required to enter the state park, and there is a small fee to rent the rowboats.

For travelers in Luce County who want to spend their nights in comfort at an inn or hotel, two interesting places are located on the northeast corner of Manistique Lake near the Mackinac County line. The first is the **_Helmer House Inn_**, reached by heading north from US 2 on County Road H 33 and then onto County Road 417. The inn was built in 1881 by a minister as a mission for early settlers; Gale Helmer turned it into a general store and resort six years later.

The area thrived as a summer getaway, so the federal government set up a post office in the inn, appointed Helmer postmaster, and named the spot, for lack of a better name, Helmer.

The post office lasted only nineteen years, and eventually the building was abandoned. Rob Goldthorpe and his wife renovated the lodge and reopened it in 1982. Today the inn is a state historic site and offers five guest rooms, all furnished with antiques. The lodge is probably better known, however, for its wraparound porch that has been glassed in and turned into a delightful little restaurant. Every table has a view of the rural setting outside, and the menu includes steaks, fish, and, occasionally, stuffed trout.

Overnight guests are treated to a full breakfast in the morning as well as a soft bed at night. Rooms, with shared bathrooms, range from $35 to $60 for singles or doubles. The restaurant is open from 3:00 to 9:00 P.M. daily from May through June and September through mid-October and noon to 9:00 P.M. daily in July and August. For room reservations write to the Helmer House Inn at McMillan 49853, or call (906) 586–3204.

The other interesting place to stay is **Chamberlin's Ole Forest Inn** right on H 33, a mile north of the blinker light to Curtis. Built in the late 1800s, it was originally a railroad hotel near the Curtis depot. The railroad stopped service in 1909, and fifteen years later the building was moved to its present location on a high bluff overlooking Manistique Lake.

The classic nineteenth-century hotel features a wraparound veranda overlooking the lake; a sprawling lobby complete with wicker chairs, deep sofas, and a 6-foot stone fireplace; and ten rooms with a unique turn-of-the-twentieth-century decor. Room rates for the Ole Forest Inn (800–292–0440) range from $85 to $130 per night and include a full breakfast in the morning.

Another pleasant spot in Luce County to spend a night is **Muskallonge Lake State Park** at the north end of County Road H 37 in the northwest corner of the county. The park is actually a strip of land between Muskallonge Lake, known for its pike, perch, and smallmouth bass fishing, and Lake Superior. You can camp on a site overlooking the small lake and then wander over to Lake Superior to enjoy its seemingly endless sandy shoreline. There is a vehicle fee to enter Muskallonge Lake State Park (906–658–3338) and an overnight fee of $16 for one of its 179 campsites.

Alger County

Grand Marais, a booming lumber town of 2,500 at the turn of the twentieth century, is a sleepy hamlet of 400 today and the gateway for the eastern half of Pictured Rocks National Lakeshore.

One spot to see within the national lakeshore is the **Grand Sable Banks and Dunes.** To reach the sandy hills, follow County Road H 58 west of town, first passing the parking lot and short side trail to Sable Falls and then the Grand Sable Visitor Center. From both places there are half-mile trails that lead to the Grand Sable Dunes. Or you can continue following the county road a mile past the visitor center. On one side of the road are the picnic area and beach of Grand Sable Lake, and on the other side is a huge dune. No more than 50 yards separate the lake and this mountain of sand. Visitors first tackle the heart-pounding scramble up the dune, where the top offers a magnificent view of the windswept sand, Grand Sable Lake, and Lake Superior off in the distance. Then it's a mad dash down the steep bank of sand and usually right into the lake to cool off.

The dunes are a four-square-mile area of sandy hills about half as high as Sleeping Bear Dunes in the Lower Peninsula, but no less impressive. They end with the Grand Sable Banks, steep sandy bluffs some 300 feet tall that tower right above the Lake Superior shoreline. The best view is obtained by turning off H 58 onto a marked side road for the **Log Slide** located 8 miles west of Grand Marais. A short boardwalk leads to a breathtaking overlook 300 feet above Lake Superior, where Au Sable Point Lighthouse to the west is silhouetted against the water and the banks to the east curve 5 miles back toward Grand Marais. Down below is the 500-foot wooden slide that loggers used in the 1800s to send trees into Lake Superior on their way to town.

To see shipwrecks without swimming in frigid Lake Superior, continue along County Road H 58 to Hurricane River Campground. East of the campground, Lakeshore Trail becomes an old access road to **Au Sable Lightstation,** and near its trailhead is a SHIPWRECKS sign pointing down to the beach. These ruins lie in the water and are hard to spot when the lake is choppy. But walk another mile and a half up the trail, and you'll see a second shipwreck sign that directs you to three sets of ruins half-buried in the sandy beach.

The lighthouse, which was built in 1874, has been renovated by the National Park Service and makes a perfect place to lunch before heading back to the campground.

You could continue along H 58, although only about half of it is paved, and end up in **Munising.** The scenic town is the gateway to the **Pictured Rocks,** sandstone cliffs that rise 50 to 200 feet above Lake Superior and stretch for 15 miles to the east. They are one of the top attractions in the U.P., and a **Pictured Rock Boat Cruise** is the best way to view them.

The three-hour cruises depart from Munising City Harbor, swing past Grand Island, and then skirt the most impressive stretch of Pictured Rocks. Along the way you view such noted formations as Miner's Castle, Battleship

Michigan's Most Beautiful Hike

The Lakeshore Trail in Pictured Rocks National Lakeshore is one of Michigan's most popular backpacking treks, a 42.8-mile hike from Grand Marais to Munising with most of it strung along Lake Superior. But if you don't have four days to spare or the desire to haul a backpack for that long, the Chapel Loop is the perfect alternative.

This hike begins and ends at Chapel parking lot, 14 miles east of Munising via County Road H 58 and then north on Chapel Road. The entire loop is a 10.2-mile walk over generally level terrain, making it a long day hike, but there are many ways to shorten it.

The first leg of the loop is hiking to Lake Superior along Chapel Falls Trail, an old road that heads north into the woods and in 1.4 miles reaches Chapel Falls, one of the most impressive in the park. Two observation decks provide a good view of the 60-foot waterfall that hurls itself over the sharp edge of a cliff into a steep-sided canyon.

In another quarter mile you reach Lake Superior and Chapel Rock, a striking pair of sandstone pillars with a large pine growing on the top of them. Just to the west is Chapel Beach, a half mile of wide, sandy shoreline framed in at one end by colorful sandstone cliffs and at the other by a waterfall where Chapel Creek leaps into Lake Superior.

At this point most people return to the parking lot, following the Chapel Lake Trail for a 6.1-mile loop. Big mistake.

By heading east on Lakeshore Trail, you'll see the most impressive scenery of the day. For the next 4.5 miles, the trail skirts Lake Superior and passes numerous overlooks of the promontories and formations that make up the Grand Portal cliffs. There is no shoreline in Michigan more beautiful than this stretch, where the orange-reddish sandstone contrasts vividly with the deep blue of Lake Superior.

The most interesting spot is a sandy beach just past Grand Portal Point, 4.6 miles into the loop. Only this beach is on top of the cliffs, almost 200 feet above the cold waters of Lake Superior.

From Grand Portal Point you continue along Lake Superior, passing more views of the Pictured Rocks and breaking out at another cliff-top beach, before arriving at Mosquito River.

Mosquito Falls Trail, one of the newest trails in the park, will return you to the parking lot in 2.7 miles and along the way pass several waterfalls.

Rock, Indian Head, Rainbow Cave, and the Colors Caves, along with waterfalls that leap into Lake Superior and kayakers bobbing in and out of sea arches.

Pictured Rock Boat Cruises (906–387–2379) offers daily trips at 10:00 A.M. and 2:00 P.M. Memorial Day through June and September through mid-October, and daily trips at 9:00 and 11:00 A.M. and 1:00, 3:00, and 5:00 P.M. from July

Michigan's Smallest State Park

The smallest unit of the Michigan State Park system is Wagner Falls Scenic Site. The day-use park is only twenty-two acres and consists of a small parking area along M 94, 2 miles south of Munising, and a 200-yard trail that ends at an observation deck. The park is small but beautiful as the deck overlooks Wagner Falls, a 20-foot cascade that splashes down several rock ledges.

through August. The best time for a trip is in late afternoon when the sun setting in the west makes the cliffs even more colorful. The cost is $27 for anyone age twelve or older, $12 for children ages six to eleven, and free for kids age five or younger.

Waterfalls abound in the Munising area, some right on the edge of town. One of them is **Munising Falls.** From H 58 head up Sand Point Road a short way to the National Park Visitor Center, where a quarter-mile path takes you into the woods and up a shaded sandstone canyon. The first viewing platform provides a fine overview of the 50-foot cascade that tumbles straight down a sandstone cliff; a nearby stairway lets you walk up to the falls for a most unusual view of the falling water.

Munising is also on the edge of another park, the Alger Underwater Preserve, a graveyard of shipwrecks that date to the 1800s and early 1900s. The preserve and especially the waters around Grand Island are a haven for scuba divers, who view the wrecks that lie 10 to 100 feet below the surface.

But nondivers can also enjoy the treasures of Lake Superior through **Grand Island Shipwreck Tours.** The company uses a 42-foot vessel with a specially designed hull glass viewing area to let passengers see wrecks in Lake Superior. The two-hour tours depart from Munising daily during the summer and glide over three wrecks as well as sail past the historic lighthouse and the intriguing rock formations of Grand Island.

The most intriguing wreck is the *Bermuda*. The wooden schooner was loaded with 488 tons of iron ore when it left Marquette in 1870 and sank in Grand Harbor during a fierce storm. In 1884 a Canadian salvage company raised the ship, removed its cargo, and resank it in Grand Island's Murray Bay. The *Bermuda* lies only 10 feet below the surface, and in the clear, protective waters of the bay, you can glide right over it and view an entire nineteenth-century ship.

"Everything is still there," says one guide, "everything except the sails and the crew."

Grand Island Shipwreck Tours (906–387–4477) departs from the Munising Dock 1.5 miles west of downtown off M 28. Tours are offered at 10:00 A.M. and 1:00 P.M. daily from June through September, weather permitting. In July and August there is also a 4:00 P.M. trip. The cost is $23 for adults and $10 for children ages six to twelve (five and under are free).

Schoolcraft County

Blaney Park is the town that refuses to die. It's been foreclosed on, boarded up, even auctioned off building by building, but today the village is surging back as a quiet resort with an ideal location for touring the Upper Peninsula. No more than ninety minutes from this one-road hamlet are the U.P.'s most popular attractions: Tahquamenon Falls, Pictured Rocks, the historic town site of Fayette, and miles of Lake Michigan's sandy shoreline.

Originally a logging camp, Blaney and the area around it were logged out by 1926, so its owners searched for another endeavor for the town's residents. With all the lakes and sandy beach nearby, recreation was the answer, and soon Blaney became Blaney Park. Tourists began arriving from all over the Midwest to spend their vacations on the Upper Peninsula. The resort featured a nine-hole golf course, tennis courts, riding stables, daily excursions to Lake Michigan beaches, and a lighted swimming pool for those who preferred to stay close to their cottages. A lumber baron's mansion was renamed Celibeth and was described in one brochure as "a beautiful club-type hotel." The boardinghouse where loggers had lived was turned into a twenty-one-room lodge, and in 1934 the Blaney Inn was built, a huge dining facility that featured stone fireplaces, walls paneled in knotty pine, and seating for 400.

Improved roads in the Upper Peninsula were Blaney Park's downfall. The family that owned the town tried twice to sell it, only to end up with it again when the buyers defaulted on their payments. The last tourist season was in 1972, after which many of the buildings were boarded up, and Blaney Park finally was auctioned off in 1985.

Today Blaney Park has come back to life again as a tourist destination. It can be reached from the Mackinac Bridge by following US 2 west for 66 miles and then north on M 77 for 1 mile.

The twenty-two room **Celibeth** is a beautiful bed-and-breakfast with seven rooms decorated in antiques and furnishings from the resort era of the 1920s. There is an enclosed porch that overlooks the front lawn and features a row of rocking chairs and a sunroom in the back where breakfast and afternoon tea are served. The bed-and-breakfast (906–283–3409) is open from May through October, and the rooms range from $85 to $100 per night.

The loggers' boardinghouse just down the street is now *Blaney Lodge* (906–283–3883), offering budget accommodations. Rooms in the historic lodge are $39 a night, cabins in the back $69. The price includes a breakfast of homemade muffins and fruit in the sunporch in the morning and fresh pie in the evening.

For dinner head over to *Blaney Inn* (906–283–3417), the resort's former dining hall and clubhouse. Dinners range from steaks to seafood fettucine and are priced from $12 to $18. The restaurant is open from June to Labor Day, Thursday through Sunday.

The heart of Schoolcraft County, some 96,000 acres, has been preserved as the largest wildlife refuge east of the Mississippi River. The *Seney National Wildlife Refuge* was established in 1935 by the U.S. Fish and Wildlife Service to provide a habitat for wildlife, primarily waterfowl migrating to nesting grounds in Canada. The refuge surrounds the Great Manistique Swamp, which endured rough treatment beginning in the 1870s when loggers were intent on stripping every tree from the area. Fires were then set deliberately to clear away the debris of the lumbering operation, preventing new forests from taking root. Finally a land development company came through, drained acre after acre of the swamp, and sold the land to farmers for agriculture in 1911. The farmers lasted about a year before discovering they had been swindled—the soil would grow little.

Seney was a wasteland that nobody wanted. The state ended up with it, and during the Great Depression, deeded it to the federal government with the recommendation that it be turned into a refuge. Civilian Conservation Corps workers came in and built dikes, dug ditches, and used other water-control devices to impound 7,000 acres of water in twenty-one major ponds, almost miraculously restoring the marsh. Seney again became a habitat for waterfowl when 332 Canada geese were released in 1936 and established its present nesting flocks. Still more geese and other species of birds depend on the area as an important rest stop on their long migration to and from nesting sites in Canada.

Other wildlife—timber wolves, deer, black bears, moose, and coyotes—live in the refuge, but the Canada goose has clearly become the symbol of Seney's return to wilderness. You will see the "honkers" the minute you drive into the parking lot of the visitor center, as a few tame ones are always around looking for a handout from softhearted tourists. The center overlooks one of the many ponds in the refuge, and a telescope at its large viewing window lets you search the marsh area for some of the more than 200 species of birds that can be found here. The center has displays, a children's touch table, and an auditorium that hosts nature movies and slide programs each hour. It is open from mid-May through mid-October from 9:00 A.M. to 5:00 P.M. daily.

The best way to view the wildlife is to follow the 7-mile **Marshland Wildlife Drive** in your car as it winds its way among the ponds, starting near the center and ending at M 77 just south of the refuge entrance. Pick up a free guide that points out items of interest at a number of marked stops, including an active bald eagle nest that can be seen clearly from the drive. Timing is important for spotting wildlife, and it is best to follow the drive either in early morning or at dusk when the animals are most active. Often during the peak of the tourist season, the refuge will stage guided evening tours that depart around 6:00 P.M. and last for almost two hours. Call the visitor center (906–586–9851) for information about the auto tours.

Another unique way to view more remote areas of the refuge is to paddle the handful of rivers that flow through it. **Northland Outfitters** (906–586–9801), located in nearby Germfask, offers canoe rentals for the area. It will supply canoes, paddles, life jackets, and transportation to the Manistique River, which runs through the southeast corner of Seney. The trips are self-guided, last either two or four hours, and offer the possibility of spotting beavers, deer, otters, and a variety of birds or of fishing for walleye or pike in the river.

On the opposite scale of parks is Palms Brook, a state park of only 388 acres located 12 miles northwest of Manistique on M 149. The park may be small, but it's equally intriguing because of **Kitch-Iti-Kipi,** Michigan's largest spring. The natural spring pours out more than 10,000 gallons of water per minute from fissures in the underlying limestone, and

strange as it sounds

Manistique boasts a bridge "below the level of the river." Built in 1919, the 300-foot-long Siphon Bridge crosses the Manistique River and is actually below the river because water is atmospherically forced under it. The bridge became famous when it was featured in the "Ripley's Believe It or Not" newspaper series. The bridge is on M 94 at the north end of the downtown area.

has created a crystal clear pool 200 feet wide and 40 feet deep. Visitors board a wooden raft with observation holes in the middle and pull themselves across the spring to get a good view of the fantasy world below. Between the swirls of sand and ghostly bubbles rising up, you can view ancient trees with branches encrusted in limestone, huge brown trout slipping silently by, and colors and shapes that challenge the imagination. The spring is especially enchanting in the early morning, when a mist lies over the water and the trout rise to the surface. Palms Brook has a picnic area but no campsites, and there is a vehicle fee to enter. The raft is free.

Delta County

In the mid-1800s iron ore was shipped from the Upper Peninsula mines to foundries in the lower Great Lakes area at a tremendous cost to companies. The high price of shipping was due to the inefficient method of transportation coupled with the nearly 40 percent waste the ore contained. Fayette Brown, general manager of the Jackson Iron Company, studied the problem and decided the solution was to build a company-owned furnace not far from the mine, where the ore could be smelted into pig iron before it was shipped to the steelmaking centers. The town he planned to build at the smelter had to be a reasonable distance from the Escanaba ore docks, possess a natural harbor, and be near large amounts of limestone and hardwood forests to smelt the iron ore. In 1866 Brown chose a spot on the Garden Peninsula overlooking Big Bay de Noc, and the town of Fayette was born.

A year later work began on the furnace and charcoal kiln, and by Christmas the first iron from Fayette was cast. Quickly a town emerged. There were the superintendent's house on a bluff overlooking the harbor, a company office, nine frame dwellings for the engineers and skilled workers, and forty log cabins for the laborers. Eventually Fayette featured a machine shop, a small railroad, barns, a blacksmith shop, a hotel, and even an opera house. It was a total community that in 1884 had a population of almost 1,000 and turned out 16,875 tons of iron. Toward the end of that decade, however, Fayette's fate was sealed. The price of pig iron fell, and newly developed coke blast furnaces produced a higher-quality iron at a much cheaper cost. In 1891 the company closed down the furnaces, and within a few years Fayette became a ghost town.

Charcoal Kiln in Fayette State Park

A Hemlock Cathedral

When we entered the cathedral it was quiet, a little dark, and almost spiritual. It was a place to ponder, maybe even meditate, but this was no church. It was a stand of hemlocks that somehow survived the logging era Michigan experienced at the turn of the twentieth century.

Today the Hemlock Cathedral is part of the Little Bay de Noc Recreation Area, and it's where you go to see what a 300-year-old tree looks like. Trees that old are so tall you can't see the tops of them, so big that two people can't link arms around them, so rare that all that's left are pockets scattered across a state that was once blanketed by them.

In Escanaba residents could see the giant hemlocks on the other side of Little Bay de Noc, and by the late 1800s the spot was a popular weekend retreat known as Maywood. When a small resort hotel was built there in 1904, this pocket of old growth was preserved from the loggers advancing down the Stonington Peninsula.

Today the Hemlock Cathedral in the Little Bay de Noc Recreation Area is as quiet and impressive as it was a century ago. The virgin hemlocks are seen by hiking the Maywood History Trail, an easy half-mile loop that includes almost a dozen interpretive plaques.

The recreation area also includes a sandy beach, picnic area, thirty-six rustic campsites, and two other trails. The Hiawatha National Forest facility is on County Road 513, 7 miles south of US 2 on the Stonington Peninsula. There is a vehicle entry fee and a nightly fee for camping. For more information call the Rapid River Ranger Station at (906) 474–6442.

Fayette changed hands several times; at last the state of Michigan obtained the area in 1959 and turned it into *Fayette State Park.* The town booms again now as a scenic ghost town overlooking Snail Shell Harbor, with its towering white cliffs. The 365-acre park is reached from US 2 on County Road 483 and contains an interpretive museum with information, guide maps, and a scale model of Fayette during its heyday. From there you leisurely wander among twenty-two existing buildings, of which nine are open. The renovated structures, which are furnished, include the company office, the hotel, the opera house, and a home of one of the skilled employees. More will be opened up in the future.

Fayette State Park (906–644–2603) also has eighty campsites, a beach and picnic area, and boat-launching facilities. The museum is open daily mid-May through June and September to mid-October from 9:00 A.M. to 5:00 P.M. and in July and August from 9:00 A.M. to 9:00 P.M. There is a vehicle fee to enter the park and a per-night fee to camp.

Another spot worth searching out on the Garden Peninsula is **Portage Bay State Campground,** which is reached from County Road 483 (before the state park) by turning off on County Road 08 and carefully following the signs. Getting to the rustic campground (no electricity, pit toilets) is a bumpy 5-mile ride along dirt roads, but the camping area is worth it: You pitch your tent or park your trailer among the pine trees that border the sandy beach of the bay. You can stroll along the beach, follow the hiking trails in the area, or take a dip in the clear water of Lake Michigan.

A delightful picnic area in Delta County is **Peninsula Point Lighthouse,** the guiding light at the very tip of the Stonington Peninsula that was built in 1865. Congress authorized the funds the year before, because the wooden sailing ships hauling lumber, iron ore, and fish from Escanaba and Fayette were no match for the treacherous shoals and reefs that separated Big Bay de Noc from Little Bay de Noc. The light went out for the last time in 1936, and the house portion of the lighthouse burned to the ground in 1959. But the view from the point was so spectacular that the Forest Service made it into a public picnic area in 1937.

strangeasitsounds

Gladstone, a small town just north of Escanaba, is home to the world's largest manufacturer of pet caskets. Hoegh Industries Inc., 317 Delta Street, produces a line of pet caskets that range in price from $15 to more than $300. You can tour the small plant and "learn the history of the pet burial phenomenon" weekdays from 8:00 A.M. to 4:00 P.M. Among the things you learn is that pet caskets are also used by amputees to bury their severed limbs. Call Hoegh Industries in advance at (906) 428–2151 to arrange a tour.

Climb the forty steps to the top of the square brick tower and you're greeted with a 360-degree panorama that includes the Escanaba waterfront to the west, the limestone bluffs of Fayette State Park to the east, and the length of Lake Michigan in front of you. You can either hike to it or drive in. The 1.5-mile hike is a scenic walk, while the final mile to the nineteenth-century light is a narrow, winding, and very bumpy one-lane road not recommended for vehicles more than 16 feet long or 8 feet high.

To reach the lighthouse from Rapid River, head east on US 2 to the Stonington exit. Go south 19 miles on County Road 513 to Stonington, and then take Forest Road 2204. The RV parking area and trailhead are reached before the forest road turns into a narrow, one-lane road in the final mile.

Places to Stay in the Eastern Upper Peninsula

AU TRAIN

Pinewood Lodge Bed and Breakfast,
M 28,
(906) 892–8300

BLANEY PARK

Celibeth House Bed & Breakfast,
M 77,
(906) 283–3409

ESCANABA

Fishery Pointe Beach Cottages,
E5041 M 35,
(906) 786–1852

Terrace Bay Resort,
US 2 and M 41,
(906) 786–7554

MACKINAC ISLAND

Chippewa Hotel,
Main Street,
(800) 241–3341

Grand Hotel,
West Bluff Road,
(800) 334–7263

La Chance Cottage,
Huron Street,
(906) 847–3526

Mission Point Resort,
Lakeshore Road,
(800) 833–7711

Murray Hotel,
Main Street,
(800) 462–2546

MANISTIQUE

Comfort Inn,
726 East Lakeshore Drive,
(906) 341–6981

Northshore Motor Inn,
East US 2,
(906) 341–2420

MUNISING

Best Western Munising,
M 28,
(906) 387–4864

Super 8 Motel,
M 28 and County Road H 13,
(906) 387–2466

NEWBERRY

Comfort Inn,
M 123 and M 28,
(906) 293–3218

PARADISE

Birchwood Lodges,
8442 North Whitefish Point Road,
(906) 492–3320

SAULT STE. MARIE

Comfort Inn,
4404 I–75 Business Loop,
(906) 635–1118

La France Terrace Motel,
1608 Ashmun Street,
(888) 458–1144

Ojibway Hotel,
240 West Portage,
(800) 654–2929

ST. IGNACE

Aurora Borealis Motor Inn,
635 I–75 Business Loop,
(906) 643–7488

Days Inn,
1074 North State Street,
(800) 732–9746

Places to Eat in the Eastern Upper Peninsula

AU TRAIN

Brownstone Inn
(American),
M 28,
(906) 892–8332

BLANEY PARK

Blaney Inn (American),
M 77,
(906) 283–3417

BRIMLEY

Wilcox's Fish House (fish),
1232 South Wilcox Lane,
(906) 437–5407

ESCANABA

Delona (American),
7132 US 2,
(906) 786–6400

Hereford & Hops
(brew pub),
624 Ludington Avenue,
(906) 789–1945

GRAND MARAIS

Lake Superior Brewing Company (brew pub),
M 77,
(906) 494–2337

MACKINAC ISLAND

French Outpost
(outdoor dining),
Cadotte Avenue,
(906) 847–3772

Governor's Dining Room (fine dining), Island House Hotel, (906) 847–3347

Pilot House Restaurant, Lake View Hotel, (906) 847–3384

MANISTIQUE

Sunny Shores (American), US 2, (906) 341–5582

MUNISING

Camel Riders, 5609 North Camel Rider Drive (Wetmore), (906) 573–2319

Dogpatch (American), 325 East Superior Street, (906) 387–9948

NEWBERRY

Pickelman's Pantry (American), M 123 and M 28, (906) 293–3777

PARADISE

Tahquamenon Falls Brewery (brew pub), Tahquamenon Falls State Park, (906) 492–3300

SAULT STE. MARIE

Antlers (American), 804 East Portage, (906) 632–3571

Freighters (fine dining), Ojibway Hotel, 240 West Portage, (906) 632–4211

Studebaker's (American), 3583 I–75 Business Spur, (906) 632–4262

ST. IGNACE

Galley Restaurant (American), 241 North State Street, (906) 643–7960

SELECTED CHAMBERS OF COMMERCE AND TOURISM BUREAUS

Bays de Noc Visitors Bureau, P.O. Box 614, Escanaba 49829; (800) 533–4386; www.deltafun.com

Mackinac Island Chamber of Commerce, P.O. Box 451, Mackinac Island 49757; (800) 454–5227; www.mackinacisland.org

Newberry Area Tourism Association, P.O. Box 308, Newberry 49868; (800) 831–7292

Sault Convention and Visitors Bureau, 536 Ashmun Street, Sault Ste. Marie 49783; (800) 647–2858; www.saultstemarie.com

St. Ignace Tourist Association, 560 North State Street, St. Ignace 49781; (800) 338–6660; www.stignace.com

OTHER ATTRACTIONS

Grand Island Recreation Area,
Munising

Mackinac Island Carriage Tours,
Mackinac Island

Paulson House Museum,
Au Train

Sand Point Lighthouse,
Escanaba

Tahquamenon Logging Museum,
Newberry

Western Upper Peninsula

Michigan's most remote and rustic region is the rugged western Upper Peninsula. Two small ranges located here constitute the only true mountains in any of the Great Lakes states; between Baraga and Marquette lie the Huron Mountains, and along the Lake Superior shoreline, from west of Ontonagon to Copper Harbor, is the Copper Range. Within these rugged hills are Mount Arvon, the highest point in Michigan at 1,979 feet above sea level, and the Porcupine Mountains, between whose ridges and peaks lies the stunning Lake of the Clouds.

It was in these hills of the western U.P. that the great iron and copper mines flourished from the 1800s to the 1940s, bringing boatloads of immigrants from Norway, Finland, and Italy to work in the shafts. Today the remnants of the mining era are ghost towns, abandoned mines, and communities with strong ethnic heritage and pride.

For most Michigan residents, this region of the state is a remote, distant place; driving to Copper Harbor from Detroit is the same distance as traveling to Washington, D.C. But once it is "discovered," travelers marvel at the western U.P.'s natural wonders. More than for its mines, pasty shops, and historical museums, you come to this region of Michigan for the beauty

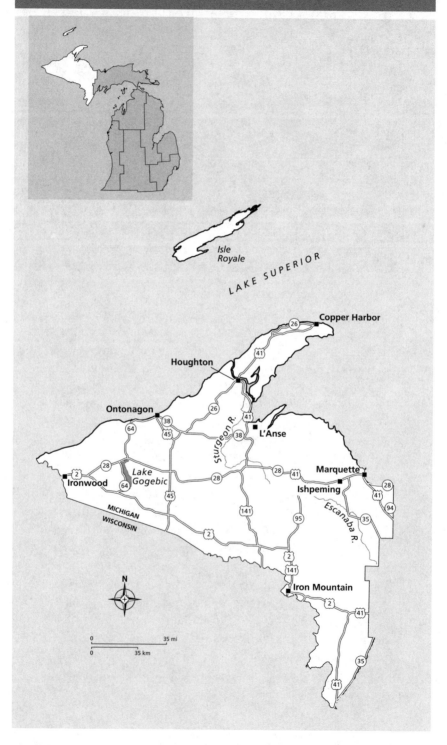

Isle
Royale

LAKE SUPERIOR

Copper Harbor

Houghton

Ontonagon

L'Anse

Marquette

Ishpeming

Ironwood

Lake
Gogebic

Sturgeon R.

Escanaba R.

MICHIGAN
WISCONSIN

Iron Mountain

N

0   35 mi
0   35 km

of nature's handiwork: cascading waterfalls, panoramas of forested wilderness, a lake set in a sea of reds, yellows, and oranges painted by autumn leaves.

Marquette County

The largest county in Michigan consists of 1,873 square miles, 1,800 lakes, 73 miles of Lake Superior shoreline, and Marquette, the largest (and, some say, only) city in the Upper Peninsula. The city of 23,000 became a spot on the map with a post office in 1849, and it bloomed the following decade as the port and shipping center for the nearby iron mines and logging camps. The lumber and mining barons graced the streets of Marquette with mansions, many still standing today. From Front Street turn east onto Ridge Street and you'll head toward Lake Superior, passing one late-Victorian home after another until you end up in the parking lot of the ***Marquette Maritime Museum*** on the waterfront.

The museum is housed in the red sandstone Old Water Works Building and features displays on shipwrecks, antique outboard motors and boats, commercial fishermen who worked the area, and other facets of the city's maritime days, which fed many and made some (from the look of their homes) incredibly wealthy. The museum (906–226–2006) is open from mid-May through October from 10:00 A.M. to 7:00 P.M. Monday through Thursday and 10:00 A.M. to 5:00 P.M. Friday through Sunday. There is a small admission fee.

AUTHOR'S TOP TEN PICKS

Black River Harbor Drive,
Bessemer;
(906) 667–0261

Canyon Falls and Gorge,
L'Anse;
(906) 524–7444

Fort Wilkins,
Copper Harbor;
(906) 289–4215

Hanka Homestead,
L'Anse;
(906) 334–2601

Iron County Museum,
Caspian;
(906) 265–2617

Lake of the Clouds,
Silver City;
(906) 885–5275

Michigan Iron Industry Museum,
Negaunee;
(906) 475–7857

Piers Gorge,
Norway;
(906) 774–2002

Quincy Mine,
Hancock;
(906) 482–3101

Sand Hills Lighthouse Inn,
Eagle River;
(906) 337–1744

The largest and most interesting structures on Marquette's waterfront are the iron ore docks that load the rock into Great Lakes freighters for a journey south. The Lake Superior and Ishpeming Railroad docks are still operating today, and the best vantage point is *Presque Isle Park.* The 328-acre city park is not an island but a peninsula that juts out into Lake Superior on the north side of Marquette. A road circles the park shoreline, beginning on the south side, where you can see the ore docks and, if your timing is right, watch a freighter take on its load (one to three times a week).

The drive continues and passes the steep red cliffs of Lookout Point and then the view at Sunset Point, where residents gather to watch the end of another day. The park also has an outdoor band shell with weekly events, a small zoo, a beach and bathhouse, picnic areas, and bicycle paths. Hiking trails crisscross the forested interior of Presque Isle and become a favorite spot for Nordic skiers during the winter. The park is open daily from 7:00 A.M. to 11:00 P.M., and perhaps the best time of year to visit it is the last weekend in July during its Art-on-the-Rocks Festival, when local artists gather to display and sell their work in this picturesque setting.

In Marquette's Lower Harbor are the Old Ore Docks, no longer operating, which have been designated a state historic site. An excellent place to view the docks is from a table in the *Vierling Saloon* at Front and Main Streets. The saloon was opened in 1883 by Martin Vierling, an art lover and saloonkeeper who headed north with his paintings after running an establishment in Detroit. Later the art lover's bar became just another cafe during Prohibition, but the present proprietors, Terry and Christi Doyle, have turned back the clock by renovating the interior and returning the building to its original function as a saloon, brew pub, and fine restaurant. The brick walls inside once again feature paintings and prints, as the owners exhibit the works of a different artist every month. There are also old photographs and artifacts of early Marquette, and the large windows in the rear of the restaurant overlook the iron ore docks. A pair of binoculars hangs on the back wall for anyone wanting a closer look at the massive structure.

The fare is "geared to healthy food," and the dinner menu features several shrimp and chicken entrees and Rogan Josh, an Indian spiced red stew served with yellow rice and chutney. The Vierling Saloon (906–228–3533) is open daily except Sunday from 11:00 A.M. to 10:00 P.M. Dinner is served after 4:00 P.M., and prices range from $11 to $16.

For an excellent view of all of Marquette, head north of town on County Road 550 for a few miles and turn into the dirt parking lot marked by the large SUGAR LOAF sign. This is the start of the *Sugar Loaf Recreation Trail,* a wide and easy path that winds 0.6 mile up the peak of the same name. You actually climb 315 feet through forest and over granite ridges by a series of steps until you reach the rocky knob marked by a stone monument. The view is spectacular on a clear day, a 360-degree panorama that includes the city, Lake Superior, the rough coastline, and the many offshore islands.

By continuing north on County Road 550 for another 26 miles, you reach its end in the small village of Big Bay on the shores of Lake Independence. Big Bay is best known as a place where scenes for the 1959 film *Anatomy of a Murder,* starring Jimmy Stewart and Lee Remick, were shot. The story is true, though the murder really took place at the Lumberjack Tavern, a classic north woods bar that was used for one scene in the movie. Other footage was shot in the Big Bay Hotel, which is now the *Thunder Bay Inn.*

A Cabin in the Woods

The most unusual lodging accommodations in Marquette County come without a flush toilet, a shower, or any plumbing, for that matter. There are no mattresses, telephones, or televisions with HBO. Heat is a stack of logs and a wood-burning stove. Hopefully you brought some matches.

But what a view!

From the porch of Cabin No. 3 in the Little Presque Isle State Forest Recreation Area, you can watch the rays of an early morning sun spread across Harlow Lake. In the background is the rocky crown of Hogsback Mountain, and when the rising sun paints it in a light shade of pink, it's the closest thing we have to alpenglow in Michigan.

Built in 1996, the six rustic cabins are scattered in Little Presque Isle, a 3,040-acre tract located 5 miles northwest of Marquette and split in the middle by County Road 550. You can't drive to them, but the walk in is not far. Cabins No. 1, 2, and 3 are a mere 200 yards from where you park the car. Cabin No. 5, the farthest from the trailhead, is only a half mile away.

Yet for the price of a little boot leather and the $35-per-night rental fee, you're ensured of solitude and peace of mind in one of the most picturesque settings in the Upper Peninsula. To reserve the cabins or obtain a brochure on Little Presque Isle State Forest Recreation Area, call the Department of Natural Resources office in Marquette at (906) 228-6561.

TOP ANNUAL EVENTS

Noquemenon Ski Marathon,
Marquette, January;
(906) 486–4841

U.P. 200 Sled Dog Championship,
Marquette, February;
(800) 544–4321

Winter Carnival,
Houghton, January;
(800) 338–7982

Art on the Rocks,
Marquette, July;
(800) 544–4321

Pine Mountain Classic,
Iron Mountain, February;
(800) 236–2447

U.P. Championship Rodeo,
Iron River, July;
(906) 265–9938

Snowburst,
Porcupine Mountains Wilderness
State Park, February;
(906) 885–5275

Ore to Shore Mountain Bike Epic,
Ishpeming, August;
(906) 486–4841

The large inn was built in 1911 as a company store and warehouse and then turned into a hotel. In 1943, Henry Ford purchased it along with the mill at the north end of the lake to produce the wooden parts for his cars. The industrialist extensively remodeled the hotel and reshaped the landscape in front of it. So obsessed was Ford with being able to see his factory from his hotel that he had the town's railroad depot moved and County Road 550 rerouted. It was in 1958, under different owners, that several short scenes of the famous murder mystery were filmed in the hotel's lobby, dining room, and bedrooms upstairs. Eventually the facility was abandoned and sat empty for ten years.

In 1985 Darryl Small bought the hotel, and he opened the first of twelve rooms two years later. Today the large inn is an interesting place to stay or have dinner. All the rooms have been renovated. (You can even stay in Ford's Room.) Guests begin their day with coffee and rolls served on the second-floor balcony, which is furnished with wicker and overlooks the lake and, yes, Ford's old factory. Room rates for double occupancy range from $65 to $109. For reservations call (906) 345–9376 or write Thunder Bay Inn, P.O. Box 28, Big Bay 49808.

An equally interesting place to stay in the area is the ***Big Bay Point Lighthouse,*** the secluded retreat 3.5 miles north of town on Lighthouse Road. The light at Big Bay was built and put into service in 1896 and included a two-story, redbrick dwelling with eighteen rooms. The house was divided in half, with the lightkeeper living in one half and his assistant in the other. The Coast

Guard automated the light in 1941 and then sold the structure in 1961 after building a new steel tower nearby.

In 1986 the lighthouse became a unique bed-and-breakfast offering guests the rare opportunity to stay overnight in one of its six bedrooms. The lights stand high above Lake Superior on a rocky point in the middle of forty wooded acres that include 2 miles of trails. You can climb the narrow staircase to the top of the tower for a splendid view of the area, catching a sunrise over Lake Superior at daybreak, a sunset over the Huron Mountains at dusk, or possibly the Northern Lights at night. The interior has been completely renovated and refinished, showing its natural wood and brick, and the various rooms include a delightful sauna.

The lighthouse (906–345–9957) is open year-round, with special rates for the off-season, weekdays, and package stays. The basic rate for the summer ranges from $165 to $185 for rooms that sleep from two to four people. For reservations write Lighthouse, P.O. Box 3, Big Bay 49808.

The railroad depot that Henry Ford moved in Big Bay is yet another addition to the unusual lodgings found in this small town. After being salvaged in 1988, the **Big Bay Depot** is now offering history, natural beauty, and a comfortable bed.

The depot has five large rooms available, featuring private baths, kitchens, and sitting areas. Best of all, every room on the second floor leads out to

Mountain Biking in the Huron Mountains

There is some great mountain biking in the Big Bay area along old logging roads and two-tracks into the foothills of the Huron Mountains. Bisected by County Roads 550 and 510, this scenic area is a rugged forest laced with trout streams, waterfalls, and miles of old logging roads and obscured two-tracks.

Unlike most southern Michigan trails, there are no directional arrows, mileage markers, or cute names for technical sections in the woods north of Marquette. Before heading out purchase the most detailed topographical maps the U.S. Geological Survey produces on the area, the 7.5-minute quadrangle series of Silver Lake Basin, Negaunee NW, and Buckroe. Then pack a compass, plus a few pieces of survival gear in case you get totally lost and have to spend the night in the woods, and head down County Road 510 from Big Bay, stopping at the first two-track that looks inviting.

Great Northern Adventures offers both day trips for mountain bikers out of Big Bay and multiday packages with accommodations at the Thunder Bay Inn. Contact the tour company at (906) 225–8687 or www.greatnorthernadventures.com for a brochure.

another deck with a panorama of the lake, anglers jigging for perch, and Ford's old mill.

From Marquette, head north on County Road 550 for 25 miles to Big Bay. The driveway to the Big Bay Depot (906–345–9350) is across County Road 550 from the Lumberjack Tavern. Rooms are $55 a night.

The newest Michigan historical museum is tucked away in the woods near Negaunee and is probably passed up by many visitors. That's a shame. The ***Michigan Iron Industry Museum*** is an interesting stop that lets you leisurely explore the history of the Upper Peninsula's iron industry. The museum lies in the forested ravines of the Marquette Iron Range and overlooks the Carp River, where the first iron forge in the Lake Superior region was built in 1848. The U.P.'s iron deposits had been discovered four years earlier when William Burt, leader of a U.S. Geological Survey party near the area, noticed the magnetic needle of his compass jumping wildly about. He instructed his men to search the ground, and they immediately turned up outcroppings of almost pure iron among the roots of pine trees. The iron era of the U.P. had begun, and in 1846 the Jackson Mine, the first operation in the U.P., was opened near Negaunee.

The museum does an excellent job of leading you through the history of iron, from its beginnings to its most robust era to the decline of the industry in the 1960s. Inside are several levels of displays, a reconstructed mine shaft to walk through, and an auditorium that presents a short introductory program. Outside are more artifacts, including a mine locomotive, and trails leading to the old forge site on the Carp River. The museum (906–475–7857) is reached from US 41 by turning onto County Road 492 about 3 miles east of Negaunee and is open daily from 9:30 A.M. to 4:30 P.M. from May through October. Admission is free.

To view a real working iron mine, join a ***Tilden Mine Tour*** near Ishpeming. The popular, two-and-one-half-hour tours give visitors a firsthand look at how iron ore is mined from open pits and includes a walk through the plant where the ore is processed and pelletized. You leave with souvenir taconite pellets from the processing plant.

The tours are offered once a day, Tuesday through Saturday, from mid-June through August, with a bus leaving the Lake Superior Community Partnership office at 501 South Front Street in Marquette at noon and the U.S. National Ski Hall of Fame in Ishpeming at 12:30 P.M. Reservations are highly recommended and can be made by calling (906) 486–4841 or (888) 578–6489. The cost is $9.00 per person.

Though it might surprise a few people, especially avid skiers, Ishpeming is home of the ***U.S. National Ski Hall of Fame.*** The hall was established here in 1954 because the Ishpeming Ski Club is "the oldest active ski club in the country."

Formed in 1887, the club was founded by Scandinavians who had emigrated to the U.P. to work the Marquette Range iron mines and brought their love of skiing with them. They were soon hosting ski jumping tournaments and in 1926 moved their ramps and competition site to a large bowl owned by Cleveland-Cliffs, Inc. When a skier badly injured himself in practice that first year, a local reporter dubbed the area "Suicide Hill" and the name stuck, much to the alarm of club officials who were trying to promote the new jumps.

In the early 1990s the Hall of Fame was relocated to a new building in Ishpeming that features an impressive roofline in the shape of a ski jump. Inside are exhibits and displays that detail the history of skiing from medieval times to the latest Winter Olympics. All three forms of skiing are included—Nordic, Alpine, and ski jumping—and many visitors are amazed to learn that Alpine skiing is a relatively new version of the sport.

The Ski Hall of Fame (906–485–6323) is on US 41 between Second and Third Streets and is open from 10:00 A.M. to 5:00 P.M. Monday through Saturday. There is a small admission fee.

Baraga County

Most roadside rest areas in the Upper Peninsula consist of little more than picnic tables, a pair of pit toilets, and a hand pump for water. Then there is the one on US 41, 8 miles south of L'Anse. It consists of picnic tables, a pair of pit toilets, a hand pump for water, and one of the most beautiful canyons in Michigan. The state's Department of Transportation maintains the tables and the toilets, but it was forestry students from Michigan Technological University who built the wooden boardwalks and observation platforms that make **_Canyon Falls and Gorge_** such a pleasant stop.

From the large display map in the rest area, the path departs into the woods, crosses a bridge over Bacco Stream, and within a half mile comes to the impressive Canyon Falls formed by the Sturgeon River. The falls mark the beginning of the canyon by thundering over a rock ledge to the river 30 feet below. Handrails have been erected here, and you can lean over the top of the cascade to listen to its roar or to feel the mist the falling water creates.

At this point there is a TRAIL ENDS sign, but the best part of the area, the gorge itself, can be seen only by following the original path, which snakes around a huge rock face. This path hugs the half-mile-long canyon and lets you view the Sturgeon River, a stretch of roiling white water that rushes through sheer rock walls 50 feet high. All visitors, especially families with young children, should be extremely careful if they choose to continue to the end of the old trail, a mile-long one-way hike. The original log handrails are

Strange As It Sounds

Highpointers are a group of adventurers whose mission in life is to stand on the highest point in all 50 states. They used to come to L'Anse from every corner of the country looking for Mount Curwood, which for two decades was thought to be Michigan's highest point at 1,996.4 feet. They would fly to Marquette, drive to Baraga County, and then search out some local for detailed directions on how to follow a maze of logging roads to the top of the peak.

Imagine their shock when the Department of the Interior conducted a survey in 1982 and concluded that Mount Curwood is really only 1,978.34 feet in elevation and actually the second highest spot in the state. Michigan's loftiest peak is nearby Mount Arvon, which at 1,979.238 feet above sea level is 11 inches higher than Curwood.

Many highpointers, who had climbed Mount Curwood 15 or 20 years earlier, were forced to return to Michigan and climb Mount Arvon. And when they finally reached the peak, what did they see? Most of the time nothing more than the trees at the top. The exception is in late fall after the leaves have dropped and a view through the trees is possible.

What there is on the summit of Arvon is a USGS brass marker verifying the elevation. There is also a small yellow mailbox containing a logbook so you can document your achievement of not getting lost as well as noting how many other highpoints you have reached.

still up, but they're flimsy and weak in places, and after they end there is nothing between you and the sharp edge of the gorge.

To reach the roof of the state, you have to find **Mount Arvon** in the Upper Peninsula, which at 1,979 feet is 21 feet short of being a true "mountain" but still the highest point in Michigan. The outing involves following unmarked logging roads in a remote section of Baraga County and hoping you can find your way back. Once on top there is no majestic view, just a yellow box in a forest with a register book inside.

But enough people undertake this adventure that the Baraga County Tourism and Recreation Association (906–524–7444) publishes a map and a set of detailed directions to the highpoint. The association visitor center is right off US 41 as you enter L'Anse from the east. It has irregular hours.

Although serious research on the subject has never been done, many say the largest and best sweet rolls in the state are found at the **Hilltop Restaurant,** on US 41 just south of L'Anse. One roll is an ample breakfast for most people since it measures more than 5 inches across and 3 inches thick and arrives filled with cinnamon and dripping in glaze. The restaurant is operated by Judy Jaeger and Vivian Delene, but its sweet-roll fame was already established when they bought the business in 1975. On a good weekend they will serve more than a thousand. The eatery also has other items on its menu (including good pastries), but who has room for anything else after devouring its sticky specialty with a cup of fresh-brewed coffee? The Hilltop is open from 6:00 A.M. to 8:00 P.M. daily.

One of Baraga County's most interesting attractions is the **Hanka Homestead,** a "living outdoor museum" where visitors learn about and see the lifestyle of the early Finnish farmers who immigrated to what was then a remote and isolated region of the state. The farm dates back to 1896, when the Hanka family applied for a homestead on two forty-acre parcels along the military road to Fort Wilkins at the tip of the Keweenaw Peninsula. The first thing Herman Hanka built was an 18-by-24-foot log house. But he was Finnish, so the second thing he constructed was his *savu,* or smoke sauna. Eventually he added barns, a self-cooling milk house that straddles a small spring, a horse stable, a blacksmith shop, and a granary.

The amazing thing about the farm is that it's never been wired for electricity, even though the youngest son, Jalmer Hanka, lived there until 1966. It was added to the National Register of Historic Places in 1984 and opened to the public the next year. Today there are ten buildings and a root cellar to explore, each filled with the Hanka possessions. From US 41 in L'Anse, head north toward Houghton, and in 12 miles turn west on Arnheim Road. Follow the small museum signs. If you pass Otter Lake, you've gone too far west. The homestead (906–334–2601) is open Tuesday, Thursday, Saturday, and Sunday from noon to 4:00 P.M. from Memorial Day to Labor Day. There is a small admission fee.

Houghton County

One of the most spectacular areas of the U.P.'s interior is relatively unknown to travelers who are hesitant to leave paved roads. The **Sturgeon River Gorge Area** is located just inside Houghton County along its border with Baraga County south of M 3838. The wilderness area includes the gorge cut by the Sturgeon River, which in some places is more than 400 feet deep, making it the largest and deepest in the Great Lakes states. For the best view of it, follow M 3838 west of Baraga and turn south onto Prickett Dam Road (also called Forest Road 193), marked by a national forest sign. Within 11 miles the road merges into Sturgeon Gorge Road (Forest Road 191), and a few hundred yards to the right there is a sharp 90-degree curve. At this bend an extremely rough Jeep trail leads west to the edge of the gorge. It is best to walk the quarter mile that ends at one of the most beautiful panoramas in the U.P. You see the deep gorge below and miles of forested ridges and hills to the west.

Before reaching Sturgeon Gorge Road, you will pass a directional sign for *Silver Mountain.* Located on the edge of the Sturgeon River Gorge Wilderness in Houghton County, Silver Mountain is a 1,312-foot peak, once the site of a fire tower. At a small parking lot, you'll find a long stairway—long as in 250 steps—but once on top you'll see the foundation of the old fire tower, two USGS markers, and a view that includes miles of the rugged Sturgeon River Gorge Wilderness.

There are a handful of mine tours in the Upper Peninsula, but the best one is at the *Quincy Mine.* The Quincy Mining Company was organized in 1846 and for almost 100 years it mined the Pewabic copper lode located just north of Hancock. It was such a moneymaker that the mine was nicknamed Old Reliable, and today it is part of the new Keweenaw National Historical Park.

The two-hour tour begins with the world's largest steam hoist, a giant spool that holds 13,200 feet of cable and lowered workers into Shaft No. 2 of the underground mine to a depth of 9,200 feet. You then board a cog tram for a journey down the steep Quincy Hill to the entrance of Shaft No. 5. Here tractor-drawn wagons take you a half mile into a horizontal tunnel 400 feet below the surface.

Exhibits and videos in the hoist house round out a visit to the mine. The Quincy Mine (906–482–3101) is open from mid-May to Labor Day, and full tours are $12.50 for adults and $7.50 for children. Summer hours are 8:30 A.M. to 7:00 P.M. Monday through Saturday and 12:30 to 7:00 P.M. Sunday.

In nearby Lake Linden, right downtown on Calumet Avenue, is *Lindell's Chocolate Shop.* Joseph Bosch had the building erected in 1893 for his Bosch Brewing Company, but in 1918 it was refurbished with wooden ceiling fans, twenty high-backed oak booths, a nickelodeon, leaded glass windows, and a 6-foot-long marble food preparation table that took four people to lift. It became the Chocolate Shop, and though the entire building was moved down the street in 1928, little of the interior has changed since then.

The menu has, however, as the shop no longer makes candy but specializes in homemade ice cream. The 1943 ice-cream maker is still proudly displayed in the front window. You can arise at 4:00 A.M. any day and watch the

funfacts

In Laurium, where Tamarack Street joins M 28, is the George Gipp Memorial. Better known as "the Gipper," Laurium's most famous son went on to become a football star at Notre Dame University. Legend has it that from his deathbed, he uttered the famous line to coach Knute Rockne, "Tell the boys to win one for the Gipper." The part of the Gipper and the deathbed scene gave Ronald Reagan his most memorable movie role.

Toledo for the Upper Peninsula

By 1835 Michigan had grown sufficiently to qualify for statehood, but Congress held it up because of a boundary controversy with Ohio over a sliver of land that included Toledo. The so-called Toledo War resulted in both states' calling out their militias but, fortunately, no bloodshed. When Michigan gave up claims to the city, it was awarded the Upper Peninsula and statehood, becoming the 26th state in 1837.

ice cream being made, or come by at a more reasonable hour and taste the frozen treat.

Lindell's Chocolate Shop (906–296–0793) is also a restaurant and bar with a full menu, but unquestionably it is the ice cream and the malts, milk shakes, sundaes, and banana splits that are its most popular items. The shop is open Monday through Thursday and Saturday from 6:30 A.M. to 7:00 P.M. and Friday from 6:30 A.M. to 8:00 P.M.

Keweenaw County

Under the forceful will of President Andrew Jackson, Michigan became a state in 1837, when it grudgingly accepted the entire U.P. in exchange for surrendering Toledo to Ohio. In only six years, this "worthless wilderness" became a land of incredible wealth after Douglas Houghton, the first state geologist, explored the Keweenaw Peninsula and reported finding chunks of pure copper. Miners began arriving by 1841, and within two years there was a lively copper rush to this small section of the U.P., forcing the U.S. Army to build Fort Wilkins in Copper Harbor (today a state historical park) to maintain law and order. As in all stampedes for a precious metal, many mines quickly died, and thousands of miners went home disillusioned and broke. Nevertheless, substantial lodes of copper were uncovered, and by the 1860s this area was producing 15 million pounds annually, or almost 90 percent of the national total. Two of the most profitable mines were Calumet and Hecla, and near them sprang up the town of Red Jacket. Later renamed Calumet, this city of 66,000 in 1898 had wealth, importance (it was considered as a new site for the state capital), and a peculiar problem.

Because of large contributions to the city budget from the mines, the council found itself with a surplus of funds. Already the community had paved streets, electric lights, and telephones, so the town decided to build an opera house, the grandest theater in the Midwest, one that would rival the stages of

Calumet Opera House

the East Coast. The **Calumet Opera House** was built in 1899 at Sixth and Elm Streets, and no expense was spared. It was designed in an Italian Renaissance style and inside featured two balconies, private viewing chambers along the walls, and rococo plaster ornamentation of gilt, cream, and crimson. The acoustics were nearly perfect: An actor could whisper on the stage and be heard in the last row of the top balcony.

On March 20, 1900, the first performance was given to a packed house of 1,100 and was described by the *Copper Country Evening News* as "the greatest social event ever known in the copper-dome's metropolis." A string of legendary performers arrived at the famed opera house, including John Philip Sousa, Sarah Bernhardt, Douglas Fairbanks, and Lillian Russell. Eventually the theater, like the town, fell upon hard times. The local mines, the last to operate in the Keweenaw Peninsula, were closed for good because of a labor strike in 1968; by then Calumet's population had dwindled to 1,000.

The mines are still closed, but the opera house has reopened. Declared a National Historic Site in 1974, it was fully restored, and its opulence can be viewed on a guided tour from mid-June through mid-October. Tours are offered from 11:00 A.M. to 2:00 P.M. Tuesday through Sunday; it's $4.00 for a peek into Calumet's past. The building has also returned to live theater after a stint showing motion pictures of the 1920s and 1930s; major performances are scheduled from March through October. Call (906) 337–2610 for information.

Next door to the opera house is **Shute's Bar,** which features what many say is the oldest wooden bar and back bar in the state. Both date to 1893 when Marco Curto, an immigrant miner who had saved his pay, opened up Curto's Saloon. One of forty-six in the area, it was a place where immigrant miners could always find somebody who spoke their native tongue. The bar is massive and polished to a gleam as is the back bar, which includes a huge mirror, wooden coolers, a metal cash register, and two intriguingly carved liquor cabinets that are 10 feet tall. The whole unit is crowned by a spectacular colored glass canopy. The long, narrow saloon also has the original booths and a ceiling and archway featuring classic trim and plasterwork. Shute's is not just a place to have a beer; it's a proper complement to the historic opera house next door.

At one time or another in the late 1800s, there were fourteen active copper mines in the Keweenaw Peninsula, and today a number of them have been preserved, offering a glimpse of the underground world of the miners. The least promoted but perhaps the most intriguing is the **Delaware Mine** on US 41 between Calumet and Copper Harbor. To reach it you pass through Delaware, a ghost town of a few abandoned buildings and a sobering reminder that when the copper ran out, so did the lifeblood for boomtowns throughout the peninsula.

Interest in the copper at Delaware began in 1845 and involved one early investor by the name of Horace Greeley. The famous newspaper editor actually made a trip to the Keweenaw Peninsula but never traveled much farther than Eagle River. A mining company was organized in 1848, and actual mining began the following year. From 1849 to 1851 the mine produced 522,541 pounds of copper, but the Northwest Copper Mining Company lost almost $100,000 on the operation. The mine was sold again and again to new investors, with one company building a huge hoist house in 1870 to pull the cars out of the deep shafts that were being dug. Despite all efforts, the Delaware never really turned a profit, and the shafts were sealed for good in 1887. The town of Delaware, which in 1879 had 300 residents, also disappeared.

Now a tourist attraction, the Delaware offers two different tours during the summer. A forty-minute tour takes you down a 100-foot staircase into Shaft No. 1 to the first level. The top level is 900 feet of tunnel from which other passages, shafts, and a huge cavern can

funfacts

Lake Superior is the largest and deepest of the Great Lakes, and its 31,700 square miles make up the largest surface area of any body of freshwater in the world. Measuring 383 miles long and 160 miles wide, Superior holds half of all the water in the Great Lakes.

be viewed. The Rustic Lantern Tour goes deeper into Shaft No. 3—without the aid of a staircase—and usually lasts ninety minutes. There is still plenty of copper lying around in this level, and in the information center visitors are told how to recognize and search for it in the mine. They are also given tips afterward on cleaning any metal they find.

The Delaware Mine (906–289–4688) is open from mid-May through mid-October from 10:00 A.M. to 6:00 P.M. daily. Admission is $8.00 per adult, $4.00 per child.

The men who actually worked the mines were often immigrants from the Cornwall area of England or from Finland or Norway, and they brought to

Copper Country their strong ethnic heritages. Traces of that heritage can be seen in the Cornish pasties that are sold throughout the U.P. and in the popularity of Finnish saunas. For years the sauna took the place of bathtubs and showers in homes, as early settlers would build their sauna huts first and worry about their cabins later. A good sauna begins with a shower to open up the pores, followed by a stay in a cedar-paneled room where a small pile of rocks is heated. As water is tossed on the rocks, a dry heat emerges that makes the body perspire profusely, flushing out dirt and grime from the skin. The temperature ranges from 160 to 180 degrees, and the old miners used wicker sticks to beat their backs to get the blood moving. The entire ordeal ends with a cold shower to close the pores.

In Copper Harbor you can experience this Finnish ritual at *Finnish Sauna House,* operated by the Harbor Hide-A-Way Motel in the heart of town on US 41. The public sauna is across the street from the resort and consists of four private suites. Each is completely paneled in cedar and features a dressing area, shower, and sauna that will seat four to six people. The building is not that far from Lake Superior, and occasionally a local resident will finish the sauna with a mad dash into the chilly lake, a tradition most visitors pass up.

The Finnish Sauna House (906–289–4741) is open daily from May 15 through October 15 from 1:00 to 10:00 P.M. The price includes use of a room, towel, soap, and a wicker stick if you request it. Call for specific rates.

The copper rush of the Keweenaw Peninsula began in 1843, and Copper Harbor quickly became the center of exploration parties, newly formed mining companies, and a "rough population of enterprising prospectors, miners, and speculators." Because of the seedy nature of the miners and the constant threat of Chippewa Indians wanting to reclaim their lost land, Secretary of War William Wilkins dispatched two companies of infantry to the remote region of Michigan. They arrived in late May of 1844, and by November *Fort Wilkins* was built.

The threat of Indian hostilities never materialized, and the troops discovered the Upper Peninsula winters were long and cold. Isolated from the rest of the world with little more than duty and drill to occupy their time, the garrison of 105 men ran into problems of boredom, low morale, and illegal whiskey. The following year half the troops were transferred to Texas in preparation for the Mexican War, and in 1846, less than two years after it was built, Fort Wilkins was abandoned. In 1921 Fort Wilkins was recognized as a historic landmark by the state, and in 1923 it was designated a state park. Today the structure is noted for being one of the few surviving wooden forts east of the Mississippi River.

Although the fort was insignificant militarily, it's an outstanding example of a mid-nineteenth-century frontier outpost, with twelve of its sixteen buildings from the original structure. You can wander through the fort year-round, even ski through it in the winter, but the buildings are open mid-May through mid-October. Ranging from kitchen and mess room to the bakery, company barracks, and hospital, many contain restored furnishings and artifacts depicting the rough life troops endured here. From mid-June through Labor Day, interpreters in period dress give tours daily from 9:00 A.M. to 5:00 P.M., adding a touch of realism to the fort.

The main entrance to the park and the fort is a mile east of Copper Harbor on US 41. A vehicle pass is required to enter the park and the fort. For more information on Fort Wilkins or on camping in the state park, call (906) 289–4215.

Keweenaw is the smallest county in the U.P., but it has more than its share of scenic drives, where every curve reveals another striking view. The most famous is the ***Brockway Mountain Drive,*** a 10-mile stretch to Copper Harbor that is the highest above-sea-level drive between the Rockies and the Alleghenies. Less traveled but almost as scenic in its own way is the ***Sand Dune Drive*** between Eagle River and Eagle Harbor. From Eagle River this portion of M 26 heads west along the Lake Superior shoreline, climbing high above the water along sandy bluffs. The road provides sweeping views of the Great Lake on the horizon and the sandy shoreline below, and the best turnoff looms above Great Sand Bay. The road returns to the lake level at Cat Harbor, a delightful beach for sunning and swimming if you can handle Superior's chilly waters, and then swings through Eagle Harbor, passing the picturesque ***Eagle Harbor Lightstation,*** which is now a museum open to the public.

Sand Hills Lighthouse Inn

Built in 1919, Sand Hills Lighthouse is one of the largest along the Great Lakes and had enough rooms to house three lightkeepers and their families. The lighthouse was so big that the U.S. Coast Guard used it as a training base during World War II and housed 200 guardsmen on the grounds.

In 1954 Sand Hills' beacon was made obsolete by new navigational technology, and the building was abandoned. In 1961 Bill Frabotta purchased the three-story brick building and its seven-story beacon tower, and after 30 years of careful renovation, opened it up as the Sand Hills Lighthouse Inn. The bed-and-breakfast offers eight guests rooms, a hearty breakfast in the morning, and more than 3,000 feet of Lake Superior shoreline from which to watch both sunrises and sunsets. Or you can climb the tower and enjoy the panoramic view from its walk-out roof.

Sand Hills Lighthouse Inn (906-337-1744) is 4 miles west of Eagle River at Five Mile Point. Rooms range from $125 to $185 per night. Make reservations well in advance if planning a trip from May through October.

Built in 1871, the lighthouse and the lightkeeper's residence have been renovated and furnished to reflect an early-twentieth-century lightstation. Next door is a small museum that contains, among other things, a display on Keweenaw's prehistoric copper culture. Signs from M 26 lead you to the lighthouse, which is open daily from noon to 5:00 P.M. mid-June through September. Admission is $3.00 for adults and free for children.

From Eagle Harbor M 26 continues east, first passing the junction to Brockway Mountain Drive and then returning to the edge of Lake Superior, whose shoreline becomes a rugged mass of red sandstone gracefully carved by the pounding waves. Along this segment you will pass *Devil's Wash Tub,* a huge depression in the shoreline that echoes the waves crashing in and out of it.

Ontonagon County

Three miles west of Silver City is *Porcupine Mountains Wilderness State Park,* a preserve of 58,000 acres of primitive forests, secluded lakes, and the rugged "Porkies." For most visitors, this state park is a quick drive to the end of M 107, where they follow a short wooded path to the escarpment overlooking *Lake of the Clouds,* a watery gem between the peaks and ridges of the mountains. Those willing to don a pair of hiking boots can enjoy some of the most unusual accommodations found in the U.P. with a night in one of the park's rustic cabins.

Within the Porkies is a trail network of more than 85 miles, and scattered along the footpaths are sixteen wilderness cabins, each located in a scenic setting along a stream or lake or on the shore of Lake Superior. You can reach them only on foot, and some take an all-day hike while others lie only thirty or forty minutes from the nearest parking lot. The cabins have no electricity, running water, or toilets that flush. Modern conveniences are replaced by candles, woodstoves, and an outhouse up the hill—ideal for anybody who wants to spend a night in the woods without having to "rough it" in a tent, sleeping on the ground.

funfacts

The Porcupine Mountains and the Huron Mountains to the east are the only ranges in Michigan formed by volcanic activity.

The cabins provide bunks, mattresses, cooking utensils, and for those on an inland lake, a small rowboat. You must provide sleeping bag, clothing, and food. The park rents the cabins, which hold from four to eight people, from April through November at $35 to $45 per night. Stop at the park visitor center just off South Boundary Road (open daily from 10:00 A.M. to 6:00 P.M. from mid-May through mid-October) for maps and a list of open cabins. Call (906) 885–5275 or write ahead for information and a cabin reservation to Porcupine Mountains Wilderness State Park, 412 South Boundary Road, Ontonagon 49953.

Thanks to a rich history of loggers and miners, Michigan is blessed (cursed?) with a scattering of ghost towns throughout the state. Fayette is the most famous and most visited, but **Old Victoria** can be an equally interesting stop. The Ontonagon County town was originally named Cushin and established in 1849 after the discovery of an ancient miner's pit that still contained a mass of copper. In 1858, a new group of investors came in and renamed the mine town Victoria, and the company town grew to more than 2,000 residents.

Victoria became a ghost town when the copper ran out. Most of the buildings date to the late nineteenth century. There are classic hand-hewn log cabins, ruins of a rock house, and mining equipment lying all over the place. Old Victoria (906–886–2617) is located 4 miles west of Rockland in Ontonagon County, with an entrance road that is clearly posted on US 45. Historical tours are given from Memorial Day through fall colors in October daily from 10:00 A.M. to 6:00 P.M. There is a small admission fee.

Upper Tahquamenon Falls in Luce County is the largest waterfall in the state, but many cascade connoisseurs think **Bond Falls** in southern Ontonagon County near Paulding is much more beautiful. The cascade is a drop of more than 50 feet where the Middle Branch of the Ontonagon River fans out and leaps down a series of steplike rocks and around a small island of large boulders in the middle. It's the constantly tumbling water that makes Bond Falls so alluring.

From US 45 in Paulding turn east onto Bond Falls Road and in 3.2 miles you'll come to the trailhead to the cascade and a small parking area. The falls are a half-mile hike that includes numerous stairways, some steep, and boardwalks. Nearby are a picnic area, beach, and campground.

Gogebic County

Waterfalls of every type and description are the gems of the Upper Peninsula, and there are more than 150 of them scattered across this region of Michigan. For example, **Black River Harbor Drive** (also known as Black River Road and County Road 513) in Gogebic County is virtually a parkway of whitewater splendor. The 15-mile road departs from Bessemer on US 2 and enters Ottawa National Forest, ending at scenic Black River Recreation Area on Lake

Wolf Mountain

This is a peak for those with short legs. The trek to the top of Wolf Mountain is only a half mile from the trailhead. The trail, which is located southeast of Wakefield in the Ottawa National Forest, can be reached by turning north onto Forest Road 9300 from US 2.

On Forest Road 9300 you cross Little Presque River and then see the mountain before reaching the trailhead at the end of the road. The hike is a stiff climb—no pain, no gain, right?—but within fifteen minutes or so, you're on a rocky knob looking at a 180-degree panorama.

The scenery is a rugged ridgeline to the west while to the south is an endless sea of pines that stretches into Wisconsin. It's such a great sunset-watching spot that some hikers have made a rustic "lounge chair" out of logs here. For more information on Wolf Mountain or a map, call the Ottawa National Forest Headquarters in Ironwood at (906) 932–1330.

Superior. Heading north you first pass ***Copper Peak Ski Flying Hill,*** the largest artificial ski slide in the world and the site of 500-foot jumps during the winter. In the summer visitors take the chairlift and elevator to the top for a view of three states and Canada.

From Copper Peak, Black River Road enters the heart of the national forest and winds near five waterfalls, each lying at the end of a trail from a marked turnoff. Gorge and Potawatomi Falls are among the most spectacular and easiest to reach. The two falls are within 800 feet of each other and only a five-minute walk from the parking lot. Potawatomi is the larger, with a 130-foot-wide cascade that drops 30 feet into the Black River. Gorge, smaller with a 24-foot drop, is encased in a steep and narrow red rock canyon—a spectacular setting. A well-marked path with stairs and observation decks leads you past both falls.

At the end of the road, you can camp at Black River Harbor Recreation Area, or those who want a little more luxury can rent a log cabin at ***Bear Track Inn*** nearby. The small resort has been around since the 1930s, when it catered to lumbermen and commercial fishermen. Its name came from a hungry bear who wandered in one night while the main cabin was being built and walked in the wet cement of the front steps. The name stuck, and the tracks can still be seen today. The inn has only three cabins for rent, but two are authentic log structures, and all three feature natural wood interiors, woodstoves and stone fireplaces, and kitchen facilities. The large cabin can sleep ten, the others hold four people each, and during the summer the rates range from $60 to $70 per night for double occupancy. For reservations call the inn at (906) 932–2144 or write Bear Track Inn, 15325 Black River Road, Ironwood 49938.

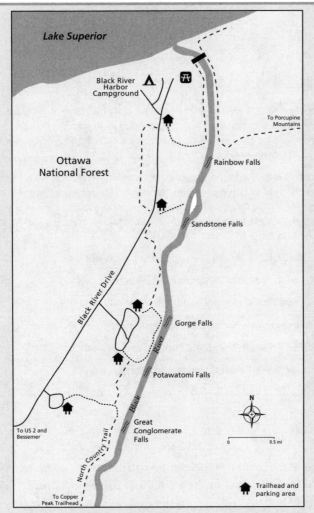

Black River Drive—The Waterfall Road

Departing from Bessemer, Black River Drive (also labeled CR 513) heads north for 15 miles to end at Black River Harbor, one of the few access points to Lake Superior and the site of a National Forest campground. It's a scenic drive past five waterfalls all located a short walk from the road.

The cascades are linked together by a portion of the North Country Trail, which hikers can walk from Cooper Peak Ski Flying Hill to the campground, a 5.5-mile trip. But it's more convenient if you drive the road, stopping at the trailhead of each individual falls. The hikes are short, the longest being a 1.5-mile round-trip, but do include a number of long staircases.

The first cascade, Great Conglomerate Falls, is reached 12 miles north of Bessemer and is followed by Potawatomi Falls, Gorge Falls, Sandstone Falls, and Rainbow Falls. The drive to view the falls makes an excellent side trip any time of the year, even in the winter, but the fall, especially from late September through early October, is by far the most spectacular time to go.

Camping in Michigan

With more than 14,000 campsites, the Michigan state park system ranks first in the country for total number of sites. Add almost 5,000 more sites in its national and state forests, and it's easy to understand why camping holidays are a time-honored tradition in Michigan, especially in the Upper Peninsula.

I prefer rustic campgrounds because they are smaller and more remote. For a list of and directions to all public campgrounds in the U.P., pick up a copy of the U.P. Travel and Recreation Association's Four Season Travel Planner. It's free and can be obtained by calling the association at (800) 562-7134. Here are my favorite rustic campgrounds in the U.P.:

Norway Lake National Forest Campground, Iron County

Gene's Pond State Forest Campground, Dickinson County

Big Knob State Forest Campground, Mackinac County

Big Eric's Bridge State Forest Campground, Baraga County

Mouth of Two-Hearted River State Forest Campground, Luce County

Kingston Lake State Forest Campground, Alger County

Iron County

Perhaps the U.P.'s largest and least-known historical complex is the ***Iron County Museum,*** located in the village of Caspian on County Road 424, 2 miles south of US 2 at Iron River. The grounds include almost twenty buildings, many a century old, in a Greenfield Village–like setting that lacks some of the polish of the famous Dearborn attraction but is no less interesting. The park occupies the site of the Caspian Iron Mine, and the head frame that hoisted cars out of the mine in the 1920s still towers over the complex. The main museum is the former engine house, which has been considerably enlarged and today is a maze of displays and three-dimensional exhibits. The favorite is the iron ore mining model that, for a nickel, will automatically run through the process of the rocks being rinsed from the mine and loaded into railroad cars above ground. Other interesting exhibits are the renovated saloon, blacksmith shop, and schoolroom, and a hand-carved model of a logging camp that fills an 80-foot display case with hundreds of figures and pieces.

Outside you can wander through one historic building after another: a logging camp bunkhouse with a table set for supper and mackinaw shirts (made of a heavy plaid wool) still hanging up near the door, a barn filled with plows and threshers of the 1800s, a completely furnished homesteaders' cabin, and many other exhibits. You could easily spend an entire day exploring this fascinating folk-life complex. The Iron County Museum (906–265–2617) is open from June through September from 9:00 A.M. to 5:00 P.M. Monday through Saturday and 1:00 to 5:00 P.M. Sunday. There is a small admission fee.

Dickinson County

As in the copper fields, many workers in the iron mines were immigrants from Europe. At Iron Mountain, many Italians came to work the Chapin Mine, which opened in 1879 and went on to become the second-leading ore producer in the U.P. You can learn about the miners' life and work at the Menominee Range Historical Museum and see the huge water pump that was built for the exceptionally wet mine at the *Cornish Pump Engine and Mining Museum.*

The pump engine was built for the Chapin Mine and while Chapin led iron ore production in the Menominee Range, it was also one of the wettest mines ever worked. To dry things out, the E.P. Allis Company of Milwaukee was

Pine Mountain Ski Jump

Known as the King of Hills, Pine Mountain Ski Jump is an awesome sight. Built in 1938 as a Works Progress Administration project and upgraded several times since, the 90-meter ski ramp features a 186-foot-high scaffold and a 381-foot slide. It sits majestically on top of a landing hill with a vertical drop of another 349 feet. Add it all up and you have a 1,440-foot run that sends skiers through the air at speeds of 55 to 65 miles an hour. In Iron Mountain they tell you it's like jumping off a twenty-nine-story building, of which there is none in the U.P.

Jumpers use skis that are wide, heavy, and often 265 centimeters or longer. Both their boots and bindings are much more closely related to Nordic skiing than Alpine, especially with the ability to lift the heels off the skis.

The jumpers are able to defy gravity by basically turning themselves into airplane wings when they lift out of the back of their bindings on takeoff and lean forward until their bodies are almost parallel to the skis. In 1994, an Austrian set a U.S. record at Pine Mountain when he leaped 400 feet.

If you're around Iron Mountain in mid-February, you can see the jumpers in action during the annual Pine Mountain Classic, which draws almost 20,000 spectators. In the summer you can climb the 280 steps to the top of the jump and be rewarded with a panoramic view that includes seven lakes.

To reach the ski jump from US 2, turn west on Kent Street and follow it past the Cornish Pump Engine and Mining Museum. Turn north on Upper Pine Mountain Road, which will wind to the ski ramp at the top of the hill.

Going Underground in the Upper Peninsula

Mining has had a long and colorful history in the Upper Peninsula, and there are many places where you can experience from a miner's point of view what it was like to go underground. Some of the following mines are covered in greater detail in this chapter:

Iron Mountain Iron Mine: Guided tours that begin on a rail tram (miner's train) take you through 2,600 feet of underground drifts and tunnels in this iron mine on US 2 in Vulcan, east of Iron Mountain; (906) 563–8077, www.ironmountainironmine.com.

Minong Mine: A 1.5-mile walk from McCargoe Cove Campground on Isle Royale National Park is this copper mine that was staked out in 1872, and once produced a 6,000-pound nugget of copper. Even if you're not backpacking across this wilderness island in the northwest corner of Lake Superior, you can still visit the site and see the open pits, and piles of tailings and metal work left over from the mining days. Forever/NPS Resorts (906–337–4993), which operates the Rock Harbor Lodge at the park, also offers day tours on its boat, MV *Sandy*. The North Shore trip is an eight-hour cruise that includes stopping at McCargoe Cove and hiking into the mine.

Delaware Mine: Located in Keweenaw County east of Mohawk on US 41, this is the only mine offering a self-guided tour into its shafts. You descend 110 feet into the mine and then follow a horizontal shaft where you can look for nuggets of pure copper. Find any and they're yours; (906) 289–4688.

Quincy Mine: This is the best mine tour in the Upper Peninsula. The Houghton County copper mine is just a mile north of Hancock on US 41 and includes an underground tour 400 feet into the No. Two Shafthouse and a scenic ride on a rail tram; (906) 482–3101, www.quincymine.com.

Tilden Mine Tour: This is the only tour in the Upper Peninsula of a working mine. Tilden Mine is an open-pit iron mine near Ishpeming in Marquette and includes walking more than a mile on steel grating around the gigantic pit and viewing the taconite processing plant; (906) 486–4841 or (888) 578–6489.

commissioned in 1889 to build a pumping system for the excess water. The centerpiece of the museum is the 725-ton steeple compound condensing engine that rises 54 feet from the floor and features a 40-foot flywheel. It has been documented as the largest steam-driven pumping engine in the United States.

There are also photos and exhibits on the underground mining days of Iron Mountain and an intriguing exhibit on Henry Ford's World War II gliders, which were manufactured in the area and used to secretly deploy troops behind enemy lines. The museum (906–774–1086) is in downtown Iron Mountain, 1 block west of US 2 on Kent Street. Hours are 9:00 A.M. to 5:00 P.M. Monday through Saturday and noon to 4:00 P.M. Sunday from Memorial Day to Labor

Day. Admission is $4.00 for adults or $7.00 for a ticket that includes the Menominee Range Historical Museum.

The Menominee River forms almost half of the border between Wisconsin and Michigan's Upper Peninsula, beginning west of Iron Mountain and extending to its mouth on Green Bay. Two miles south of Norway, the river flows through Piers Gorge, a whitewater area of large falls, holes, and swirls as the river tumbles through a scenic forested canyon. The gorge picked up its name in the 1840s when loggers built piers along this section of the river to slow the current and prevent logs from jamming and splitting on the jagged rocks. You can view this spectacular stretch of wild water by heading south of Norway on US 8; just before its bridge across the Menominee, turn left onto Piers Gorge Road. The paved road quickly turns into a dirt one, and then after 0.6 mile it ends at **Piers Gorge Nature Trail.** The trail is a round-trip of 3 miles but swings past a series of viewing points above the falls.

During the summer you can also experience the gorge and what many rafters call the "Midwest's premier whitewater river" through **Kosir's Rapid Raft.** The company offers a three-hour raft trip that takes you through Piers Gorge and over its falls. On Saturday and Sunday, the rafters meet nearby and then proceed to the river with their large inflated rafts. It's a wild ride, one that will leave you soaking wet but exhilarated. The company provides the rafts, guides, helmets, life jackets, and a paddle for each passenger.

Kosir's Rapid Raft (715–757–3431) is based in Wisconsin. The raft trips, which also can be set up during the week by advance reservation, cost $44 per person.

Menominee County

One of the products of Michigan's white pine era was hardwood floors by the IXL Company of Hermansville. Established by C. J. Meyer in the 1870s as part of his Wisconsin Land and Lumber Company, IXL became world-renowned for its floors after machines were invented in Hermansville that could precision-manufacture tongue-and-groove hardwood flooring in one operation. By the early 1900s IXL had the largest such plant in the country, and its flooring could be seen (and walked on) in the main lodge at Yellowstone National Park and the Mormon Temple in Salt Lake City.

In 1881 Meyer erected a huge office building to manage his sprawling lumber operation, and today it's one of the most intriguing museums in the Upper Peninsula. The **IXL Office Museum** is literally a step into a nineteenth-century business office. On the first floor visitors wander through the payroll and accounting departments as well as the private offices of the company executives. All are fully furnished and appear as if the workers had just stepped out for

IXL Office Museum

lunch. In one room are dictaphones, mimeographs, typewriters, and other machines complete with instruction booklets, while across the hall beautiful roll-top desks and an ornate walk-in vault can be seen. On the second floor several rooms are devoted to the machinery and equipment used in the flooring industry, and on the third floor visitors can still flip through original payroll records and see what a worker earned each week (along with deductions) in the 1890s.

The museum is located in the heart of Hermansville, a small town on US 2, 26 miles west of Escanaba and 30 miles east of Iron Mountain. The museum is open from June through Labor Day from 1:00 to 4:00 P.M. daily. There is a small admission fee.

Places to Stay in the Western Upper Peninsula

BIG BAY

Big Bay Point Lighthouse,
3 Lighthouse Road,
(906) 345–9957

Thunder Bay Inn,
County Road 550,
(906) 345–9376

BLACK HARBOR

Bear Track Inn,
15325 Black River Road,
(906) 932–2144

CALUMET/LAURIUM

Americinn,
5101 South Sixth Street,
(800) 634–3444

Laurium Manor Inn Bed and Breakfast,
320 Tamarack Street,
(906) 337–2549

COPPER HARBOR

Keweenaw Mountain Lodge,
US 41,
(906) 289–4403

Lake Fanny Hooe Resort,
US 41,
(800) 426–4451

EAGLE RIVER

Eagle River Inn,
M 26,
(800) 352–9228

Sand Hills Lighthouse Inn,
Five Mile Point,
(906) 337–1744

HOUGHTON

Charleston House Inn,
918 College Avenue,
(800) 482–7404

Franklin Square Inn,
820 Shelden Avenue,
(888) 487–1700

King's Inn,
215 Shelden Avenue,
(906) 482–5000

IRON MOUNTAIN

Comfort Inn,
1555 North Stephenson
Avenue,
(906) 774–5505

Edgewater Resort Cabins,
N4128 US 2,
(800) 236–6244

Woodlands Motel,
N3957 US 2,
(800) 394–5505

IRONWOOD

Comfort Inn,
210 East Cloverland Drive,
(906) 932–2224

Sandpiper Motel,
1200 East US 2,
(906) 932–2000

KEARSARGE

**Belknap's Garnet House
Bed and Breakfast,**
238 US 41,
(906) 337–5607

MARQUETTE

Cedar Motor Inn,
2523 US 41,
(906) 228–2280

Landmark Inn,
230 North Front Street,
(888) 752–6362

Nordic Bay Lodge,
1880 US 21,
(800) 892–9376

Super 8 Motel,
1275 US 41,
(906) 228–8100

SILVER CITY

Mountain View Lodges,
M 107,
(906) 885–5256

**Porcupine Mountain
Lodge,**
120 Lincoln Avenue,
(906) 885–5311

Places to Eat in the Western Upper Peninsula

BIG BAY

Thunder Bay Inn
(American),
County Road 550,
(906) 345–9376

SELECTED CHAMBERS OF COMMERCE AND TOURISM BUREAUS

Dickinson Area Partnership,
600 South Stephenson,
Iron Mountain 49801;
(906) 774–2002;
www.dickinsonchamber.com

Keweenaw Tourism Council,
326 Shelden Avenue,
Houghton 49931;
(866) 304–5722;
www.keweenaw.org

**Marquette Country
Convention and Visitors Bureau,**
2552 US 41 West,
Marquette 49855;
(800) 544–4321;
www.marquettecountry.org

**Upper Peninsula Travel and
Recreation Association,**
P.O. Box 400,
Iron Mountain 49801;
(800) 562–7134;
www.uptravel.com

**Western U.P. Convention and
Visitor's Bureau,**
P.O. Box 706,
Ironwood 49938;
(906) 932–4850;
www.westernup.com

CALUMET/LAURIUM

Toni's Country Kitchen
(American),
79 Third Street,
(906) 337–0611

COPPER HARBOR

**Keweenaw Mountain
Lodge** (fine dining),
US 41,
(906) 289–4403

Pines Restaurant
(American),
US 41,
(906) 289–4222

EAGLE RIVER

Fitzgerald's Restaurant
(lakeview dining),
M 26 in the
Eagle River Inn,
(906) 337–0666

HOUGHTON

Library Restaurant
(brew pub),
62 North Isle Royale Street,
(906) 487–5882

Suomi Home Bakery
(Finnish),
54 North Huron Street,
(906) 482–3220

IRON MOUNTAIN

Fontana's (Italian),
115 North Stephenson
Avenue,
(906) 774–0044

Gathering Place
(bakery and cafe),
427 South Stephenson,
(906) 774–8757

IRON RIVER

Alice's (Italian),
402 West Adams Street,
(906) 265–4764

IRONWOOD

Manny's (Italian),
316 East Houk Street,
(906) 932–0999

Mike's (American),
US 2 and Lowell Street,
(906) 932–0555

ISHPEMING

Jasper Ridge Brewery
(brew pub),
US 41 West,
(906) 485–6017

L'ANSE

Hilltop Restaurant
(American),
US 41,
(906) 524–7858

MARQUETTE

Jean Kay's (pastries),
1639 Presque Isle,
(906) 228–5310

Landmark Inn
(fine dining),
230 North Front Street,
(800) 752–6362

Northwoods Supper Club
(fine dining),
260 Northwoods Road,
(906) 228–4343

Sweet Water Cafe
(espresso and bakery),
517 North Third Street,
(906) 226–7009

Vierling Saloon
(brew pub),
119 South Front Street,
(906) 228–3533

MENOMINEE

Harbor House Gallery
(American),
1821 First Street,
(906) 863–7770

OTHER ATTRACTIONS

**Menominee Range
Historical Museum,**
Iron Mountain

**Marquette County
Historical Museum,**
Marquette

Coppertown USA,
Calumet

World's Tallest Indian,
Ironwood

Old Depot Park Museum,
Ironwood

**Menominee County
Historical Museum,**
Menominee

Indexes

Entries for Museums and Parks and Natural Places also appear in the special indexes beginning on page 217.

MUSEUMS

PARKS AND NATURAL PLACES

About the Author

Jim DuFresne is a Detroit-based travel and outdoor writer whose syndicated columns, "Travels in Michigan" and "Kidventures," appear in daily newspapers across the state. Formerly a sports and outdoors editor for the *Juneau Empire* in Alaska, DuFresne published his first travel book, *Tramping in New Zealand,* in 1982. His other books include *Isle Royale National Park; Voyageurs National Park; Alaska: A Travel Survival Kit; Glacier Bay National Park: A Backcountry Guide to the Glaciers and Beyond; Michigan State Parks;* and *Michigan's Best Hikes with Children.*